DOW JONES INDUSTRIAL AVERAGE

HISTORY AND ROLE IN AN INVESTMENT STRATEGY

DOW JONES INDUSTRIAL AVERAGE

HISTORY AND ROLE IN AN INVESTMENT STRATEGY

RICHARD J. STILLMAN
PROFESSOR EMERITUS
UNIVERSITY OF NEW ORLEANS

DOW JONES-IRWIN
Homewood, Illinois   60430

ISBN 87094-586-6

Library of Congress Catalog Card No. 85–73873

Printed in the United States of America

1 2 3 4 5 6 7 8 9 0 MP 3 2 1 0 9 8 7 6

To
My Daughter
Ellen

PREFACE

The Dow Jones Industrial Average (DJIA) is the dean of stock market indicators. It first appeared in *The Wall Street Journal* in 1896 and has come to occupy center stage of the investment community. But what do we know about the DJIA? And can it be helpful in the development of an investment strategy?

The purpose of this book is to provide answers to these two questions. Hopefully the historical background and investment strategy will be useful in arriving at your investment decisions. George Santayana, poet and philosopher, reminded us that "Those who cannot remember the past are condemned to repeat it." The long history of the Dow Industrials (1896 to present) permits us to profit from its experiences in peace and war; in prosperity and depression; and in democratic and republican administrations. Study the historical background on the DJIA and note how this information can be useful in establishing an investment strategy.

I first became interested in the Dow Industrials after taking courses in investments and security analysis from Dr. James A. Close at Syracuse University from 1949 to 1950. For the past 35 years I have followed the Dow and charted its progress along with significant political, military, technological, and economic events. This material has been used for many years in classroom lectures. Last year I published this chart (35 × 18 inches) and sold it locally in New Orleans. Sales of over 5,000 copies pointed up the interest in this subject. Furthermore, my research over the years indicated the need for a book written exclusively on the Dow Jones Industrial Average. Surprisingly, none had been written to this date.

This book is the outgrowth of my research. It covers the entire life and times of the Dow Jones Industrial Average as well as how the DJIA may be used in an investment strategy. Charts are provided that permit the reader to plot the Dow's progress in comparison with individual stocks as well as to make projections based on the DJIA's monthly movement since 1896. A number of publications discuss the Dow, but no writer has related the DJIA to its environment and indicated how to use it as part of a total money management program. My goal is to assist the reader in arriving at sound decisions in the selection of his/her portfolio.

Work on this text has given me a better understanding of Charles H. Dow's achievements: Dow Theory, Dow Averages, and founder of Dow, Jones & Company (with Jones and Bergstresser). He was a journalist, author, historian, economist, and entrepreneur. High on the list should be his entrepreneurial skills. He was the prime organizer of Dow, Jones & Company and its flagship publication, *The Wall Street Journal.* Thanks primarily to his *Journal,* the DJIA has become a household term. He wisely encouraged reader interest with his concept on market forecasting and daily averages. Shortly before his death, in 1902, he furthered prospects for the growth of Dow, Jones & Company by selling it to Clarence W. Barron, a successful Boston businessman and publisher. Dow was not only a leader but also an able manager. His many talents and good fortune have given Charles H. Dow, and his Dow Jones Industrial Average, immortality.

ACKNOWLEDGMENTS

I would like to thank the individuals who have previously labored long in the Charles Henry Dow vineyard. All have made helpful contributions to the Dow body of knowledge and made my research efforts easier. In particular, I am grateful to Samuel Armstrong Nelson, William Peter Hamilton, Robert Rhea, George Wesley Bishop, Jr., Lloyd Wendt, Maurice L. Farrell, and Phyllis Pierce. Librarians James R. Smith, Gregory P. Spano, and Evelyn H. Chandler at the University of New Orleans provided much needed assistance. Mrs. Claire R. French, librarian, Sterling Public Library, Orenco, Conn., and Ms. Susan Edgar of the News Library, the Providence *Journal-Bulletin*, furnished early background material on Dow. The New York Public Library, Library of Congress, and the Dow Jones Library proved to be helpful sources. A score of other libraries throughout the country loaned me their rare books.

The early editions of *The Wall Street Journal* that included Dow's editorials were indispensable.

Without the invaluable typing and administrative skills of Ellen, my daughter, this book would have been delayed. Thomas, my younger son, was in England attending law school the past year. His research produced stock market material with a European perspective. Darlene, my wife, and Richard, my older son, offered valued advice. Helen Stillman Fisher has been a successful investor for over 40 years. Her wise counsel was sought frequently.

This writing project has occupied the bulk of my time for the past 18 months. My primary relaxation was working out three times a week with my good friends at the YMCA Health Center. Joseph A. Martin, Robert A. DeMarco, Sidney J. Comer, and Robert Williamson offered continuing encouragement and made our two-mile runs pass quickly with "war stories" of every description. Each Saturday we would continue our storytelling at a New Orleans restaurant: Galatoire's, Pontchartrain Hotel (Caribbean Room), Windsor Court Hotel, Commander's Palace, Royal Orleans Hotel (Rib Room), and Upperline.

I wish to thank Donald Mesler, a reviewer of the manuscript, for his excellent recommendations. I also owe a debt of gratitude to bookstore buyers, librarians, and professors who took time to select my book from the many available. Also a nod to the media who enabled me to publicize it. Most important, I salute all of you who read my book. I hope it will be helpful and welcome your comments. My address is 2311 Oriole Street, New Orleans, LA 70122.

Richard J. Stillman

CONTENTS

LIST OF FIGURES

PART ONE

History: How the Dow Jones Industrial Average Has Evolved

There is much more to the history of the Dow Jones Industrial Average than the addition and deletion of various stocks. The history of the DJIA is also the story of its founder. It is affected not only by the rise and fall of various companies but also by the person in charge of the composition of the stock list, by the general growth (or decline) in the economy, and by what events are occurring in the United States and the world.

1

Origin: 1884–1896

However plentiful silver dollars may become, they will not be distributed as gifts among the people.
—*Grover Cleveland (March 4, 1885)*

INITIAL LIST OF STOCKS

The forerunner of *The Wall Street Journal* was a two-page financial bulletin entitled *Customer's Afternoon Letter* (see Figure 1–1). The first Dow Jones Average came into being when Charles Henry Dow presented his initial market average on July 3, 1884, in this *Letter*.[1] It was composed of 11 stocks—9 of this group were railroad companies. The two industrials were Pacific Mail Steamship and Western Union (see Figure 1–2). On February 16, 1885, the list of stocks was increased to 14 (see Figure 1–3). The St. Paul Railroad was deleted, but four other rails were added.[2] No change was made in the two industrials.

The list was modified twice between 1886 and 1894. On January 2, 1886 two railroads were removed (Central Pacific and Central Railroad of New Jersey), returning the total number of stocks used by Dow to 12 (see Figure 1–4). In 1894, eight years later Dow substituted three issues in his 12-stock average with the only two nonrailroads being American Sugar and Western Union (see Figure 1–5).[3] It was not until May 26, 1896, that Dow compiled a list consisting only of industrial stocks.[4]

RAILROAD'S DOMINANT ROLE

The railroads dominated the list of stocks in Dow's average during the period from 1884 to 1896 because Dow wanted his list to include

FIGURE 1–1 First Page of the *Customer's Afternoon Letter*

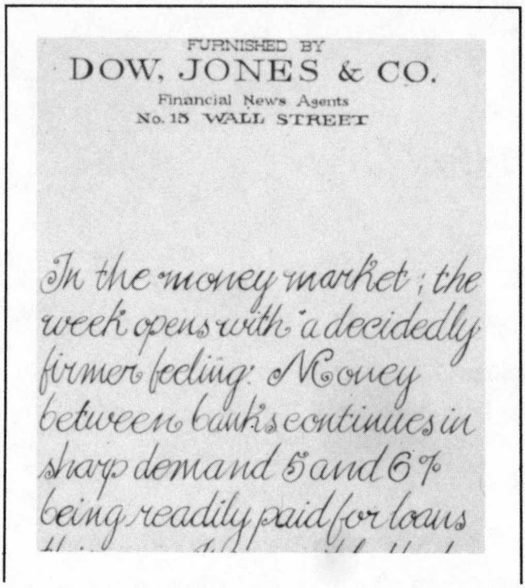
FURNISHED BY
DOW, JONES & CO.
Financial News Agents
No. 15 WALL STREET

In the money market; the week opens with a decidedly firmer feeling: Money between banks continues in sharp demand 5 and 6% being readily paid for loans

First published by Dow, Jones & Company on July 3, 1884. This paper later included Dow's first published stock average.

companies that were being actively traded. At that time, the railroads were the big play—there were very few other companies that were bought and sold in volume on a daily basis.[5] After all, railroads were the primary source for long distance travel. (The horse was still the principal mode of short distance transportation.) The predominance of railroads can be seen in Dow's description of his itinerary from Jersey City to Leadville, Colorado:

> The plan is to start from Jersey City, in a special hotel car, at 7 o'clock this evening, and go by the New York, Lake Erie and Western road to Chicago: thence by the Chicago and Alton Railroad to Kansas City; thence on the Kansas Pacific Railway to Denver, Colorado. The hotel car will be left at Denver and the journey continued by the Denver and South Park narrow gauge railroad to Webster, a distance of between 70 and 80 miles. Stages run from Webster to Leadville, a distance of about 40 miles, across the South Park. It will take six days to reach Denver and six days to return. Two or three days are to be spent at the mines.[6]

FIGURE 1–2 Dow's Initial 11 Stocks (July 3, 1884)

Stocks

Chicago & North Western
Delaware, Lackawanna & Western
Lake Shore
Louisville & Nashville
Missouri Pacific
New York Central
Northern Pacific preferred
Pacific Mail Steamship
St. Paul
Union Pacific
Western Union

Dow Average (July 3, 1884)

$$69.93\left(\frac{769.23}{11}\right)$$

These 11 stocks were selected by Dow for his initial average and appeared in the *Customer's Afternoon Letter,* July 3, 1884.

FIGURE 1–3 Dow's 14-Stock Average (February 16, 1885)

Stocks

Central Pacific
Central Railroad of New Jersey
Chicago Milwaukee & St. Paul
Chicago & North Western
Delaware & Hudson Canal
Delaware, Lackawanna & Western
Lake Shore Railroad
Louisville & Nashville
Missouri Pacific
New York Central
Northern Pacific preferred
Pacific Mail Steamship
Union Pacific
Western Union

Dow Average (February 16, 1885)

$$62.76\left(\frac{878.64}{14}\right)$$

This 14-stock average was prepared by Dow and appeared in the *Customer's Afternoon Letter,* February 16, 1885.

FIGURE 1–4 Dow's 12-Stock Average (January 2, 1886)

Stocks

Chicago, Milwaukee & St. Paul
Chicago & North Western
Delaware & Hudson Canal
Delaware, Lackawanna & Western
Lake Shore Railroad
Louisville & Nashville
Missouri Pacific
New York Central
Northern Pacific preferred
Pacific Mail Steamship
Union Pacific
Western Union

Dow Average (January 2, 1886)

$$86.26\left(\frac{1035.12}{12}\right)$$

This 12-stock average was prepared by Dow to appear in the *Customer's Afternoon Letter*, January 2, 1886.

FIGURE 1–5 Dow's 12-Stock Average (April 9, 1894)

Stocks

American Sugar
Chicago, Burlington & Quincy
Chicago, Milwaukee & St. Paul
Chicago & North Western
Chicago Rock Island & Pacific
Delaware & Hudson Canal
Delaware, Lackawanna & Western
Louisville & Nashville
Missouri Pacific
Northern Pacific preferred
Union Pacific
Western Union Telegraph

Dow Average (April 9, 1894)

$$78.27\left(\frac{939.24}{12}\right)$$

This 12-stock average was prepared by Dow and appeared in *The Wall Street Journal*, April 9, 1894.

THE 1884–1896 ERA

Dow's average of railroads and industrials did not change much during the period from 1884 to 1896. Figure 1–6 indicates that it varied less than 40 points over this 12-year time frame. Its lowest point was 61.49 in July 1885, and the Dow high approached 100 (99.14) in May 1890. Even the financial panic of 1893 saw this stock barometer drop to only 61.94. While it may seem surprising that very little variation occurred over a 12-year period, there were three reasons. First, all but two issues in the Dow were major railroads that produced solid growth and good annual earnings. Second, it was a *relatively* peaceful era of economic development, and third, the divisor had not been diluted and thus changes reflected the actual increase or decrease.

While it was an era of *relatively* peaceful economic development, not all was tranquil (see Figure 1–6). There were three violent strikes and two panics. Dow himself wrote about two economic crises during the period. He regarded the 1884 panic as primarily related to the stock market whereas he thought that the 1893 panic was more pervasive.

> The year 1884 brought a Stock Exchange smash but not a commercial crisis. The failure of the Marine Bank, Metropolitan Bank, and Grant & Ward in May was accompanied by a large fall in prices and a general check which was felt throughout the year. The Trunk Line War, which had lasted for several years, was one of the factors in this period.[7]

> The panic of 1893 was the outcome of a number of causes—uncertainty in regard to the currency situation, the withdrawal of foreign investments, and the fear of radical tariff legislation. The anxiety in regard to the maintenance of the gold standard was undoubtedly the chief factor, as it bore upon many others.[8]

LIFE AND TIMES OF CHARLES H. DOW

Early Years

Now let us look more closely at the life and times of Charles Henry Dow. What do we know about the man who conceived the most famous of market indicators? Dow, son of a farmer, was born in Sterling, Connecticut, on November 6, 1851. Young Charles' early years were spent on the family farm. When he was six, his father died and the boy was required to work very hard in order to help

FIGURE 1–6 Dow Railroad and Industrial Average, 1884–1896 (with Stillman's significant political, military, technological, and economic events)

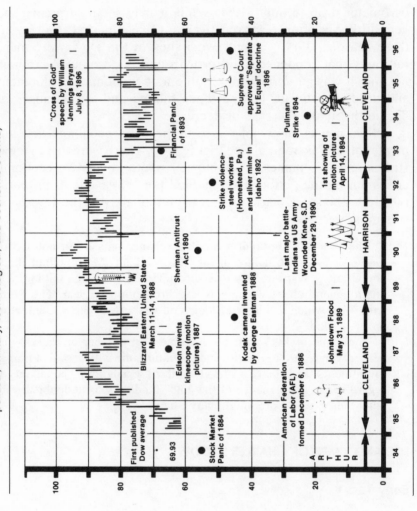

his mother maintain her small acreage. To supplement the family income Dow held a variety of jobs, more than 20 according to his own recollection. He soon found out that manual chores on the farm (and elsewhere) were not to his liking. However, writing did appeal to him, and—like other young men of this time—he admired the works of the American author, Horatio Alger, Jr. (1832–1899), who published *Ragged Dick* in 1867.

Dow's journalistic experience began at age 18, when he obtained a position in Springfield, Massachusetts with the *Springfield Republican*. He was fortunate to come under the guidance of its highly respected editor, Samuel Bowles III. He remained in Springfield for six years before moving to Providence, Rhode Island to write for several newspapers.[9] Again he worked for a leader in the newspaper business. A *Wall Street Journal* article reported that "he went to Providence and after a short experience on the *Press* and *Star,* he virtually by sheer originality and forceful persistence created a place for himself on the *Providence Journal,* when that paper was in the hands of George W. Danielson, himself one of the newspaper giants in those days. His experience on this paper was similar in kind, but his success was even more marked than it was at Springfield.[10]

First Major Publication

Dow's first "book" was published in 1877 while he was working for the *Providence Journal.*[11] It was titled *History of Steam Navigation between New York and Providence,* and covered the years from 1792 to 1877. More a pamphlet than a book, the 29-page publication was written under the direction of D. S. Babcock, president of the Providence & Stonington Steamship Company.[12] Babcock's primary purpose for distributing the book was to publicize the company's four steamers—the Massachusetts, Rhode Island, Narragansett, and Stonington (see Figures 1–7A and 1–7B).

The book provides an excellent account of the growth of steamers traveling the waters between Providence and New York during an 85-year period. Dow pointed out the popularity of boat excursions during this era and the actions of people aboard the ships:

> The excursions themselves were very much like what they are now. The reports of them indicate that there was, proportionately, about the same number as now of elderly ladies who constantly expected an explosion; of young people who sought the uttermost parts of the

FIGURE 1–7A Advertisement Appearing in Dow's *History of Steam Navigation between New York and Providence*

THE

Providence & Stonington S. S. Co.

Commencing with the Summer season of 1877, there will be two first-class passenger and freight lines, owned and operated by this Company.

The Providence Line

will consist of the new and magnificent steamers

MASSACHUSETTS

—AND—

RHODE ISLAND,

which will run direct between Providence and New York, leaving Providence from FOX POINT WHARF at 7.15 P. M., and New York from PIER No. 29, NORTH RIVER at 5 P. M.

New and elegant cars will run over the BOSTON & PROVIDENCE R. R., leaving BOSTON at 6 P. M., and making the run to Providence in one hour, and making direct connections with the boats. A train will leave Providence for Boston each morning, about 6 o'clock, or on the arrival of the boat.

HORSE CARS will run between the RAILROAD STATION in Providence and FOX POINT.

The Stonington Line

will consist of the well-known and favorite steamers

Narragansett —AND— Stonington,

which will run as heretofore between Stonington and from PIER No. 33, NORTH RIVER, New York, connecting with the cars of the New York, Providence & Boston R. R. Co. at Stonington.

☞ Arrangements are being perfected for making close connections for the WHITE MOUNTAINS, and other principal points in the interior of New England.

FIGURE 1–7B Picture of Steamer Massachusetts in Dow's *History of Steam Navigation between New York and Providence*

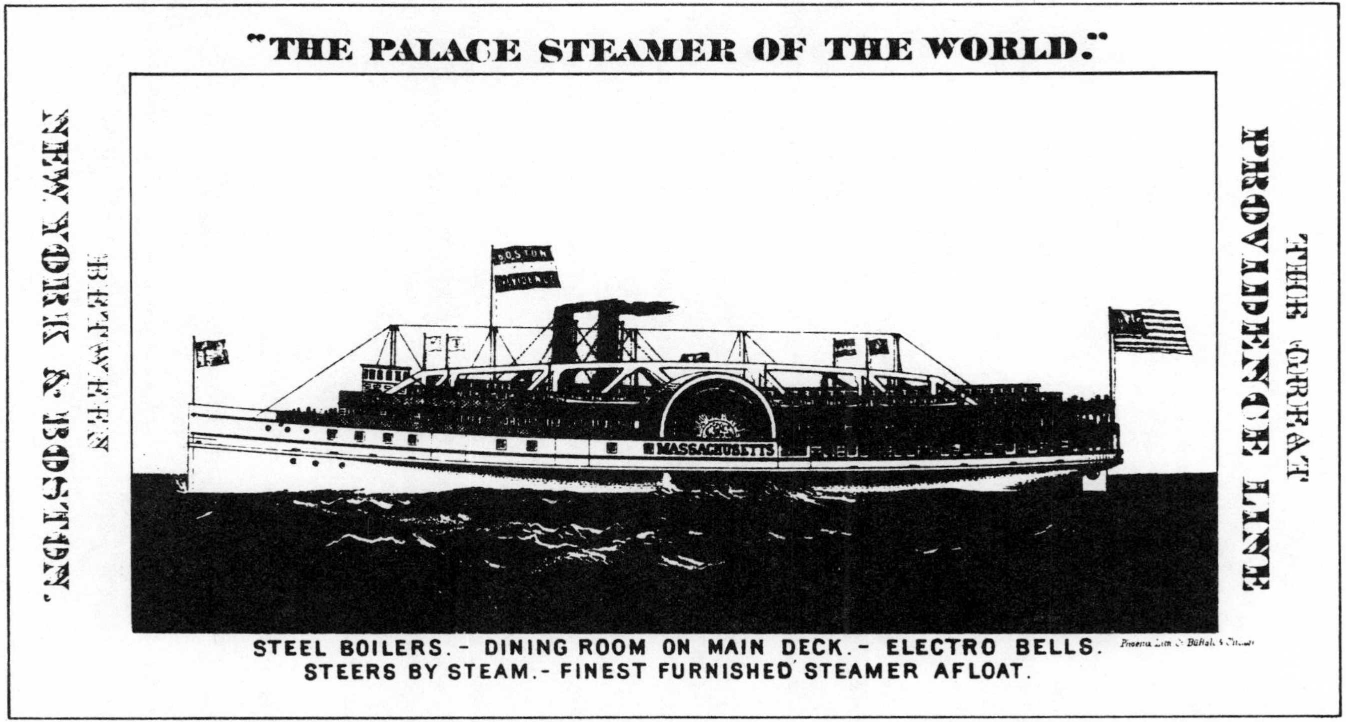
"THE PALACE STEAMER OF THE WORLD."
THE GREAT
PROVIDENCE LINE
BETWEEN
NEW YORK & BOSTON.
BOSTON
MASSACHUSETTS
STEEL BOILERS. - DINING ROOM ON MAIN DECK. - ELECTRO BELLS.
STEERS BY STEAM. - FINEST FURNISHED STEAMER AFLOAT.

The Masschusetts might be described as ''The Love Boat'' cruise of that era. She was 325 feet long, had a 46-foot beam and 16-foot hold. Her engine was a 90-inch cylinder and had a 14-foot stroke. There were several family apartments, 200 rooms, and 220 berths for passengers.

boat and sat quite unnecessarily close together, considering the amount of room that there was to spare; of rampageous lads, who unceasingly rushed from one end of the boat to the other; and of quiet people, who watched the rest and had a good deal of fun.[13]

Leadville Experience

Charles Dow did not focus his writing efforts on business news until he was assigned by the *Providence Journal* to cover the dynamic silver mining activities in Leadville, Colorado. From May to June of 1879 he wrote nine articles that have been referred to as "The Leadville Letters."[14] See Figure 1–8 for a copy of his first letter.

The Leadville experience pointed Dow in the direction of his primary interest—financial journalism. In the fall of 1879 he went to New York to find a job, and his success was apparent from this *Journal* editorial:

> Practically unknown in New York and with no backers of any kind, he came down into Wall Street and sought employment as a reporter, on mining stocks. He obtained a position at a small salary with one of the daily papers, his duties at once bringing him into intimate connection with the financial world. His work here was characteristic. The men of the Street soon learned that this reticent, quiet-speaking man who took shorthand notes on his cuffs could be relied upon to quote them absolutely and without embellishment and moreover, that it was safe to tell him news in confidence. He was never satisfied to do work merely well; nothing but the best contented him, and soon developed what was at the outset a mere routine reporting task into what may be called, without exaggeration, highly expert criticism. His editorial articles in the *Mail* and *Express,* when that was owned by Mr. Cyrus W. Field, were practically the first examples of real financial criticism in the daily press.[15]

Founded Dow, Jones & Company

Dow next accepted a position as financial reporter for the Kiernan News Agency. Here he worked with Edward D. Jones and Charles M. Bergstresser. They left Kiernan a few months later to found Dow, Jones & Company in November 1882. It was a news agency that provided daily bulletins on financial matters to its subscribers. In addition, beginning in November 1883, the company distributed a two-page newspaper titled *Customer's Afternoon Letter* (see Figure 1–1).[16] *The Wall Street Journal* was an expansion

FIGURE 1–8 Dow's First Leadville Article

PROVIDENCE JOURNAL

MONDAY MORNING, MAY 26, 1879.

EN ROUTE FOR LEADVILLE.

A Proposed Visit to the Phenomenal City of Southern Colorado.

Correspondence of the Providence Journal.

NEW YORK, May 21, 1879.

I have had several ardent wishes: one has been that I might see the Great Sunset land; another that I might go to Europe; another that I might be truly good. I have hesitated somewhat about mentioning the last named wish, on account of the incredulous sentiments to which it may give rise, but a correspondent is nothing if not truthful. As for Europe and the West, they have looked to me only like microscopic possibilities. Suddenly the possibility has become a reality, and all through the good luck of the Little Pittsburgh Consolidated Mining Company. I stop here to mention that if the programme to which I shall presently allude is a fair specimen of the way in which the Little Pittsburgh Consolidated Mining Co. do things, I should like to become intimately acquainted with the managers of the Little Pittsburgh Consolidated Mining Co. It may or may not be a household truth among the circles of delightful people who always take the JOURNAL, that the Little Pittsburgh Consolidated Mining Company own the finest mining property in that new marvel of the west, Leadville, Colorado.

The story of Leadville may be briefly told here. The town which in twenty months has grown from nothing to be a place of 15,000 or 20,000 inhabitants, is in California Gulch, on the bank of the Arkansas river, about one hundred and forty miles southwest of Denver. California Gulch was a rich mining district fifteen or twenty years ago. Oro City was the metropolis of those days, and the miners took out between $3,000,000 and $4,000,000 in placer mining. The "rush" left Oro City in 1864, but mining has been carried on in the Gulch every summer with tolerably satisfactory results. The miners have always been troubled with a sort of heavy sand that kept getting into the sluice boxes, but they never considered it of the slightest value.

In 1877 it was discovered that the sand was composed of lead carbonates and was enormously rich in silver. Leadville came into prominence at once, and, if half that is said of the wealth of the region is true, the Leadville mines are bonanzas of the most satisfactory kind. Various mines have been located and several companies have been organized for developing these new fields of wealth. A Colorado company secured four of the most valuable mines, and have achieved the most astonishing results in the way of earnings and dividends. The mines have produced in the last five months, a net profit, over and above all expenses, of $100,000 a month. The net proceeds from ore now being mined average $10,000 a day, and, when smelting facilities are increased, the profits, the Company declare, will be greatly increased also.

The magnitude of the "find" drew the attention of New York capitalists to the mines, and arrangements were made last November by means of which the Little Pittsburgh Consolidated Mining Company organized under the laws of the State of New York, with a capital of $20,000,000—200,000 shares at $100 per share—and chose a Board of Directors, composed of the following-named gentlemen: Jerome B. Chaffee, H. A. W. Tabor, J. M. A. Griswold, Henry Howard, Henry Havemeyer, Charles L. Perkins, C. C. Dodge, James L. Soutter, M. L. Potter, J. C. Babcock, J. D. Smith, A. J. Dam and D. H. Moffat, Jr. The President of the Company is Jerome B. Chaffee, and the Secretary George C. Lyman.

The astonishing reports from the mines, during the past winter, have aroused in the minds of the directors a desire to see a property paying such fabulous dividends. Quite a number of New York capitalists, too, wanted to see the mines and the country, and so the Little Pittsburgh folks have arranged an excursion to the mines. The party is composed of the following-named persons:

Messrs. Brayton Ives, President of the Stock Exchange; M. L. Potter, E. H. Potter, J. L. Soutter, Com. S. N. Kane, James D. Smith, John Smith, A. J. Dam, Charles C. Dodge, S. B. Elkins, J. C. Babcock, Prof. Raymond, U. S. Grant, Jr., David Draper, Charles L. Perkins, H. W. Gray, R. F. Hill, E. S. Bowen, Dr. C. L. Bissell, of New York; Jas. H. Chace, of Providence; Prof. Marsh of Yale College; M. B. Crowell, of New Bedford; D. H. Moffatt, Jr., of Denver, Col.; George H. Fryer, of Leadville, Col.; Mr. White, of the New York Tribune; a representative of the New York Herald; Alphonso Ross of the Boston Advertiser, and the JOURNAL correspondent.

Mr. Chaffee, who, by the way, is ex-United States Senator Chaffee, intended to be one of the party; but ill health keeps him in New York. Senator Blaine also was going, but at the last moment, was obliged to give up the trip. The party goes in charge of Mr. Moffat, one of the leading owners in the mines. The plan is to start from Jersey City, in a special hotel car, at 7 o'clock, this evening, and go by the New York, Lake Erie and Western road to Chicago; thence by the Chicago and Alton Railroad to Kansas City; thence on the Kansas Pacific Railway to Denver, Col. The hotel car will be left at Denver and the journey continued by the Denver and South Park narrow-gauge railroad to Webster, a distance of between 70 and 80 miles. Stages run from Webster to Leadville, a distance of about 40 miles, across the South Park. It will take six days to reach Denver and six days to return. Two or three days are to be spent at the mines. Prof. Raymond, the widely-known geologist, goes as an expert, to assure the capitalists, of whom the company is quite largely composed, that the "testimony of the rocks" and of the miners does not deceive them.

Every one is predicting a remarkably blissful time, although some of the "old stagers" have uttered ominous words about "being tired," "shaken to death," "stopping over a day to rest," "dreadful cold on the mountains," "fearful dusty on the plains," etc.: but those who have never made the trip feel as if that was all prejudice and as if anybody could ride a week in a hotel car. I will let you know who was right after a few days' experience.

of the *Customer's Afternoon Letter,* which discontinued upon publication of *the Journal.* An article appearing in the 50th anniversary edition said:

> The Wall Street Journal,, strictly speaking, was not established until 1889. It is an amplification, however, of the *Customer's Afternoon Letters,* consisting of two single-column pages, 10½ by 8 inches, which the Messrs. Dow and Jones began publishing in 1883, when their office was at 15 Wall Street. Dow Jones did its own printing for the first time in 1885; and in 1886, after removal to 26 Broad Street, increased the size of its "Letters" to 15½ by 10½ with two-column instead of one-column pages. The first issue of *The Wall Street Journal* under that name was an evening edition published July 8, 1889, at the 26 Broad Street address. Later that year the offices were moved to 41 Broad Street and still later, April 18, 1893, to No. 44.[17]

First Edition of the WSJ

The first edition of *The Wall Street Journal,* appeared July 8, 1889—(nearly seven years after the founding of Dow, Jones & Company (see Figure 1–9). A yearly subscription cost $5, an individual copy cost 2 cents, and advertisements were 20 cents a line. Published daily at 3:15 PM. except Sundays and Stock Exchange holidays, the paper contained four pages of financial news and statistical data. The quantitative material took more than a page and included bond and commodity quotations, active stocks, railroad earnings, and bank and U.S. Treasury reports. The bond quotations took the most space—requiring over two columns. The listed and unlisted stocks are shown on facing page.

The paper's purpose and principles were reported as follows:

> The Wall Street Journal is another step in the development of our business. Its object is to give fully and fairly the daily news attending the fluctuations in prices of stocks, bonds, and some classes of commodities. It will aim steadily at being a paper of news and not a paper of opinions. It will give a good deal of news not found in other publications, and will present in its market article, its tables, and its advertisements a faithful picture of the rapidly shifting panorama of the Street.
>
> We believe that such a paper will be of use to operators, bankers, and capitalists who can find in its columns essential statistics compiled so that their pith and bearing can be easily remembered; also, the events which have moved or are moving prices, together with the drift of opinion in the Street. Our bond table is unique in that it gives

The Opening, Highest, Lowest, and Closing Prices of Active Stocks on the New York Stock Exchange Today

Stock	Op'g.	High	Low	Clos.
Atch., Top. & S.F.	38 1/4	38 1/4	36 7/8	37 5/8
Burling. & Quincy	98	98 3/8	97 3/4	98 1/2
Central Pacific	55	58	—	—
Canada Southern	52 3/4	55	52 1/2	52 3/4
Ches. & Ohio	20 1/8	20 7/8	—	—
Chi. & E. Ill. Com.	44 1/8	44 1/8	—	—
Chi. & E. Ill. pfd.	102 3/4	102 3/8	99	102 1/4
Chicago Gas	59 5/8	59 3/4	59	59 3/4
Colorado Coal	29	29	—	—
Consol. Gas	86 1/2	86 1/2	86	86
Delaware & Hudson	145	145	144 3/4	144 3/4
Del. Lack. & W.	144 3/8	144 3/8	143 3/8	144 5/8
East Tenn. 2d	10	26	—	—
Erie	26	26	25 1/2	25 3/4
Lake Shore	101 3/4	101 3/4	100 3/4	101 1/2
Louisville	68 1/2	68 1/2	67 1/2	67 7/8
Manhattan	96	96	96	96
M. L. S. & W. pfd.	114 1/2	114 1/2	—	—
Missouri Pacific	69 1/2	69 1/2	68 3/8	68 5/8
New England	49 1/2	49 3/4	49	49 5/8
N. Y. Central	105 1/2	105 1/2	105	105 1/2
N. Y. Ont. & W.	17 1/4	19	—	—
Northern Pac. com.	27 1/4	27 1/8	27 1/8	27 1/8
Northern Pac. pref.	64	64 1/8	63 1/4	63 1/8
Northwest	105 1/4	105 3/4	104 3/4	105 1/2
Omaha com.	32 1/2	38	32 1/4	32 1/4
Oregon Trans.	33 3/8	33 3/8	33	33
Reading	46 1/8	46 1/8	45 3/8	45 7/8
Richmond Terminal	23 1/2	23 1/4	23 1/4	23 5/8
Rock Island	92 3/8	92 1/2	92	92 3/4
St. Paul	67 5/8	67 5/8	66 1/4	67 1/4
Texas Pacific	19 1/2	19 1/2	18 3/4	19 1/4
Union Pacific	58 1/2	58 1/8	56 1/2	57 1/2
Wabash com.	—	—	—	—
Wabash pref.	38 1/2	30 3/8	28	28 1/2
Western Union	85 3/8	—	85	85 1/4
Wheel & L. E. pfd.	67 5/8	69 1/2	—	—
UNLISTED				
Cotton Oil	56	58 3/4	55 3/4	56
Lead Trust	32 1/2	32 1/2	31 1/2	32 1/8
Sugar Trust	115	116	114 3/8	116 3/8

Total sales of stocks: listed, 283,703 shares, unlisted, 40,028 shares—total of both, 323,731 shares.

SOURCE *The Wall Street Journal,* July 8, 1889, p.2.

the yield as well as the price, and enables the observer to observe the return on one issue compared with another, without laboriously consulting tables of investments.

* * * * *

The fundamental principles in carrying on our news business, are these:

To get the news.

To publish it instantly, whether bull or bear.

FIGURE 1–9 Front Page of *The Wall Street Journal's* First Edition

THE WALL STREET JOURNAL.

VOL. 1.—NO. 1.	NEW YORK, MONDAY, JULY 8, 1889.	PRICE TWO CENTS.

This is the first page of the initial copy of The Wall Street Journal, *published by Dow, Jones & Company on July 8, 1889. Dow was editor-in-chief. His "Average Movement of Prices" was featured on the front page.*

No operator controls or can control our news. Any prominent man can say in our columns substantially what he pleases over his own name.

We are proud of the confidence reposed in our work. We mean to make it better, and we mean to have the news always honest, intelligent, and unprejudiced.[18]

It is interesting to note that in the first edition of the *Journal* Dow made his 12-stock average a lead item on the front page:

Average Movement of Prices.

The bull market of 1885 began July 2, with the average price of 12 active stocks 61.49.

The rise culminated May 18, 1887, with the same twelve stocks selling at 93.27.

Prices gradually declined for about a year, reaching the next extreme low point April 2, 1888, the 12 stocks selling at 75.28. The movement since then, counting from one turning point to another, follows:

Last low point	Apr. 2,	1888,	75.28
Rallied to	May 1,	"	83.54
Declined to	June 13,	"	77.12
Rallied to	Aug. 8,	"	85.95
Declined to	Aug. 18,	"	83.76
Rallied to	Oct. 1,	"	88.10
Declined to	Dec. 5,	"	81.88
Rallied to	Feb. 18,	1889,	87.77
Declined to	Mar. 18,	"	83.59
Rallied to	June 12,	"	91.38
Closed Sat. night	July 6,	"	87.71

SOURCE *The Wall Street Journal*, July 8, 1889, p. 1.

Computation of Initial Average

To compute his initial average, Dow added up the current market price of all the stocks in his average and divided the total by the number of issues. For example, on February 20, 1885, Dow's average contained 14 companies (12 railroads and 2 industrials). The closing prices of the 14 stocks totaled 892.92. This aggregate was then divided by 14 to provide a result of 63.78. As the previous day's close was 64.73, it could be said that the market, based on Dow's average, was down for the day. The Dow average was down nearly a point from the February 19, 1885, close.

The method used by Dow to obtain his daily average is mathematically an unweighted arithmetic mean. That is, he merely added up the price of each stock and divided the aggregate by the number of corporations.[19] He gave no extra weight to the largest corporation in the average nor did he adjust for the smallest.

The formula used to compute the daily average is as follows:

$$\frac{\text{Sum of the current market prices of all issues}}{\text{Current divisor}}$$

or

$$\frac{\Sigma\,P}{D} = DA$$

where

Σ = sum
P = price of each stock comprising the Dow Average
D = divisor (number of issues in the DA).

Founders Jones and Bergstresser

Although all the averages carry the name of Edward Davis Jones (1856–1920) coequal with Dow, there is no record that he made any contribution to their development. Jones, who was with the company from 1882 to 1899, provided considerable managerial and editorial talent to the early success of Dow, Jones & Company. Charles Milford Bergstresser (1859–1923), as founding partner, furnished valuable editorial skill and had excellent contacts with business leaders during his 23 years with the firm from 1882 to 1905. Dow had little formal education and respected the academic background of his two youthful colleagues. Jones attended Brown and Bergstresser was a Lafayette College graduate.

John C. Gerrity, in 1948, wrote a letter to *The Wall Street Journal* (Figure 1–10) describing his early experiences working for Dow, Jones & Company beginning June 6, 1884. He provides an excellent description of the three founders and their responsibilities in the company during its formative years.

Dow's Death

Dow held the position of editor-in-chief of *The Wall Street Journal* from July 8, 1889, until his death on December 4, 1902. He died at his home in Brooklyn, New York "after a short illness that followed an attack of nervous prostration."[20] Edward D. Jones wrote the following tribute about his longtime associate:

Messrs. Dow, Jones & Co.:

Gentlemen—May I offer a brief tribute to the memory of your senior partner, Mr. Charles H. Dow, with whom I worked as an editor 28 years ago in Providence, Rhode Island, and whose partner I was in Dow & Jones and Dow, Jones & Company, until three years ago. He was always a ceaseless searcher for facts, and the best way to tell and to distribute them. He was a tower of strength in our early struggles to force reluctant railroad managers to furnish reports which told something, to protect the speculating public from swindlers in and out of Wall Street, and to praise where praise was due. His honesty was rugged, his industry was prodigious, his integrity unsullied, and his home life ideal.

Financial journalism loses one of its best and certainly one of its most honest exponents, his family mourns a devoted, loving son, husband, and father, and Wall Street parts with a most conscientious, forceful, and able critic. I do not think his place here can be filled.

Very truly yours,
Edward D. Jones[21]

OBSERVATIONS

Charles H. Dow created and published the first U.S. stock market average in 1884. He was 32 years old and had been an owner of Dow, Jones & Company less than two years. Dow came along at the right time—there was need for a market barometer. Trading volume in U.S. stocks approximated 250,000 shares daily and the number of issues *actively* traded exceeded 35. More important, there were hundreds of small publicly held companies that were lightly traded but had potential growth. Dow provided the financial community with an indicator reflecting the general movement of U.S. stocks.

How did Dow come to recognize the need for a market average? Unfortunately, he left no records revealing this fact. The paucity of information on the early days of Dow, Jones & Company is surprising. Even its opening date in November 1882 is not available.

FIGURE 1–10 Worker Describes the Early Days of Dow Jones

News Gathering in 1884

Editor, The Wall Street Journal

Every time I hear on the radio the statement "Dow Jones Averages" my mind goes back to that great and eventful day, June 6, 1884 when, having graduated from elementary school, my formal education was completed and it was up to me to get out and face the world and earn a living

A family friend, Mr. Thomas Manning, had already arranged for me to call at Dow, Jones & Company and ask for Mr. Bergstresser.

Living at 35th Street, between 8th and 9th Avenues, I took the 9th Avenue horse-drawn stage coach running from 37th Street to the Battery. (The fare on the elevated was 10 cents—the stage 8¢ cents). My instructions were to get off at Trinity Church and look for 15 Wall Street.

That number was on a little ramshackle building, next door to the entrance of the Stock Exchange. I think it was only two stories and basement. A flight of stairs led me down to a basement soda fountain, beside the serving counter of which was a narrow passageway to the rear of the building—in here was Dow, Jones & Company! As I started into the passageway, I met a man coming out and I informed him that I was looking for a Mr. Bergstresser. He informed me that my search was over, for he was my man. I told him why I was there and we then proceeded together back to the domain of Dow, Jones & Company.

As we entered, my mind flashed back to my reader at school which had contained an excerpts from Dickens' "Nicholas Nickleby" recording the first time Squeers brought Nicholas into the school—thus: "It was such a crowded scene that at first Nicholas saw nothing at all. By degrees, however, the place resolved itself into a bare hole

with a few forms, a detached desk for Squeers. . . ."

This was, indeed, a small dark room (lights on all day) without any attempt at painted walls or floor covering. On one side of the room, a little space was walled off by a few plain pine boards which gave privacy of a sort to two desks—one for Mr. Dow and the other for his assistant, Mr. Henderson. Mr. Jones' desk was at the far end. If Mr. Bergstresser had a desk I never knew where it was. The center of the room was taken up by the copywriters. We boys—well, we were just there.

My recollection of the members of the firm is quite clear even after the passing of 64 years.

Mr. Dow was probably over 6 feet tall, though noticeably round-shouldered and must have been well over 200 pounds, though he could not be termed "fat." He had jet-black hair and a full beard. We boys never thought of him as part of the business as he passed in and out of his cubbyhole without paying any attention to what might be going on. I think it was in that year, or in 1885, that he started the Stock Exchange firm of Goodbody, Glenn & Dow with offices at 30 Broad Street.

Mr. Jones—very tall and very slim—I was going to say "lank"—yes, I think I will leave it at that. He wore a long flowing red moustache and sat (or rather reclined) in a lean-back chair with his feet up on the desk the entire day, and from that position he dictated the news to the manifold writers. We boys considered Mr. Jones the boss. He knew each of us by name and tried to keep us in some kind of order, but when you think of the capabilities of a dozen or more "gentlemen" ranging in age from 14 to 16 years, you can readily see the tough job he had. In order to cope with the situation he instituted a system of fines

---

John C. Gerrity, at age 14, worked as a messenger for Dow, Jones beginning June 6, 1884. His six-day-a-week job paid him $5. Gerrity recounted his early experiences in this letter to The Wall Street Journal *64 years after his initial employment. It was published August 27, 1948.*

to be applied to those guilty of breach of the peace. He would mark the fine against the offender on a piece of scrap paper and put it on his file. These fines were supposed to be deducted from the erring youth's pay at the end of the period. But whatever became of those slips will never be known, because I've never heard of any boy getting a split pay envelope. (Wages $5.00 per week).

Mr. Bergstresser—not as large or tall as either of his partners. Like Mr. Dow, he had jet-black hair and a beard. He had a quiet disposition, but carried much weight with the boys. He knew each of us, and when Mr. B. told anyone to do anything, that thing was done. His duties were outside, gathering news.

All three could be called young men, with the ages running down in the order of names—Dow, Jones, Bergstresser.

Mr Bergstresser and a Mr. James King were the chief news gatherers But any other person could bring in any story they heard and Mr. Jones would send either Mr. Bergstresser of Mr. King to verify it. There were four or five manifold writers to whom Mr. Jones dictated. They wrote on books of tissue paper with carbon paper between each two sheets (the carbon paper had carbon on both sides). They used agateware stencils and produced around 26 copies a writing.

Each writer had his own boys assigned to him and arranged the news sheets according to the number of customers on the various routes. As soon as we came in from a delivery we looked on our place and, if there were more sheets we immediately started out again. A route covered from 8 to 12 customers.

A 4-page printed news sheet was delivered the last thing each day. This letter could be subscribed for separately at $1.50 per month—the full news service was (I think) $15. A commission of 50c was given for receiving a subscriber to the letter—$15 commission for the full news (?)

I was always mad at Jim King, because I secured Mr. Morton of Morton, Bliss & Co. for the letter and was trying him out

for the news when I learned that Jim King had landed that commission.

An instance of how news came in—The Wall Street Bank, or Bank of Wall Street was situated at the Mills Building, 15 Broad Street, and the boy who delivered on that route noticed a man closing the door of the bank. He waited for no further information but dashed into our office to Mr. Jones with just that news. Jones jumped up, yelling "Hey, Buggy—Hey, King—get out there quick." The boy was right. The bank was closed.

Railroad earnings were items of very great importance. Each month the various front line roads reported their earnings for that period. As that news came in a shout of "earnings!" caused everyone to drop what he was doing and turn to his part of getting out "Earnings" as a "rush". (Incidentally, I don't think there was anything on the ticker at that time but railroad bonds and stocks.)

Grover Cleveland was elected President in November 1884—the first Democrat in 24 years, and—as election returns were not compiled as promptly as they are today, we had a very busy and hectic session the day after election.

~~You will notice that at no time have I~~ mentioned "telephone"—We had none

By the way, there was another news agency at the corner of Broad and Wall. No. 2 Broad Street — the Kiernan News Company Mr. Kiernan was then, or had been, a member of the New York State Senate from Brooklyn. However, we paid very little attention to Kiernan's, since they paid the boys only $4 per week.

One customer I delivered to for a while, was R. P. Flower & Company, Exchange Court Building at Broadway and Exchange Place. I mention this because in 1891, the year of my first vote, I cast it for Mr. R. P. Flower who was elected Governor of New York State—and I very proudly notified my friends that I was personally acquainted with the new Governor.

JOHN C. GERRITY.

New York City

There were also no by-lines for the articles appearing either in the *Customer's Afternoon Letter* or the early editions of *The Wall Street Journal*. The anonymity surrounding Dow and his publications may be due in part to a desire to avoid possible legal action.

Edward D. Jones, his partner, pointed out that the type of reporting could cause problems. In writing of Dow, Jones said: "he was always a ceaseless searcher for facts, and the best way to tell and to distribute them. He was a tower of strength in our early struggles to force reluctant railroad managers to protect the speculating public from swindlers in and out of Wall Street."

Lloyd Wendt's book discussed the sale of Dow, Jones & Company to Clarence W. Barron in 1902. Wendt noted that Dow owned only 10 shares of his company stock in contrast to his wife's 3,400 shares.[22] Wendt comments: "Many owners of stocks at the time 'judgment proofed' themselves by putting their company ownerships in their wive's names. Thus, should the company lose a lawsuit for damages, only the company and its assets would be risked, since the wife owned no other tangible property."[23] A further indication of concern for secrecy is the fact that even the names of the senior executives did not appear in *The Wall Street Journal* until after the Barron transaction. Immediately following the sale on March 14, 1902, the *Journal* masthead listed four names:

Charles H. Dow

Charles M. Bergstresser

Thomas F. Woodlock

J. W. Barney, Business Manager[24]

In spite of the secrecy, there is sufficient evidence to support Dow's sole authorship of the averages as well as his theory on forecasting market moves. Two individuals who personally knew Dow and his writings published books about his contributions. William Peter Hamilton, fourth editor of *The Wall Street Journal*, was hired by Dow, Jones & Company in 1899. In 1922 he wrote: "It has been my lot to discuss these averages in print for many years past, on the tested theory of the late Charles H. Dow, the founder of *The Wall Street Journal*.[25] Hamilton wrote of his relationship with Dow, "Knowing and liking Dow, with whom I worked in the last years of his life."[26]

Dow himself never gave a name to his market concepts. It was S. A. Nelson who coined the term *Dow's Theory*. In the preface of his 1902 book on stock speculation, Nelson pointed out that efforts were made to have Dow write about his views "dealing with the principles governing stock speculation":

> Following the publication of *The ABC of Wall Street* there were many requests for a book dealing with the principles governing stock speculation. If there is one man better qualified than another to produce such a book that man is Mr. Charles H. Dow. Several attempts were made to have him write the desired volume but they were unavailing. From time to time in his Wall Street career, extending over a quarter of a century, Mr. Dow has carefully evolved his theories of successful stock speculation.[27]

Thomas F. Woodlock, second editor of *The Wall Street Journal*, also pointed out Dow's interest in the stock market. He worked with him from 1892 until Dow died in 1902. Woodlock, in a 1932 article, said, "Dow attended to the stock market end of the news and wrote the stock market gossip. He was well and favorably known in all of the important stockbroker offices of the day." The entire article recounting the early days of Dow, Jones & Company appears in Appendix E and is titled "Pioneer Financial News Trio Recalled By Sole Survivor of 1892 Local Staff."[28]

What enabled Dow to be so productive in his chosen field? We are all imprisoned to a degree by our life spans—we are locked into the economic, political, military, and technological events that shape the times. An examination of Figure 1–11 indicates that Charles H. Dow's life of 51 years was relatively short, based on today's standards. His formal schooling was limited. But he could write well and concentrated at a young age on his lifetime profession—journalism. Dow was fortunate to come under the tutelage of two distinguished New England editors for a 10-year period beginning in 1869.

The 10-year apprenticeship in Providence and Springfield gave Dow the credentials to launch his successful career in New York City. Just before leaving Providence in 1879, he visited the Colorado silver mines. This experience sparked his interest in financial affairs as apparent from the "Leadville Letters" appearing in the *Providence Journal*.

Dow created and published his first stock average five years after arriving in New York. And the Dow Jones Industrial Average was born in 1896. Three years later he printed the first article in *The Wall Street Journal* on his market concepts. He nursed his theory and averages through infancy but he died before either became well known.

FIGURE 1–11 Life Span of Charles H. Dow 1851–1902, Pictorial Highlights (with Stillman's significant political, military, technological, and economic events)

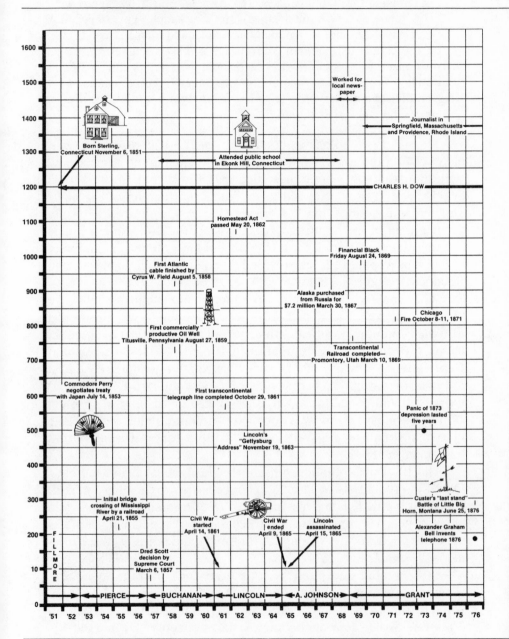

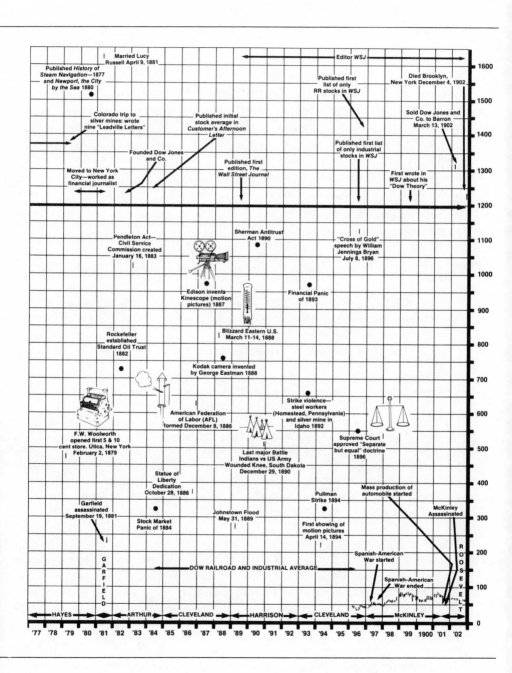

Married Lucy
Russell April 9, 1881

Published *History of
Steam Navigation*—1877
and *Newport, the City
by the Sea* 1880

Editor *WSJ*

Published first
list of only
RR stocks in *WSJ*

Died Brooklyn,
New York December 4, 1902

Colorado trip to
silver mines: wrote
nine "Leadville Letters"

Published initial
stock average in
*Customer's Afternoon
Letter*

Sold Dow Jones and
Co. to Barron
March 13, 1902

Founded Dow Jones
and Co.

Published first list
of only industrial
stocks in *WSJ*

Moved to New York
City—worked as
financial journalist

Published first
edition, *The
Wall Street Journal*

First wrote in
WSJ about his
"Dow Theory"

Pendleton Act—
Civil Service
Commission created
January 16, 1883

Sherman Antitrust
Act 1890

"Cross of Gold"
speech by William
Jennings Bryan
July 8, 1896

Edison invents
Kinescope (motion
pictures) 1887

Financial Panic
of 1893

Rockefeller
established
Standard Oil Trust
1882

Blizzard Eastern U.S.
March 11-14, 1888

Kodak camera invented
by George Eastman 1888

Strike violence—
steel workers
(Homestead, Pennsylvania)
and silver mine in
Idaho 1892

American Federation
of Labor (AFL)
formed December 8, 1886

Supreme Court
approved "Separate
but equal" doctrine
1896

F.W. Woolworth
opened first 5 & 10
cent store. Utica, New York
February 2, 1879

Last major Battle
Indians vs US Army
Wounded Knee, South Dakota
December 29, 1890

Statue of
Liberty
Dedication
October 28, 1886

Pullman
Strike 1894

Mass production of
automobile started

Garfield
assassinated
September 19, 1881

Stock Market
Panic of 1884

Johnstown Flood
May 31, 1889

First showing of
motion pictures
April 14, 1894

McKinley
Assassinated

G
A
R
F
I
E
L
D

R
O
O
S
E
V
E
L
T

DOW RAILROAD AND INDUSTRIAL AVERAGE

Spanish-American
War started

Spanish-American
War ended

HAYES   ARTHUR   CLEVELAND   HARRISON   CLEVELAND   McKINLEY

'77 '78 '79 '80 '81 '82 '83 '84 '85 '86 '87 '88 '89 '90 '91 '92 '93 '94 '95 '96 '97 '98 '99 1900 '01 '02

1600
1500
1400
1300
1200
1100
1000
900
800
700
600
500
400
300
200
100
0

Dow deserved credit not only for his creativity but also for the ability to select qualified people who would carry on the principles he established for *The Wall Street Journal*. If we study the events which affected Dow's life (Figure 1–11) we can see he lived through the turbulence of two wars, several panics, three presidential assassinations, numerous violent strikes, and significant technological progress. His life is portrayed in Figure 1–11 as enclosed on three sides to reflect entrapment within his lifetime. However, the top of Figure 1–11 is open to reflect man's capacity to make contributions to future generations. Dow left a legacy of his theory and his averages. In the chapters ahead we shall examine both in further detail.

It is significant to recognize that the nation's political environment permitted Dow to achieve his goals. Dow could not have accomplished what he did without a free enterprise system.

NOTES

¹This forerunner of *The Wall Street Journal* has been referred to as *Customer's Afternoon Letter, Customer's Afternoon News Letter, Customers' Afternoon News Letter,* and collectively as *Dow Jones Letters.*

²The St. Paul Railroad became a part of the Chicago, Milwaukee and St. Paul Railroad.

³Chicago, Burlington and Quincy; Chicago, Rock Island and Pacific; and American Sugar replaced Lake Shore Railroad, New York Central, and Pacific Mail Steamship.

⁴Dow compiled a 20-stock average between September 23, 1889, and October 24, 1896. It consisted of 18 railroad stocks and 2 industrials. Beginning October 26, 1896, he published a list of 20 stocks containing only railroads.

⁵Daily trading volume on listed and unlisted issues varied from 100,000 to 350,000 shares. Stocks were traded six days a week.

⁶The initial article Dow sent to the *Providence Journal,* titled "En Route for Leadville," was dated from New York (May 21, 1879) and published May 26, 1879.

⁷*The Wall Street Journal,* July 9, 1902, p. 3.

⁸Ibid.

⁹*Providence Star, Providence Evening Press,* and *Providence Journal.*

¹⁰*The Wall Street Journal,* December 5, 1902, p. 1.

¹¹Three years later Dow published his only other book, titled *Newport: The City by the Sea* (Providence, R.I.: John F. Sanborn, 1880). An earlier version appeared as an article in the *Providence Journal* on May 22, 1879. This 120-page writing established Dow as a respected historian.

¹²Dow referred to his publication as an article: "Such is an outline history of steam navigation on Narragansett Bay. The *Journal* extends its thanks to those

who have taken an interest in the preparation of this article'' (p. 29). It was initially published in the *Providence Journal* on April 23, 1877.

[13]Charles H. Dow *History of Steam Navigation between New York & Providence* (Providence, R.I.: William Turner & Company, 1877), p. 28.

[14]Dow himself used the word *letter* in referring to a previous article he had written.

[15]*The Wall Street Journal*, December 5, 1902, p. 1.

[16]Dow was a partner in the brokerage house of Goodbody, Glyn & Dow from 1885 to 1891. He held this partnership while writing initially for the *Customer's Afternoon Letter* and later for *The Wall Street Journal*. Today this would be considered a conflict of interest.

[17]"New Home for 50th Birthday," *The Wall Street Journal*, June 27, 1932, section 3, p. 1.

[18]*The Wall Street Journal*, July 8, 1889, p. 3.

[19]Stock market quotes were all on a percentage basis until October 13, 1915. At that time the New York Stock Exchange required that all stocks sell on a dollar share basis.

[20]"Death List of a Day," *New York Times* obituary column on Charles H. Dow, December 5, 1902.

[21]*The Wall Street Journal*, December 5, 1902.

[22]Dow married Lucy Martin Russell on April 9, 1881. While she had a daughter by a previous marriage, they had no children together. Bergstresser married Lucy's cousin, Helen Russell, in 1889.

[23]Lloyd Wendt, *The Wall Street Journal* (Chicago, Ill.: Rand McNally, 1982), p. 80.

[24]*The Wall Street Journal*, March 15, 1902, p. 2.

[25]*The Stock Market Barometer*, (New York: Harper & Row, 1922), p. 4.

[26]Ibid. p. 22. Hamilton followed Thomas F. Woodlock (1902–05) and Sereno S. Pratt (1905–08) as editor. He remained with the Journal until his death in 1929.

[27]Samuel A. Nelson, *The ABC of Stock Speculation* (New York: S. A. Nelson, 1902), preface.

[28]*The Wall Street Journal*, June 27, 1932, section 3, p. 1. Woodlock left Dow, Jones in 1905 and returned to the firm 25 years later as an associate editor.

Charles Henry Dow (1851–1902) was a founder of Dow, Jones & Company in 1882. He created the Dow Jones Industrial Average in 1896.

Edward Davis Jones (1856–1921) was a founder of Dow, Jones & Company in 1882.

Charles Milford Bergstresser (1859–1923) was a founder of Dow Jones & Company in 1882. The designation founder is debatable. There is no question, however, that Bergstresser was a partner, along with Charles H. Dow and Edward B. Jones, during the firm's formative years.

*Clarence Walker Barron (1855–1928) bought Dow, Jones & Company from Dow
and other stockholders in 1902 for $130,000. He began publication of* Barron's *in
1921.*

Jessie Waldron Barron (1851–1918) was the wife of C. W. Barron and chairman of the board of directors of Dow, Jones & Company from 1902 to 1912. She married her husband in 1900, at age 49. Her two daughters, Jane and Martha, were adopted by Barron.

Dow, Jones & Company opened for business in November of 1882 in a one-room office at 15 Wall Street. This was its home from 1882 to 1886. John C. Gerrity wrote that it was located in "a little ramshackle building next door to the entrance of the Stock Exchange. I think it was only two stories and basement. A flight of stairs led me down to a basement soda fountain, beside the serving counter of which was a narrow passageway to the rear of the building—in here was Dow, Jones & Company!" (see figure 1–10, p. 20).

This was the second home of Dow, Jones & Company at 26 Broad Street (from 1886 to 1889).

The third building occupied by Dow Jones (at extreme right) was located at 41 Broad Street. The company occupied this building from 1889 to 1893.

Dow, Jones & Company's fourth home was at 42–44 Broad Street (from 1893 to 1931). Note the names on the building—The Wall Street Journal and Dow Jones & Co. *The company temporarily moved to 130 Cedar Street in 1931, but returned to Broad Street in 1932 and remained there until 1972 when it moved to 22 Cortlandt Street. In 1986 it relocated to the World Financial Center at 200 Liberty Street.*

Hugh Bancroft (1880–1933) married Barron's stepdaughter, Jane Waldron Barron, in 1907. He began working for Dow Jones in 1906 and became president on Barron's death in 1928. Barron and Bancroft heirs currently own a controlling interest in Dow Jones with William C. Cox, Jr., Bettina Bancroft Klink, and Martha S. Griffith on the board of directors.

Warren H. Phillips, current chairman of the board and chief executive officer Dow Jones & Company, Inc. He was named president and a Dow Jones director in 1972, chief executive officer in 1975, and chairman of the board in 1978. His present Keeper of the Dow Jones Industrial Average is Charles N. Stabler.

A rarity, this signature of Dow appeared on the title page of History of Steam Navigation between New York and Providence.

First Press Used By Dow Jones (1887)

Dow, Jones & Company initially was organized as a financial news agency in order to provide the business community with financial news in the form of bulletins. The first bulletins were written in longhand. In 1887 a press was invented that enabled Dow Jones to print a one-page bulletin that was 5 by 9 inches in size.

DOW, JONES & CO.

FINANCIAL NEWS, 26 BROAD ST.

WEDNESDAY, AUGUST 10, 1887.　　No. 20

ERIE'S FLOATING DEBT.

The Erie balance sheet June 30, 1887, shows floating debt:

Bills payable	$684,000
Interest accrued	1,017,210
Dividends unpaid	7,038
Due for wages, supplies, etc.	1,898,939
Due companies	455,098
Due account traffic	774,608
Rentals, etc.	581,536
Erie Coal Company	207,637
Total gross	5,576,064

Continued.

2

Early History: 12 Stock Series (1896–1916)

We demand that big business give the people a square deal.
—*Theodore Roosevelt (1913)*

The following toast was proposed to honor an octogenarian event in the summer of 1985:

Happy 89th birthday DJIA! You have become an international celebrity since your humble 12-stock beginning on May 26, 1896. Some of your early followers were concerned about your health in view of your initial infrequent appearances in *The Wall Street Journal*. But your vigor prevailed and daily publication of the DJIA began in the autumn of 1896.

DOW'S 1896 INDUSTRIALS

Dow published his first list composed exclusively of industrial issues in the spring of 1896 (see Figure 2–1). However, the Dow Jones Industrial Average did not appear in *The Wall Street Journal* on a regular basis until October 7, 1896.[1] At that time, Dow had a limited number of active industrial issues to select from in arriving at his list of 12 (shown in Figure 2–2 on page 42). His average at that time was 35.30 in contrast to the present one over 1,550. The only stock from this list to appear in the current DJIA without having changed its name is General Electric. The composition of the Dow Average shortly before the turn of the century included

---

FIGURE 2–1   The Initial Dow Jones Industrials, May 26, 1896 (12 stocks)

Stocks

American Cotton Oil
American Sugar
American Tobacco
Chicago Gas
Distilling and Cattle Feeding
General Electric
Laclede Gas
National Lead
North American
Tennessee Coal & Iron
U.S. Leather preferred
U.S. Rubber

Dow Average (May 26, 1896)

$$40.94 \left(\frac{491.28}{12} \right)$$

These 12 stocks were selected by Dow for his initial industrial average. The list appeared in *The Wall Street Journal*, May 26, 1896.

two preferred issues. The companies listed dealt in sugar, spirits, leather, cordage, tobacco, gas, lead, rubber, coal, iron, and electrical products.

A look at today's list finds oils, steel, aluminum, autos, food, aerospace, trucks, restaurants, chemicals, drugs, department stores, computers, cigarettes, electrical equipment, soap and paper products, communications, glass, rubber, nickel, copper, tapes, abrasives, photographic apparatus, metal containers, travel services, and banking.

It is apparent that the present mix of corporations is markedly different from issues appearing in 1896. This variation mirrors the remarkable growth of the American economy. It also reflects the movement from an agrarian to urban society. The current demands of a sophisticated populace require the latest in technological products and an abundance of services. What will the DJIA list look like in another 89 years (2074)?

MODIFICATIONS PRIOR TO DOW'S DEATH

Dow lived little more than six years after placing his average in the *Journal* on a daily basis. During these formative years he made modifications on seven occasions. In late 1896 he replaced U.S.

FIGURE 2–2   Dow Jones Industrials, October 7, 1896 (12 stocks)

Stocks

American Cotton Oil
American Spirits Manufacturing
American Sugar
American Tobacco
Chicago Gas
General Electric
Laclede Gas
National Lead
Tennessee Coal & Iron
U.S. Cordage preferred
U.S. Leather preferred
U.S. Rubber

DJIA (October 7, 1896)

$$35.30 \left(\frac{423.60}{12} \right)$$

These 12 industrial stocks were selected by Dow on August 26, 1896. The daily movement of these issues first appeared on a regular basis in *The Wall Street Journal* beginning October 7, 1896. The October 7, 1896, *Journal* listed the industrials and rails as well as their daily movement as follows:

DAILY MOVEMENT OF AVERAGES.

Following is the daily average price of twenty railway stocks and twelve industrials for thirty days last passed:

	12 Indus	20 Railroads
Tuesday, Sept. 8	$35.50	$48.55
Wednesday, Sept. 9	35.39	48.56
Thursday, Sept. 10	34.58	47.71
Friday, Sept. 11	35.30	48.27
Saturday, Sept. 12	35.02	47.86
Monday, Sept. 14	34.86	47.66
Tuesday, Sept. 15	34.13	47.22
Wednesday, Sept. 16	33.72	46.68
Thursday, Sept. 17	34.35	47.77
Friday, Sept. 18	34.81	47.82
Saturday, Sept. 19	35.03	47.91
Monday, Sept. 21	35.53	48.65
Tuesday, Sept. 22	35.59	48.43
Wednesday, Sept. 23	35.78	48.67
Thursday, Sept. 24	36.23	49.16
Friday, Sept. 25	36.61	49.81
Saturday, Sept. 26	36.75	50.21
Monday, Sept. 28	36.35	49.80
Tuesday, Sept. 29	36.33	50.21
Wednesday, Sept. 30	36.05	50.31
Thursday, Oct. 1	36.01	50.17
Friday, Oct. 2	35.88	50.00
Saturday, Oct. 3	35.82	49.86
Monday, Oct. 5	35.92	50.10
Tuesday, Oct. 6	35.91	49.71

Twelve industrial stocks used are: Sugar, Tobacco, Leather pfd., Cotton Oil, Cordage pfd., Rubber com., Chicago Gas, Tennessee Coal & Iron, General Electric, Lead, American Spirits and Laclede Gas.

The twenty active stocks used are: Erie, Kansas & Texas pfd., Chesapeake & Ohio, Minneapolis & St. Louis 2d pfd., Susquehanna & Western pfd., New York Central, Atchison, C. C. C. & St. Louis, Southern Railway pfd., Missouri Pacific, Jersey Central, Pacific Mail, Northwest, Louisville & Nashville, Western Union, Rock Island, Burlington, St. Paul, Texas & Pacific and Lake Shore.

Rubber with Pacific Mail Steamship and U.S. Cordage preferred with Standard Rope & Twine. On March 24, 1898, he replaced Chicago Gas with People's Gas. General Electric was removed in the fall of 1898 and U.S. Rubber reappeared. Seven months later he added American Steel & Wire, Continental Tobacco, Federal Steel, and General Electric. The four eliminated included American Spirits Manufacturing, American Tobacco, Laclede Gas, and Standard Rope & Twine. His final changes in the average were made more than a year prior to his death. On April 1, 1901, he deleted American Cotton Oil, American Steel & Wire, Federal Steel, General Electric, and Pacific Mail Steamship. Additions included Amalgamated Copper, American Smelting & Refining, International Paper preferred, and U.S. Steel preferred. Continental Tobacco and International Paper preferred were removed on July 1 and replaced by American Car & Foundry and Colorado Fuel & Iron. Figure 2–3 presents the differing composition of the Industrial Average between October 7, 1896, and July 1, 1901.

MODIFICATIONS AFTER DOW

After Dow's death the succeeding editors made five modifications in the list of 12 stocks during the remaining years of its existence. These changes were: U.S. Rubber first preferred replaced U.S. Leather preferred, April 1, 1905; General Electric returned to the list and Tennessee Coal & Iron was removed, November 7, 1907; Colorado Fuel & Iron was eliminated and Central Leather added, May 12, 1912; and General Motors initially appeared March 16, 1915, while U.S. Rubber first preferred was deleted. The final modification in the 12-stock average occurred July 29, 1915, when Anaconda Copper replaced Amalgamated Copper. The composition of the Dow Industrials between 1905 and 1916 is shown in Figure 2–4. Note that the July 29, 1915, list included only four of the stocks originally selected by Dow on May 26, 1896—American Sugar, General Electric, National Lead, and U.S. Rubber. The 20-year life of the 12 stock series found frequent changes in the fortunes of young industrial corporations. The result was 12 modifications in the list by the editors of Dow, Jones & Company.

IMPACT OF WORLD WAR I

The New York Stock Exchange discontinued trading after the close of business on July 30, 1914, and did not reopen until December 12, 1914. The reason for the shutdown was the disruption of finan-

FIGURE 2–3 How the Configuration of the 12 Stocks Used for the Dow Jones Industrials Changed (October 7, 1896, to April 1, 1905)

October 7, 1896*

American Cotton Oil
American Spirits
 Manufacturing
American Sugar
American Tobacco
Chicago Gas
General Electric
Laclede Gas
National Lead
Tennessee Coal & Iron
U.S. Cordage preferred
U.S. Leather preferred
U.S. Rubber

March 24, 1898

American Cotton Oil
American Spirits
 Manufacturing
American Sugar
American Tobacco
General Electric
Laclede Gas
National Lead
Pacific Mail Steamship
People's Gas
Standard Rope & Twine
Tennessee Coal & Iron
U.S. Leather preferred

April 1, 1901

Amalgamated Copper
American Smelting &
 Refining
American Sugar
Continental Tobacco
International Paper
 preferred
National Lead
People's Gas
Tennessee Coal & Iron
U.S. Leather preferred
U.S. Rubber
U.S. Steel
U.S. Steel preferred

November 10, 1896

American Cotton Oil
American Spirits
 Manufacturing
American Sugar
American Tobacco
Chicago Gas
General Electric
Laclede Gas
National Lead
Pacific Mail Steamship
Tennessee Coal & Iron
U.S. Cordage preferred
U.S. Leather preferred

September 22, 1898

American Cotton Oil
American Spirits
 Manufacturing
American Sugar
American Tobacco
Laclede Gas
National Lead
Pacific Mail Steamship
People's Gas
Standard Rope & Twine
Tennessee Coal & Iron
U.S. Leather preferred
U.S. Rubber

July 1, 1901

Amalgamated Copper
American Car &
 Foundry
American Sugar
Colorado Fuel & Iron
National Lead
People's Gas
Tennessee Coal & Iron
U.S. Leather preferred
U.S. Rubber
U.S. Steel
U.S. Steel preferred

December 23, 1896

American Cotton Oil
American Spirits
 Manufacturing
American Sugar
American Tobacco
Chicago Gas
General Electric
Laclede Gas
National Lead
Pacific Mail Steamship
Standard Rope & Twine
Tennessee Coal & Iron
U.S. Leather preferred

April 21, 1899

American Cotton Oil
American Steel & Wire
American Sugar
Continental Tobacco
Federal Steel
General Electric
National Lead
Pacific Mail Steamship
People's Gas
Tennessee Coal & Iron
U.S. Leather preferred
U.S. Rubber

These 12 stocks were used by Dow to obtain his Industrial Average from its initial *regular* appearance October 7, 1896 in *The Wall Street Journal* until his death in 1902. The July 1, 1901 list remained unchanged until April 1, 1905.

*The October 7, 1896 list was first used to compute the DJIA on August 26, 1896, but the average appeared irregularly in the *Journal* until October 7, 1896.

FIGURE 2–4 How the Configuration of the 12 Stocks Used for the Dow Jones Industrials Changed (April 1, 1905 to September 30, 1916)

April 1, 1905

Amalgamated Copper
American Car & Foundry
American Smelting & Refining
American Sugar
Colorado Fuel & Iron
National Lead
People's Gas
Tennessee Coal & Iron
U.S. Rubber
U.S. Rubber first preferred
U.S. Steel
U.S. Steel preferred

March 16, 1915

Amalgamated Copper
American Car & Foundry
American Smelting & Refining
American Sugar
Central Leather
General Electric
General Motors
National Lead
People's Gas
U.S. Rubber
U.S. Steel
U.S. Steel preferred

November 7, 1907

Amalgamated Copper
American Car & Foundry
American Smelting & Refining
American Sugar
Colorado Fuel & Iron
General Electric
National Lead
People's Gas
U.S. Rubber
U.S. Rubber first preferred
U.S. Steel
U.S. Steel preferred

July 29, 1915

American Car & Foundry
American Smelting & Refining
American Sugar
Anaconda Copper
Central Leather
General Electric
General Motors
National Lead
People's Gas
U.S. Rubber
U.S. Steel
U.S. Steel preferred

May 12, 1912

Amalgamated Copper
American Car & Foundry
American Smelting & Refining
American Sugar
Central Leather
General Electric
National Lead
People's Gas
U.S. Rubber
U.S. Rubber first preferred
U.S. Steel
U.S. Steel preferred

cial markets which occurred at the beginning of World War I. The July 30, 1914, edition of the *Journal* carried the following information on the Industrial and Railway Averages:

DAILY MOVEMENT OF AVERAGES

Following is the daily average price of twenty active railway stocks and twelve industrials for period indicated:

	12 Industrials	20 Railways
Last high point..June 10, '14,	81.84	May 27 '14, 103.64
Last low point.. July 28, '14,	76.28	July 28, '14, 96.14

		12 Ind.	Adv.	Dec.	20 R. R.	Adv.	Dec.
Monday	....July 20	80.47		.16	98.30		2.12
Tuesday	....July 21	80.76	.35	..	98.77	.47	..
Wednesday	..July 22	80.83	.07	..	98.49	..	.28
Thursday	...July 23	80.62		.21	97.95	..	.54
Friday	....July 24	79.77	..	.81	97.05	..	.90
Saturday	...July 25	79.67		.01	97.16	.11	
Monday	..July 27	79.07		.60	96.58	..	.58
Tuesday	..July 28	76.28	..	2.79	93.14		3.44
Wednesday	..July 29	76.72	.44	..	94.12	.98	..

SOURCE *The Wall Street Journal*, July 30, 1914, p. 2.

After the New York Stock Exchange reopened on December 12, *The Wall Street Journal* made the following front-page announcement:

> As a convenience to our subscribers, in view of the plan to resume stock trading on the New York Stock Exchange today, *The Wall Street Journal* reprints on pages 6 and 7 of this issue the prices of stocks on July 30, the last day on which the Exchange was open for trading in stocks, together with the transactions in detail.[2]

At the start of World War I, *The Wall Street Journal* was published Monday through Saturday. There was both a morning and evening edition. The eight-page paper published by Dow, Jones & Company cost 5 cents. The masthead listed C. W. Barron, president; Hugh Bancroft, secretary and Joseph Cushman, treasurer. The *Journal* proudly informed readers that it was "The oldest news agency in Wall Street" and had "The largest circulation of the American financial papers."[3]

Advertisements continued to appear on the front page of the *Journal* in a manner similar to Dow's first edition on July 8, 1889. Roger W. Babson, noted economist, caught the attention of readers with the lead: "Should Business Men Buy Stocks?"

Liggett & Myers Tobacco Company had the largest ad in the paper. It indicated that a pack of 20 cigarettes sold for 15 cents.[4]

The new 20-stock average did not begin until September 30, 1916. The *Journal* continued to report only the 12-stock Industrial Average until that date. Its Market Diary and Daily Movement of Averages appeared as follows:

Should Business Men Buy Stocks?

As many disagree on this question, you will be
interested to see what

ROGER W. BABSON

has to say in his reply.

It is done up in an attractive little booklet that you can keep.
Send for it, there is no charge.

Address Dept. J-6

THE BABSON STATISTICAL ORGANIZATION
Wellesley Hills, Mass.

SOURCE   *The Wall Street Journal,* December 12, 1914, pp. 1 and 2.

MARKET DIARY

1216	1915
Friday, Sept. 29—Strong	Friday, Oct. 1—Irregular

(table continues below)

1,575,890	Sales of stocks	1,496,315
40,460,443	Since January 1	116,901,617
$5,280,000	Sales of bonds	$4,444,000
$769,806,000	Since January 1	$605,087,500

Price Up Off	Sales	Stocks	Sales Price Up Off
46% ⅛	47090	Amer. Can. 37400	64% ⅛
71⅞ 5⅛	33200	Am Car & F 25500	84 2
98⅛	47605	Anaconda 28900	74 ⅛
32⅛ 3⅛	79650	Cal. Fuel 51400	62⅛ 1⅛
95⅛ 1⅛	45080	Crucible St'l 21420	104⅛
44⅛ 2⅛	54450	Gt Nor Ore 26500	48⅞ ⅛
64⅛ 1	54400	Inter. Nickel 845	210 4⅛
122⅛ ⅛	44800	Marine pf	
82½ ⅛	73000	Rep Ir & St 26850	55⅛ 1⅛
120 1%	396600	U S Steel 280400	81 1⅛
62⅜ ⅛	48190	West'house 203800	132⅛ 7⅛
110.03 .27	Average 20 railroads	97.68 .25	
156.67 1.55	Average 12 industrials	112.78 2.54	
1.34⅛ ⅛	Chicago December wheat	95⅛ * ⅛	
58⅛ ⅛	Chicago September corn	58⅛ * 1⅛	
12.82 2	New York October cotton	11 79 8	
9.30 5	New York December coffee 6.15		
2⅛⅝ ⅛	Call money renewals	2% ⅛	
2@2½%	Time money	2⅛ @3%	
3⅛@3⅜%	Commercial paper	3@4%	
4.86 7-16	Sight sterling	4.77½	
4.75 11-16	Demand sterling	4.72	
*December.		

DAILY MOVEMENT OF AVERAGES

Following is the daily average price of twenty railway stocks and twelve industrials for the period indicated:

	12 Industrials	20 Railways
Last high point	Sep. 29, '16, 156.67	Sep. 27, '16, 110.26
Last low point	July 30, '14, 71.42	Dec. 24, '14, 87.40

	12 Ind. Adv. Dec.	20 R. R. Adv. Dec.
Tues.	Sep. 26 152.24 1.46	109.25 .80
Wed.	Sep. 27 155.77 3.43	110.26 .90
Thur.	Sep. 28 155.12 .65	109.76 .50
Fri.	Sep. 29 156.67 1.55	110.03 .27

SOURCE   *The Wall Street Journal,* December 12, 1914, p. 1 and 2.

THE 1896–1916 ERA

How did Dow's 12-stock average of industrials perform during the period from 1896 to 1916? A look at Figure 2–5 indicates that it varied about 128 points over this 20-year period. Its lowest point was 28.48 on August 8, 1896, and the Dow high exceeded 156 (156.67) on September 29, 1916. The bleak financial year of 1896 saw this stock barometer drop below 30. Why was there such a marked variation during this era when there was limited change in the last period we examined? For observations on 10 years of this period (1897–1907), let us look at the views of W. P. Hamilton, an early editor of *The Wall Street Journal:*

> Only with the first election of McKinley did the country emerge into a state of sanity and light. It had tried out the Populist follies—free silver and all the rest of them—and found that they pointed in the direction of national bankruptcy. Politicians were terrified at the results of their rash enactments. For 10 years, between 1897 and 1907, the paralyzing head of politics was removed from the business of the United States. We never had such a period of prosperity, before or since. The railroad development in that time was greater than it had ever been before. It was a decade which saw the broadest and most beneficent industrial amalgamations, of which the United States Steel Corporation is the outstanding example. It was a time when the cost of living was upon the whole low, although it was rising in the latter part of the 10-year period. It was a time when wages were good, not merely in their amount as expressed in dollars and cents, but in their purchasing power.[5]

The prosperous period Hamilton spoke of came to an abrupt halt with the financial panic of 1907. As Figure 2–5 indicates, the Dow Industrials declined to 53 from a high of 103 less than two years earlier. However, by the fall of 1909 it once again broke the 100 barrier. The start of World War I found the Dow at 71. After the New York Stock Exchange reopened on December 12, 1914, the 12 stocks stood at 74.56. Less than two years later the average peaked at 156.67 (September 29, 1916). The dozen members of the Dow series closed at 155.13 on September 30, 1916. The new 20-stock series was first listed in the *Journal* on October 4, 1916, but its daily average was traced back to the reopening of the NYSE on December 12, 1914. It is apparent from a study of Figures 2–6 and 2–7 that the 12-stock average exceeded the newly expanded series.[6] *However, the up and down movement reflects similar patterns.*

FIGURE 2–5 Dow Jones Industrial Average: 1896–1916 (with Stillman's significant political, military, economic and technological events)

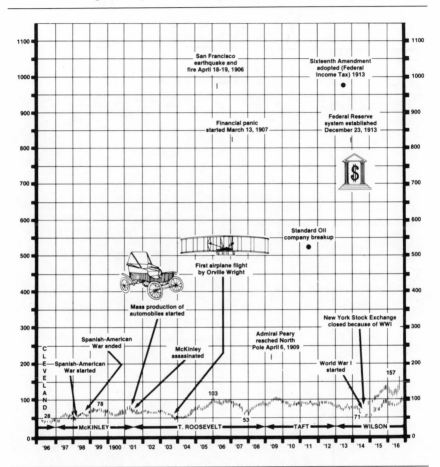

FIGURE 2–6 Monthly Highs and Lows of the 12- and 20-Stock Industrial Averages (December 12, 1914 to September 30, 1916)

	1914–20 Stocks		1914–12 Stocks		1915–20 Stocks		1915–12 Stocks		1916–20 Stocks		1916–12 Stocks	
	Low	High	Low	High	Low	High	Low	High	Low	High	Low	High
January					54.63	58.52	74.65	78.41	90.58	98.81	120.23	128.19
February					54.22	57.83	73.18	76.58	90.89	96.15	120.15	126.02
March					55.29	61.30	74.76	82.14	90.52	96.08	118.15	125.64
April					61.05	71.78	82.51	90.91	84.96	94.46	109.92	122.84
May					60.38	71.51	82.46	90.78	87.71	92.62	112.91	127.77
June					64.86	71.90	84.16	91.94	87.68	93.61	119.84	129.42
July					67.88	75.79	87.27	93.12	86.42	90.53	116.72	125.28
August					76.46	81.95	92.92	99.51	88.15	93.83	121.53	132.60
September					80.40	90.58	100.12	114.05	91.19	103.73	126.21	156.67
October					88.23	96.46	111.91	121.29				
November					91.08	97.56	116.79	127.04				
December	53.17	56.76	73.48	76.86	94.78	99.21	125.28	134.00				

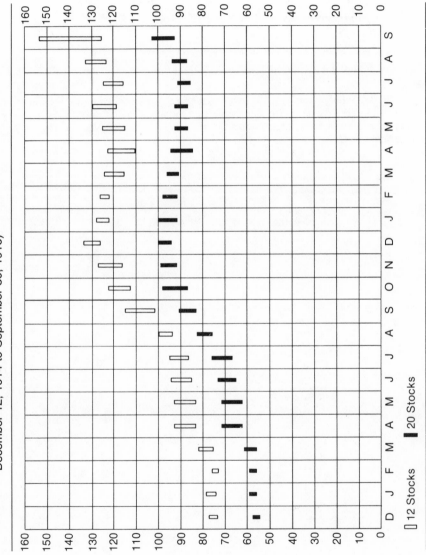

FIGURE 2-7 Comparative Monthly Movement of the Dow Industrials (12 and 20 stock series from December 12, 1914 to September 30, 1916)

☐ 12 Stocks   ▮ 20 Stocks

SOURCE © Copyright 1986 by Richard J. Stillman. All Rights Reserved.

NOTES

[1]The May 26, 1896, list of 12 stocks included Distilling & Cattle Feeding and North American. These were the first two companies to be replaced in the DJIA. They were replaced by American Spirits Manufacturing and U.S. Cordage preferred on August 26, 1896.

[2]*The Wall Street Journal,* December 12, 1914, p. 1.

[3]Ibid., p. 2.

[4]Liggett & Myers did not make the Dow Industrial list until July 18, 1930.

[5]William Peter Hamilton, *The Stock Market Barometer* (Harper & Row, 1922), p. 215.

[6]R. W. Schabacker, in 1930, wrote that "In a study of the matter over a period of several years the Harvard Economic Review has shown the old average to be very near 33⅓ percent higher than the new index" (Stock Market Theory and Practice), p. 829.

3

Mid Years: 20 Stock Series (1916–1928)

The business of America is business.
—*Calvin Coolidge (January 17, 1925)*

EXPANDED 20 STOCK SERIES

The expanded 20 stocks comprising the Dow Industrials first appeared in *The Wall Street Journal* in the fall of 1916. The new list contained 8 stocks from the old 12 stock series plus 12 new corporations (see Figure 3–1). The companies deleted from the list were General Motors, National Lead, People's Gas, and U.S. Steel preferred. The elimination of U.S. Steel preferred meant that for the first time, the list was composed exclusively of common stocks. Newcomers were American Beet Sugar, American Can, American Locomotive, American Telephone & Telegraph, Baldwin Locomotive, Goodrich, Republic Iron & Steel, Studebaker, Texas Company, Utah Copper, Westinghouse, and Western Union. Hindsight indicates that over the years the *Journal* editors have selected a cross section of long-term winners and losers. For example, if a person had followed a "buy-and-hold investment concept" in 1916 for each of the 20 industrials on the list, he would have both won rich rewards and suffered dramatic losses.

The 20 stock series appeared in the *Journal* initially on Wednesday, October 4, 1916. However, the 20 stock series was traced back to December 12, 1914 (date the NYSE reopened). On December 12, 1914, the list of 20 stood at 54.62 in comparison to 74.56 for

FIGURE 3-1   Dow Jones Industrials: Initial List of 20 Stocks Compared to the Final List of 12 Stocks

20 Stocks—October 4, 1916	12 Stocks—September 30, 1916
American Beet Sugar	American Car & Foundry
American Can	American Smelting & Refining
American Car & Foundry	American Sugar
American Locomotive	Anaconda Copper
American Smelting & Refining	Central Leather
American Sugar	General Electric
American Telephone & Telegraph	General Motors
Anaconda Copper	National Lead
Baldwin Locomotive	People's Gas
Central Leather	U.S. Rubber
General Electric	U.S. Steel
Goodrich	U.S. Steel preferred
Republic Iron & Steel	
Studebaker	
Texas Company	
U.S. Rubber	
U.S. Steel	
Utah Copper	
Western Union	
Westinghouse	

the 12 series. At the end of September, 1916 the old 12-stock average closed at 155.13 in contrast to 102.90 for the 20 stocks.

Figures 2–6 and 2–7 help explain the wide variation (during the period from December 12, 1914, to September 30, 1916) in the monthly movements of the two series. The disparity between the old and new stock series occurred because the 12-stock list contained higher-priced issues. The 12 stocks also had a slightly better growth rate during this 21½-month period (74.56 to 155.13 versus 54.62 to 102.90).[1] Even a change of one company in the Dow Industrials can make a significant difference in the average. AT&T, for instance, was substituted for IBM in 1939. If IBM had not been removed, the Dow would have been considerably higher during the 40 years it was excluded from the DJIA.[2] As a matter of fact, if IBM had not been removed, the Dow barrier of 1,000 would have been broken in 1961 instead of in 1972.

The *Journal* editors expanded the list because they felt it desirable to have a greater number of companies in the DJIA in order to represent a better cross section of the stock market. The number of actively traded issues had increased markedly since 1896. Furthermore, five major industries were not represented on the list of 12—oil, rubber, locomotives, containers, and communications. The reason for the series' overlap of 21½ months (see Figure 2–6 and 2–7) was based on a desire to provide comparative information for followers of the Dow. This overlap did not occur in actuality: the 12-stock average appeared in *The Wall Street Journal* until the new series replaced it on Wednesday, October 4, 1916. It was only later that the trace back of the 20 series occurred.[3]

THE 1916–1928 ERA

A look at Figure 3–3 indicates that Dow's 20-stock average varied about 178 points during the period from 1916 to 1928. Its low was 63.90 on August 24, 1921, and the Dow high approached 242 on September 7, 1928. In the year of the Harding administration the Dow average dropped below 64. The Dow dipped to 66 a few months after Wilson brought the United States into World War I. However, the Allied military victory in 1918 and the pent-up demand for consumer goods helped the average reach 120 in late 1919. But less than two years later it dropped to nearly half its previous high. Hamilton, editor of the *Journal* at that time, presented his views on the reasons for the sharp decline of the stock market:

> With the demoralized condition of European finance, the disaster to the cotton crop, the uncertainties produced by deflation, the unprincipled opportunism of our lawmakers and tax-imposers, all the aftermath of war inflation—unemployment, uneconomic wages in coal mining and railroading—with all these things overhanging the business of the country at the present moment, the stock market has acted as if there were better things in sight.[4]

MODIFICATIONS IN THE 20 STOCK SERIES

During the life of the 20 stock series, ordinary modifications were made on eight occasions.[5] Figure 3–2 presents the differing composition of the 20-stock list between 1920 and 1927. Besides the usual modifications, the 20-stock list was subject to another kind of modification. For the first time, the *Journal* editors were faced with stock splits in several issues of the stock series. While the editors had to acknowledge the splits, they desired to maintain the divisor at 20 for arriving at the daily DJIA. This was accomplished

March 1, 1920	May 12, 1924	December 31, 1925
American Can	American Can	Allied Chemical
American Car & Foundry	American Car & Foundry	American Can
American Locomotive	American Locomotive	American Car & Foundry
American Smelting	American Smelting	American Locomotive
American Sugar	American Sugar	American Smelting
American Telephone & Telegraph	American Telephone & Telegraph	American Sugar
Anaconda Copper	American Tobacco	American Telephone & Telegraph
Baldwin Locomotive	Anaconda Copper	American Tobacco
Central Leather	Baldwin Locomotive	General Electric
Corn Products	Du Pont	General Motors
General Electric	General Electric	International Harvester
Goodrich	Mack Trucks	Mack Trucks
Republic Iron & Steel	Sears Roebuck & Co.	Paramount Famous Lasky
Studebaker	Standard Oil of California	Remington Typewriter
Texas Company	Studebaker non-par	Sears Roebuck & Co.
U.S. Rubber	U.S. Rubber	Texas Co.
U.S. Steel	U.S. Steel	U.S. Rubber
Utah Copper	Western Union	U.S. Steel
Western Union	Westinghouse	Western Union
Westinghouse	Woolworth	Woolworth

January 22, 1924	August 31, 1925	March 16, 1927
American Can	American Can	Allied Chemical
American Car & Foundry	American Car & Foundry	American Can
American Locomotive	American Locomotive	American Car & Foundry
American Smelting	American Smelting	American Locomotive
American Sugar	American Sugar	American Smelting
American Telephone & Telegraph	American Telephone & Telegraph	American Sugar
American Tobacco	American Tobacco	American Telephone & Telegraph
Anaconda Copper	General Electric	American Tobacco
Baldwin Locomotive	General Motors	General Electric
Du Pont	International Harvester	General Motors
General Electric	Kennecott	International Harvester
Mack Trucks	Mack Trucks	Mack Trucks
Republic Iron & Steel	Sears Roebuck & Co.	Paramount Famous Lasky
Sears Roebuck & Co.	Texas Co.	Sears Roebuck & Co.
Studebaker	U.S. Realty	Texas Co.
U.S. Rubber	U.S. Rubber	United Drug
U.S. Steel	U.S. Steel	U.S. Rubber
Utah Copper	Western Union	U.S. Steel
Western Union	Westinghouse	Western Union
Westinghouse	Woolworth	Woolworth

February 6, 1924	December 7, 1925	
American Can	Allied Chemical	
American Car & Foundry	American Can	
American Locomotive	American Car & Foundry	
American Smelting	American Locomotive	
American Sugar	American Smelting	
American Telephone & Telegraph	American Sugar	
American Tobacco	American Telephone & Telegraph	
Anaconda Copper	American Tobacco	
Baldwin Locomotive	General Electric	
Du Pont	General Motors	
General Electric	International Harvester	
Mack Trucks	Kennecott	
Republic Iron & Steel	Mack Trucks	
Sears Roebuck & Co.	Paramount Famous Lasky	
Standard Oil of California	Sears Roebuck & Co.	
Studebaker	Texas Co.	
U.S. Rubber	U.S. Rubber	
U.S. Steel	U.S. Steel	
Western Union	Western Union	
Westinghouse	Woolworth	

FIGURE 3-3 Dow Jones Industrial Average: 1916–1928 (with Stillman's significant political, military, economic and technological events)

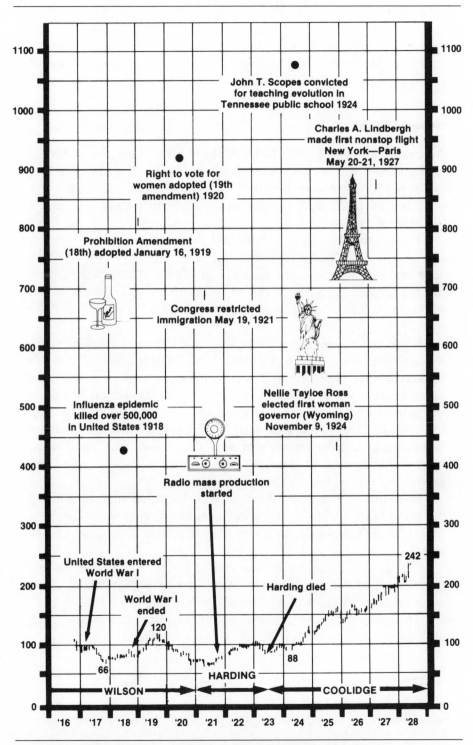

by giving extra weight to the companies that had stock splits. For example, when American Tobacco split 2 for 1, its price after the split was multiplied by two. Other weighted issues included American Can (Multiplier six), American Car & Foundry (two), General Electric (four), and Sears Roebuck & Co. (four).

THE ROARING 20S

An examination of Figure 3–3 will show that a long rise occurred in the Dow a few months after Coolidge took office. From a low of 88 in 1924 it rose to nearly 242 by September 1928. This 154 point rise in the 20 stocks took place in an environment well suited to corporate growth.

The roaring 20s were a delightful period in American history. Our country was not involved in any major military conflict. The economy was booming. Movie stars, athletes, and adventurers were the heroes and heroines of the era. Charles A. Lindbergh, at 25, made the first solo nonstop airplane flight from New York to Paris in 1927.

It was the "Golden Age" of sports. Babe Ruth reigned supreme in baseball as the "Sultan of Swat." Jack Dempsey beat all comers in boxing until Gene Tunney, the handsome ex-Marine, took the heavyweight title from him in 1926. Over 120,000 people attended the fight in Philadelphia. Gertrude Ederle became the first woman to swim the English Channel in 1925. William T. Tilden and Helen Wills dominated the tennis world. Bobby Jones was undisputed king of golfdom. Red Grange, "the galloping ghost," ruled the gridiron.

Box office attractions at the movies included such household names as Mary Pickford, Douglas Fairbanks, Gloria Swanson, Tom Mix, Charlie Chaplin, John Barrymore, Rudolph Valentino, and Al Jolson.

The political climate of the 20s provided fertile soil for big business. It was an era of laissez-faire[6]—an era personified by President Coolidge's remark that "The business of America is business."[7]

The prosperous 20s continued to be reflected in a rising DJIA after the transition from a 20- to 30-stock average.[8]

NOTES

[1]All stock quotations on the New York Stock Exchange were listed on a percentage basis through October 11, 1915. However, effective Monday, October

13, 1915, the NYSE required all listed corporate securities to be reported on a dollar per share basis.

[2]IBM did not return to the DJIA until June 29, 1979.

[3]Remember that the NYSE was closed between July 30 and December 11, 1914. Thus, it was convenient to retrace the 20 series to the reopening date of December 12.

[4]William Peter Hamilton, *Barron's*, November 5, 1921, p. 3.

[5]The first change came on March 1, 1920, when Corn Products replaced American Beet Sugar. The *Journal* made no substitutions in its list for nearly four years after that. Then on January 22, 1924, it added American Tobacco, Du Pont, Mack Trucks, and Sears Roebuck & Co. The stocks removed included Corn Products, Central Leather, Goodrich, and Texas Co. Fifteen days later Standard Oil of California replaced Utah Copper. Woolworth made the list for the first time on May 12, 1924. At this time Studebaker nonpar also replaced Studebaker $100 par. Republic Iron & Steel was eliminated. On August 31, 1925, five changes occurred. General Motors, International Harvester, Kennecott, Texas Company, and U.S. Realty replaced Anaconda Copper, Baldwin Locomotive, Du Pont, Standard Oil of California, and Studebaker. Allied Chemical and Paramount Famous Lasky were added on December 7, 1925. U.S. Realty and Westinghouse Electric were eliminated. And on the last day of 1925, Remington Typewriter replaced Kennecott Copper. The final change in the 20 series took place on March 16, 1927, when United Drug replaced Remington Typewriter.

[6]A dogma that believes the less the government interferes in economic matters the better. However, appropriate protection of property and individual rights was expected.

[7]Speech before the Society of American Newspaper Editors in Washington, D.C. on January 17, 1925.

[8]On closer examination the primary beneficiaries of the prosperous 20s were white males. Other people were often excluded from opportunities. For example, neither females nor blacks were welcomed at such diverse educational institutions as the Harvard Business School, West Point, and the University of Florida.

4

Current Period: 30 Stock Series (1928–1985)

The test of our progress is not whether we add more to the abundance of those who have much; it is whether we provide enough for those who have too little.
—*Franklin D. Roosevelt (January 20, 1937)*

THE UPDATED 30 SERIES

The present 30 stock series comprising the Dow Industrials first appeared in *The Wall Street Journal* on October 1, 1928. The new list contained 14 stocks from the old 20 stock series plus 16 new corporations (see Figure 4–1).[1]

The *Journal* editors decided to expand the list to 30 stocks in order to represent a better cross section of the stock market. The number of actively traded issues had increased markedly since 1916. Furthermore, a number of major industries were either represented inadequately or not represented at all on the old list of 20—primarily oil, aeronautical, radio and phonograph, food, steel, chemicals, cars, and electrical products. These were all industries that had come into their own in the modern American economy.

MODIFICATIONS IN THE 30 STOCK SERIES

From its inception in 1928 until 1986, the 30 stock series has been modified 15 times and has involved 36 companies. The first change came on January 8, 1929, when National Cash Register was added

60

FIGURE 4–1   Dow Jones Industrials: Initial List of 30 Stocks Compared to the Final List of 20 Stocks

---

30 Stocks—October 1, 1928	*20 Stocks—September 29, 1928*
Allied Chemical	Allied Chemical
Allied Can	American Can
American Smelting	American Car & Foundry
American Sugar	American Locomotive
American Tobacco	American Smelting
Atlantic Refining	American Sugar
Bethlehem Steel	American Telephone & Telegraph
Chrysler	American Tobacco
General Electric	General Electric
General Motors	General Motors
General Railway Signal	International Harvester
Goodrich	Mack Trucks
International Harvester	Paramount Famous Lasky
International Nickel	Sears Roebuck & Co.
Mack Trucks	Texas Co.
Nash Motors	United Drug
North American	U.S. Rubber
Paramount Publix	U.S. Steel
Postum, Inc.	Western Union
Radio Corporation	Woolworth
Sears Roebuck & Co.	
Standard Oil (N.J.)	
Texas Corporation	
Texas Gulf Sulphur	
Union Carbide	
U.S. Steel	
Victor Talking Machine	
Westinghouse Electric	
Woolworth	
Wright Aeronautical	

---

and Victor Talking Machine deleted. Figure 4–2 lists all the changes and the specific dates. Note that between March 14, 1939, and July 3, 1956, no replacements were made in the DJIA. Likewise, between June 1, 1959, and August 8, 1976, the list held firm. Figure 4–3 presents differing composition of the 30-stock list between 1928 and 1985. During this period, stock splits, stock dividends, spin offs, and the like occurred in numerous issues of the 30 stock series, requiring the *Journal* editors to modify the divisor in order to maintain the continuity of the DJIA. It stood at 16.67 on October 1, 1928, and at this writing has been reduced to 1.090. *The Wall Street Journal* reported the most recent change in the divisor, as well as modifications in the DJIA's composition, as follows:

Significant Switch Made In Dow Jones Industrials

The Wall Street Journal made a significant change in the roster of 30 companies making up the Dow Jones Industrial Average, effective with the close of stock market trading yesterday.

Philip Morris Cos. replaced General Foods Corp. on the list, and McDonald's Corp. was substituted for American Brands Inc.

The switches won't affect the statistical continuity of the market indicator, which dates to 1928. Instead, a change was made in the divisor used to calculate the average so that the differing market prices of the stocks involved won't distort the final result.

General Foods was dropped from the list because of its acquisition by Philip Morris. Standing alone, this change would overweight the indicator, which is designed to reflect price trends in the broader stock market, in the to-

bacco products and processed foods sectors. For this reason, American Brands, formerly known as American Tobacco and a component of the 30 industrials since their inception, was dropped from the list.

McDonald's, a major food services company, is among the largest companies in market value, is widely owned and will cover a previously unrepresented sector.

Effective with the opening of trading today, the new divisor for the Dow Jones Industrials is 1.090. The substitutions also will change the divisor used to calculate the 65-stock composite index. It will be 4.653.

The 30 stocks used in the Dow Jones Industrials now are:

Allied-Signal	General Electric	Owens-Illinois
Aluminum Co	General Motors	Philip Morris
Amer Can	Goodyear	Procter & Gamb
Amer Express	Inco	Sears Roebuck
Amer T&T	IBM	Texaco
Bethlehem Steel	Inter Harvester	Union Carbide
Chevron	Inter Paper	United Technol.
DuPont	McDonalds	US Steel
Eastman Kodak	Merck	Westinghouse EI
Exxon	Minnesota M&M	Woolworth

SOURCE *The Wall Street Journal*, October 30, 1985, p. 49

During the depression decade of the 1930s, the *Journal* editors made 23 changes in the DJIA.[2] The fast-declining fortunes of many companies made it difficult to retain a list of leading corporate issues. Note, for example (Figure 4–3), that American Tobacco was removed on July 18, 1930, but less than two years later reappeared replacing another Tobacco company (Liggett & Myers). The editors were also concerned with maintaining a representative list of industries. They also tried to make substitutions that caused little change in the divisor.

A look at the DJIA list of 1928 in comparison with the current members of this exclusive club (Figure 4–3) indicates that nearly half of the 1928 membership is present today. They include Allied-Signal (formerly Allied Chemical), American Can, Bethlehem Steel, General Electric, General Motors, Inco. (formerly International Nickel), International Harvester, Sears Roebuck & Co., Exxon (formerly Standard Oil of New Jersey), Texaco (formerly Texas Corporation), Union Carbide, U.S. Steel, Westinghouse Electric, and Woolworth. It is interesting to note how the 14 survivors have diversified and/or expanded their products to meet changing needs.

Allied Signal, for example diversified from chemicals to oil and gas, electronics, health and scientific products, cars, and aerospace equipment. And on September 19, 1985, it merged with Signal to cover the fields of high technology and engineering. Sears Roebuck & Co. expanded from a mail order firm to retail stores, insurance, and financial services. There has been one exception to this diversification, and/or expansion policy. International Harvester fell on hard times partially because of a farming recession. Consequently, it sold its unprofitable farm machinery division. While this has enabled the company to concentrate its efforts on the more profitable truck manufacturing division, the reduced size of I.H., its loss of market dominance, and its tenuous financial position poses a question: Will International Harvester continue to remain in the DJIA? If it is retained in the Dow Industrials there will be a name change. As part of I.H.'s agreement with Tenneco Inc. covering the sale of its agricultural equipment business, Harvester must select a new corporate name. The name selected by the management will be submitted for stockholder approval at the 1986 meeting.

THE 1928–1985 ERA

Figure 4–4 indicates that Dow's 30-stock average of industrials varied about 1423 points during the 57-year period from 1928 to 1985. During this time the Dow low was 41.22 on July 8, 1932, and the Dow high exceeded 1472 (1472.13) on November 29, 1985. Why such a marked variation during this era? The Dow bottom occurred during the depth of the Depression in the bleak summer of 1932. The Hoover administration must share some of the blame for this debacle. Similarly, the Reagan years can take some credit for the Dow's new high.

The 30-stock period (1928 to present) can be divided into seven segments based on an examination of Figure 4–4. You may wish to refer to Figure 4–4 as we look at each time frame. It can be helpful in determining the impact of significant events on the stock market.

1. 1928–29: Final fling upward.
2. 1930–39: The Depression.
3. 1939–53: War years.

FIGURE 4–2 Modifications in the Composition of the DJIA (1928–1985)

Date	Added	Deleted
January 8, 1929	National Cash Register	Victor Talking Machine
September 14, 1929	Curtiss-Wright	Wright Aeronautical
January 29, 1930	Johns-Manville	North American
July 18, 1930	Borden	American Sugar
"	Eastman Kodak	American Tobacco
"	Goodyear	Atlantic Refining
"	Liggett & Myers	General Railway Signal
"	Standard Oil of California	Goodrich
"	United Air Transport	Nash Motors
"	Hudson Motor	Curtiss-Wright
May 26, 1932	American Tobacco	Liggett & Myers
"	Drug Inc.	Mack Trucks
"	Procter & Gamble	United Air Transport
"	Loew's	Paramount Publix
"	Nash Motors	Radio Corp.
"	International Shoe	Texas Gulf Sulphur
"	International Business Machines	National Cash Register
"	Coca Cola	Hudson Motor
August 15, 1933	Corn Products Refining	Drug, Inc.
"	United Aircraft	International Shoe
August 13, 1934	National Distillers	United Aircraft
November 20, 1935	Du Pont	Borden
"	National Steel	Coco-Cola
March 14, 1939	United Aircraft	Nash Kelvinator (formerly Nash Motors)
"	American Telephone & Telegraph	International Business Machines
July 3, 1956	International Paper	Loew's Inc.
June 1, 1959	Anaconda	American Smelting
"	Swift & Company	Corn Products
"	Aluminum Co. of America	National Steel
"	Owens-Illinois Glass	National Distillers
August 9, 1976	Minnesota Mining & Manufacturing	Anaconda
June 29, 1979	International Business Machines	Chrysler
"	Merck	Esmark
August 30, 1982	American Express	Manville Corp.
October 30, 1985	McDonald's	American Brands
"	Philip Morris	General Foods

FIGURE 4–3   How the Configuration of the List of 30 Stocks Changed (January 8, 1929 to present)

January 8, 1929

Allied Chemical
American Can
American Smelting
American Sugar
American Tobacco
Atlantic Refining
Bethlehem Steel
Chrysler
General Electric
General Motors
General Railway Signal
Goodrich
International Harvester
International Nickel
Mack Trucks
Nash Motors
National Cash Register
North American
Paramount Publix
Postum, Inc.
Radio Corporation
Sears Roebuck
Standard Oil (NJ)
Texas Corporation
Texas Gulf Sulphur
Union Carbide
U.S. Steel
Westinghouse Electric
Woolworth
Wright & Aeronautical

September 14, 1929

Allied Chemical
American Can
American Smelting
American Sugar
American Tobacco
Atlantic Refining
Bethlehem Steel
Chrysler
Curtiss-Wright
General Electric
General Foods
General Motors
General Railway Signal
Goodrich
International Harvester
International Nickel
Mack Trucks
Nash Motors
National Cash Register

North American
Paramount Publix
Radio Corporation
Sears Roebuck & Co.
Standard Oil (NJ)
Texas Corporation
Texas Gulf Sulphur
Union Carbide
U.S. Steel
Westinghouse Electric
Woolworth

January 29, 1930

Allied Chemical
American Can
American Smelting
American Sugar
American Tobcco
Atlantic Refining
Bethlehem Steel
Chrysler
Curtiss-Wright
General Electric
General Foods
General Motors
General Railway Signal
Goodrich
International Harvester
International Nickel
Johns-Manville
Mack Trucks
Nash Motors
National Cash Register
Paramount Publix
Radio Corporation
Sears Roebuck & Co.
Standard Oil (NJ)
Texas Corporation
Texas Gulf Sulphur
Union Carbide
U.S. Steel
Westinghouse Electric
Woolworth

July 18, 1930

Allied Chemical
American Can
American Smelting
Bethlehem Steel
Borden

Chrysler
Eastman Kodak
General Electric
General Foods
General Motors
Goodyear
Hudson Motor
International Harvester
International Nickel
Johns-Manville
Liggett & Myers
Mack Trucks
National Cash Register
Paramount Publix
Radio Corporation
Sears Roebuck & Co.
Standard Oil of
   California
Standard Oil (NJ)
Texas Corporation
Texas Gulf Sulphur
Union Carbide
United Air Transport
U.S. Steel
Westinghouse Electric
Woolworth

May 26, 1932

Allied Chemical
American Can
American Smelting
American Tobacco
Bethlehem Steel
Borden
Chrysler
Coca Cola
Drug Inc.
Eastman Kodak
General Electric
General Foods
General Motors
Goodyear
International Business
   Machines
International Harvester
International Nickel
International Shoe
Johns-Manville
Loew's
Nash Motors
Procter & Gamble
Sears Roebuck & Co.

FIGURE 4–3 *(continued)*

Standard Oil of
  California
Standard Oil (NJ)
Texas Corporation
Union Carbide
U.S. Steel
Westinghouse Elecric
Woolworth

June 15, 1933

Allied Chemical
American Can
American Smelting
American Tobacco B.
Bethlehem Steel
Borden
Chrysler
Coca Cola
Corn Products Refining
Eastman Kodak
General Electric
General Foods
General Motors
Goodyear
International Business Machines
International Harvester
International Nickel
Johns-Manville
Loew's
Nash Motors
Procter & Gamble
Sears Roebuck & Co.
Standard Oil of California
Standard Oil (NJ)
Texas Corporation
Union Carbide
United Aircraft
U.S. Steel
Westinghouse Electric
Woolworth

August 13, 1934

Allied Chemical
American Can
American Smelting
American Tobacco B.
Bethlehem Steel
Borden
Chrysler
Coca Cola
Corn Products Refining

Eastman Kodak
General Electric
General Foods
General Motors
Goodyear
International Business Machines
International Harvester
International Nickel
Johns-Manville
Loew's
Nash Motors
National Distillers
Procter & Gamble
Sears Roebuck & Co.
Standard Oil of California
Standard Oil (NJ)
Texas Corporation
Union Carbide
U.S. Steel
Westinghouse Electric
Woolworth

November 20, 1935

Allied Chemical
American Can
American Smelting
American Tobacco B.
Bethlehem Steel
Chrysler
Corn Products Refining
Du Pont
Eastman Kodak
General Electric
General Foods
General Motors
Goodyear
International Business Machines
International Harvester
International Nickel
Johns-Manville
Loew's
Nash Motors
National Distillers
National Steel
Procter & Gamble
Sears Roebuck & Co.
Standard Oil of California
Standard Oil (NJ)
Texas Corporation
Union Carbide
U.S. Steel
Westinghouse Electric
Woolworth

March 14, 1939

Allied Chemical
American Can
American Smelting
American Telephone & Telegraph
American Tobacco B.
Bethlehem Steel
Chrysler
Corn Products Refining
Du Pont
Eastman Kodak
General Electric
General Foods
General Motors
Goodyear
International Harvester
International Nickel
Johns-Manville
Loew's
National Distillers
National Steel
Procter & Gamble
Sears Roebuck & Co.
Standard Oil of California
Standard Oil (NJ)
Texas Corporation
Union Carbide
United Aircraft
U.S. Steel
Westinghouse Electric
Woolworth

July 3, 1956

Allied Chemical
American Can
American Smelting
American Telephone & Telegraph
American Tobacco B.
Bethlehem Steel
Chrysler
Corn Products Refining
Du Pont
Eastman Kodak
General Electric
General Foods
General Motors
Goodyear
International Harvester
International Nickel
International Paper
Johns-Manville
National Distillers

FIGURE 4–3 *(concluded)*

National Steel
Procter & Gamble
Sears Roebuck & Co.
Standard Oil of Californi
Standard Oil (NJ)
Texas Corporation
Union Carbide
United Aircraft
U.S. Steel
Westinghouse Electric
Woolworth

June 1, 1959

Allied Chemical
Aluminum Co. of
    America
American Can
American Telephone &
    Telegraph
American Tobacco
Anaconda
Bethlehem Steel
Chrysler
Du Pont
Eastman Kodak
General Electric
General Foods
General Motors
Goodyear
International Harvester
International Nickel
International Paper
Johns-Manville
Owen's-Illinois Glass
Procter & Gamble
Sears Roebuck & Co.
Standard Oil of
    California
Standard Oil (NJ)
Swift & Co.
Texas Corporation
Union Carbide
United Aircraft
U.S. Steel
Westinghouse Electric
Woolworth

August 9, 1976

Allied Chemical
Aluminum Co. of
    America

American Can
American Telephone &
    Telegraph
American Tobacco B.
Bethlehem Steel
Chrysler
Du Pont
Eastman Kodak
Esmark
Exxon
General Electric
General Foods
General Motors
Goodyear
International Harvester
International Nickel
International Paper
Johns-Manville
Minnesota Mining &
    Manufacturing
Owens-Illinois
Procter & Gamble
Sears Roebuck & Co.
Standard Oil of
    California
Texas Corporation
Union Carbide
United Technologies
U.S. Steel
Westinghouse Electric
Woolworth

June 29, 1979

Allied Chemical
Aluminum Co. of
    America
American Can
American Telephone &
    Telegraph
American Tobacco B.
Bethlehem Steel
Du Pont
Eastman Kodak
Exxon
General Electric
General Foods
General Motors
Goodyear
International Business
    Machines
International Harvester

International Nickel
International Paper
Johns-Manville
Merck
Minnesota Mining &
    Manufacturing
Owen's-Illinois
Procter & Gamble
Sears Roebuck & Co.
Standard Oil of
    California
Texas Corporation
Union Carbide
United Aircraft
U.S. Steel
Westinghouse Electric
Woolworth

Current
(November 1, 1985)

Allied - Signal
Aluminum Co. of
    America
American Can
American Express
American Telephone &
    Telegraph
Bethlehem Steel
Chevron Corporation
Du Pont
Eastman Kodak
Exxon
General Electric
General Motors
Goodyear
Inco
International Business
    Machines
International Harvester
International Paper
McDonald's Corporation
Merck & Company
Minnesota Mining &
    Manufacturing
Owens-Illinois
Philip Morris Companies
Procter & Gamble
Sears Roebuck & Co.
Texaco
Union Carbide
United Technologies
U.S. Steel
Westinghouse Electric
Woolworth

FIGURE 4–4   Dow Jones Industrial Average: 1928–1985 (with Stillman's significant political, military, technological, and economic events)

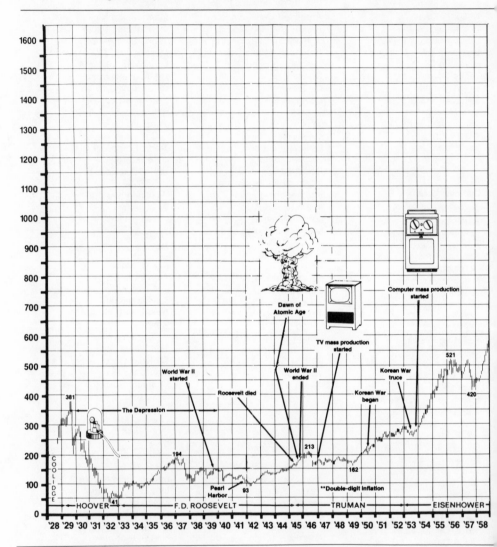

4. 1953–63: Eisenhower-Kennedy upswing.

5. 1963–74: Johnson-Nixon turbulence.

6. 1974–81: Ford-Carter malaise.

7. 1981–85: Reagan rise.

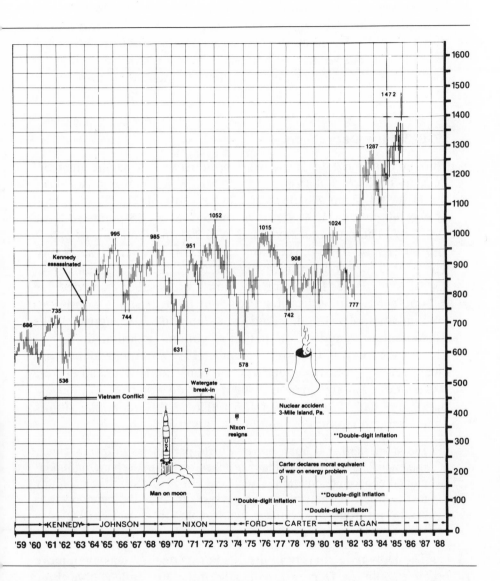

1928–29: Final Fling Upward

The bull market of the 20s had a final fling upward after the arrival of the 30 stock series. It advanced from 240.01 on October 1, 1928, to peak at 381.17 11 months later on September 3, 1929. The political climate during the years 1928 and 1929 continued to be highly favorable to business. "The less the government interfered the better" was the philosophy expounded by Herbert Hoover. In a 1928 speech he referred to "The American System of Rugged Individualism."[3] He later defined *rugged individualism* as "God-fearing men and women of honesty whose stamina and character and fearless assertion of rights led them to make their own way in life."[4]

1930–39: The Depression

Hoover continued to speak with optimism even as the financial markets began to collapse. On October 29, 1929 (Black Tuesday), the DJIA fell from a high of 252.38 to a low of 212.33—a spread of over 40 points. However, it recovered nearly 18 points to close at 230.07. The previous day's high was 295.18 with a low of 256.75 and a close of 260.64. The Dow closed on October 31 at 273.51. The spread for the month was over 120 points (352.86 high versus 230.07 low). Paper losses for the month of October exceeded $16 billion. Yet two months later President Hoover said "Conditions are fundamentally sound."[5] And a year later he told Congress, "The fundamental strength of the nation's economy is unimpaired."[6]

Hoover knew better—by December 19, 1930, the evidence was clear. Leading industries such as cars, construction, and steel were down markedly and unemployment was on the rise. Capital expenditures had slowed. The DJIA reflected this economic slump. John Kenneth Galbraith pointed out this reflection:

> The stock market is but a mirror which, perhaps as in this instance, somewhat belatedly, provides an image of the underlying or fundamental economic situation. Cause and effect run from the economy to the stock market, never the reverse. In 1929 the economy was headed for trouble. Eventually that trouble was violently reflected in Wall Street.[7]

The Dow rose sharply in the 20s but its decline was even more precipitous in the Depression decade of the 30s. In less than three years it plunged from 381.17 to 41.22—a drop of more than 89 percent. Remember, the DJIA contained the highest-rated corporations in the United States. Furthermore, the *Journal* made 18 substitutions in this time frame (from January 8, 1929 to May 26, 1932) to bolster the DJIA. Many lesser companies failed. A factor that contributed to the sharp market decline was easy credit provided by brokers and bankers that enabled individuals to purchase stocks for as little as 10 percent down. Many individuals had bought on margin and were sold out because they could not provide additional capital.

Unemployment jumped from 1.25 million in 1929 to 12 million by 1933. Figure 4–4 refers to *The Depression*. In my view there has been only one depression of this magnitude since the founding of America; in comparison, others have been recessions. Those who lived through it can recall massive bank failures, numerous plant layoffs, pay cuts, violent strikes, large-scale home and farm foreclosures, political demagogues, the Veterans Bonus March on Washington, the Dust Bowl tragedy, and able-bodied men and children selling apples on street corners for five cents.[8]

In spite of the nation's tragic plight, a few individuals like Joseph Kennedy made a great deal of money in a short period of time. They used the decline of the DJIA to their advantage—they sold short. This technique involved selling stock they did not own (borrowing it) and buying it back at a lower price. Kennedy reportedly made millions by selling short. It is interesting to note from an examination of Figure 4–4 that the market normally declines faster than it rises.

Gloom and doom pervaded the land until Franklin D. Roosevelt came on the scene. He spoke with confidence, and even the tilt of his cigarette holder reflected his positive attitude. F.D.R. personified courage by overcoming his own considerable physical handicap. Here was a man confined largely to a wheelchair as a result of poliomyelitis; yet he led the nation out of its worst economic time and successfully guided it to victory in World War II.[9] Roosevelt's bold approach was expressed in a talk at Oglethorpe University:

> The country needs and, unless I mistake its temper, the country demands bold, persistent experimentation. It is common sense to take a method and try it. If it fails, admit it frankly and try another. But above all, try something.[10]

Roosevelt did try. Among his successes were providing jobs through the WPA (Works Progress Administration) and the CCC (Civilian Conservation Corps). He established the SEC (Securities and Exchange Commission) to curb abuses in the stock market. The RFC (Reconstruction Finance Corporation) provided loans for hard-pressed farmers. FDR created the Tennessee Valley Authority and the Social Security System. He established a national minimum wage. He even tried to increase the size of the Supreme Court in order to appoint judges who hopefully would support his programs. His popularity was apparent from the fact that he was reelected three times by large majorities. But his progressive programs were not popular with the tycoons on Wall Street who viewed him as far too liberal. His efforts, however, produced positive economic results and the Dow rose from 41 in 1932 to 194 five years later. The Dow closed out the Depression 30s in the 150 range. War rumblings in Europe and the Far East by Germany and Japan were factors in its decline.

1939–53: War Years

The dominant forces affecting the stock market during the period from 1939 to 1953 were World War II and the Korean conflict. Figure 4–4 shows the reaction of the market to the Pearl Harbor defeat (December 7, 1941) and the dark days that followed. The DJIA reached its low of the 1940s early in 1942. As the Allied forces began to turn back the Axis powers, the market moved higher. By the end of the war with Japan the Dow climbed to 160. Less than a year later it approached 213.

Roosevelt died on April 12, 1945, and Harry S. Truman assumed the mantle of political leadership. He made the decision to use the atomic bomb against Japan. The Air Force implemented his decision, and Japan promptly surrendered.[11]

America at the time was the undisputed leader of the world—politically, militarily, and economically. Much of Europe, Russia, and Japan were devastated. The United States provided considerable economic assistance to war-ravaged countries. It also established a military government in Japan as well as in a sector of Germany.[12]

Peace among the wartime Allies was short lived. Russia attempted to blockade Berlin by refusing Allied supplies to enter the city by either rail or ground transport. The United States countered by providing a massive airlift (1948 to 1949) to supply the Berliners and the blockade was defeated.

The Korean War began in June 1950 and ended in a truce three years later. The outcome was a stalemate: The 38th parallel remained the dividing line between communist North Korea and U.S.-supported South Korea. The Dow reflected these uncertain times, fluctuating between a high of 290 and a low of 162.

1953–63: Eisenhower-Kennedy Upswing

During Eisenhower's first year in office a truce was achieved in Korea. The stock market reflected the relatively peaceful eight years under Dwight D. Eisenhower. The Dow moved from 288 to over 630 (634.17) upon his departure on January 20, 1961.

The youthful John F. Kennedy, age 43, provided a decided contrast to his predecessor, who left office at 70. Kennedy brought in a team of eastern intellectuals who developed the "New Frontier" philosophy attempting to emulate FDR's "New Deal." His achievements included establishing the Peace Corps, expansion of civil rights, support of mental health improvements, agreement on a limited nuclear test ban treaty with the USSR and the United Kingdom, and a successful space program. A significant failure was the defeat of a U.S.-supported invasion force by Premier Castro's communist Cuba (April 17, 1961). In October 1962 he faced up to Russia's attempt to create missile bases in Cuba by establishing a naval and air blockade of the island. Kennedy's action resulted in the USSR decision to remove its missiles from the island.

The DJIA continued its upward move after Kennedy took office, reaching a high of 735 during his first year. In mid-1962 the average slumped to 536, but it recovered promptly and the Kennedy upswing closed at 732.65 the day before he died.[13]

1963–74: Johnson-Nixon Turbulence

Lyndon B. Johnson assumed the presidency at a difficult time— after the assassination of John F. Kennedy on November 22, 1963. Although he did much to further the civil rights movement, his legacy was a deeper involvement in our nation's most unpopular war—Vietnam. Riots in Los Angeles (1965) as well as Detroit and Newark (1967) resulted in over 100 dead with thousands injured and homeless. Regular Army and National Guard troops were sent to Detroit to protect lives and property.

Nixon was elected as a backlash to the Johnson years. His major achievements were establishing detente with China and securing a cease-fire agreement with North Vietnam. Major failures included the loss of a war by the United States for the first time and the Watergate debacle. While he denied any knowledge of the June 17, 1972, burglary of the Democratic headquarters (located in the Watergate office building), when impeachment proceedings were underway in the House of Representatives, Nixon decided to resign from office. The DJIA hit an 11-year low of 578 (577.60 on December 6) a few months after Nixon resigned on August 9, 1974. Watergate, and its aftermath, was a tragic time in American history with bright young people turning away from government and military service.

1974–81: Ford-Carter Malaise

Gerald R. Ford entered the White House after Nixon's resignation. He had been selected by Nixon to be vice president and took that office October 12, 1973. Ford became the first person to gain the presidency without being elected to either that position or that of the vice presidency.

Ford's long experience in Washington, D.C. (from 1948 to 1973 as a member of the House of Representatives) served him well in keeping cordial relations with Congress. The market responded to his honest efforts to restore faith in the federal government. During 1976, his last full year in office, the DJIA exceeded 1000 in 7 of the 12 months (see Figure 4–4).

Jimmy Carter became president on January 20, 1977. His major political accomplishment was the peace negotiations that occurred between Egypt and Israel. His failures included two years of double-digit inflation and an economic recession. Carter's most significant political blunder involved U.S. hostages taken at our Embassy in Iran. His inability to obtain their release, and the futile military effort to rescue them, were factors that weighted heavily against him in his losing reelection effort. The stock market reflected the Carter malaise with the Dow dipping to 742 in 1978. It recovered to the 1000 range in the waning months of 1980 as Reagan's victory appeared imminent.

1981–85: Reagan Rise

Ronald W. Reagan became president on January 20, 1981. Under his leadership the nation moved from an outlook of malaise to one of pride in our achievements and confidence in the future.

Reagan had his share of difficulties, including heavy Marine Corps losses in Lebanon, double-digit unemployment, and being wounded in an assassination attempt. But he had the courage to follow through on his conservative philosophy. For example, he cut taxes to stimulate production, and it worked. During his first term he solved the number one problem concerning the American people. Inflation was reduced from over 10 percent to 4 percent. A look at Figure 4–4 indicates that the stock market liked what he had done. It advanced to an all-time high. The citizens responded to his achievements by reelecting him in a landslide victory. His Democratic opponent won only one state.

Reagan faces difficult problems in the years ahead. I stated some of these problems in the summer of 1984 to a *Times Picayune* reporter who wrote:

> The professor listed three problems that could play havoc with the market if they are not resolved: (1) the Third World debt that has "many American banks scared to death," (2) the huge imbalance of foreign trade, which set a record in the first quarter of 1984, and (3) the federal budget deficit.
>
> But Stillman was optimistic about the nation's and market's future, crediting President Reagan with "standing back and sizing up what had to be done to turn the country around, and then doing one hell of a good job as a leader and a master salesman."[14]

During the first year of President Reagan's second term the rate of inflation continued to decline, approaching 3 percent. The stock market maintained its upward march and by mid-December 1985 the DJIA exceeded 1550—an advance of over 770 points from its August low of 777.

OBSERVATION

The current stock series has survived for the longest period of time—from 1928 to 1985. The first three chapters represented the life span of previous averages as follows:

1884–1896: Dow's combined rails and industrials.

1896:–1916: DJIA 12 stock series.

1916–1928: DJIA 20 stock series.

As of this writing the current series has been in existence for 57 years in contrast to 44 years for all the previous averages. Is it time for another change? This question will be discussed in Chapter 5.

NOTES

[1]The companies that were removed included American Telephone & Telegraph, American Car & Foundry, American Locomotive, United Drug, U.S. Rubber, and Western Union. Newcomers were Atlantic Refining, Bethlehem Steel, Chrysler, General Railway Signal, Goodrich, International Nickel, Nash Motors, North American, Postum, Inc., Radio Corporation, Standard Oil (N.J.), Texas Gulf Sulphur, Union Carbide, Victor Talking Machine, Westinghouse Electric, and Wright Aeronautical.

[2]The largest number of changes in the DJIA occurred on two occasions. On July 18, 1930, seven companies entered the list—Borden, Eastman Kodak, Goodyear, Hudson Motor, Liggett & Myers, Standard Oil of California, and United Air Transport. Removals included American Sugar, American Tobacco, Atlantic Refining, Curtis-Wright, General Railway Signal, Goodrich, and Nash Motors.

Eight substitutions were made on May 26, 1932. Additions included American Tobacco, Drug Inc., Procter & Gamble, Loew's, Nash Motors, International Shoe, International Business Machines, and Coca-Cola. Those removed were Liggett & Myers, Mack Trucks, United Air Transport, Paramount Publix, Radio Corp., Texas Gulf Sulphur, National Cash Register, and Hudson Motor.

[3]Campaign speech in New York City on October 22, 1928.

[4]Herbert C. Hoover, *The Challenge of Liberty* (New York: Charles Scribner's Sons, 1934, p. 93.

[5]Speech December 11, 1929.

[6]Message to Congress December 2, 1930.

[7]John Kenneth Galbraith, *The Great Crash, 1929* (Boston: Houghton Mifflin, 1954).

[8]In 1933 4,000 U.S. banks failed. In contrast, the highest failure rate since the Depression was 76 in 1984.

[9]In a speech supporting FDR's bid for governor of New York, Alfred E. Smith said: "The governor of New York State does not have to be an acrobat."

[10]Franklin D. Roosevelt, Speech at Oglethorpe University, Atlanta, Georgia, on May 22, 1937.

[11]Hiroshima was bombed on August 6 and Nagasaki on August 9.

[12]Russia, United Kingdom, and France governed the other part of Germany.

[13]On November 22 (the day of Kennedy's death) the Dow high was 739.00, and the low was 710.83. It closed at 711.49.

[14]The *Times Picayune*, July 8, 1984, p. F 3.

PART TWO

How to Use the Dow Jones Industrials in Your Investment Strategy

Now that you know the history of the Dow Jones Industrial Average, it is time to discover what role the Dow stocks can play in your investment strategy. With this in mind, we will examine:

- The position of the DJIA in the marketplace as compared to other commonly used indicators.
- The Dow theory, which uses the DJIA as a tool to forecast the movement of stock prices.
- A money management concept that will allow you to make decisions while utilizing the Dow Industrials in your investment strategy.

5

How to Compute the Daily Dow Jones Industrial Average

There are a considerable number of common-stock indexes or "averages," but most studies of the earnings, dividends, prices, and other market relationships of cross-sectional groups of stocks have used the data of the Dow-Jones Industrial Average.

—*Benjamin Graham*

MARKET INDICATORS

How is the stock market doing? The answer to this question will vary, depending upon what basic information is used. The stock market, in the broadest sense, is composed of the thousands of companies that have made their stock available to the public. A complete listing of them would take in the New York, American, Midwest, Cincinnati, Pacific, Boston, and Philadelphia exchanges, various foreign exchanges, and the many unlisted equities bought and sold in over-the-counter transactions. It would be extremely difficult to incorporate all corporate stocks into one market indicator as a result of the multitude of daily purchases and sales. Therefore, limited numbers are used for the purpose of providing an answer to the question, "How is the market doing?"

There are numerous statistical compilations that are prepared by various concerns to arrive at an answer. The advent of the computer age has made it possible to compute daily the average price of all stocks listed on the New York Stock Exchange. Other well-known market indicators are those of Standard & Poor's, the American Stock Exchange, Barron's 50-Stock Average, Wilshire

5000 Equity Index, and Value Line. There are also indexes for over-the-counter issues and mutual funds. The over-the-counter index is prepared by the National Association of Securities Dealers. The index has the short title of NASDAQ (National Association of Securities Dealers Automated Quotations). The Lipper index contains 30 major mutual funds.

A number of foreign countries have their own indexes. A few of the prominent indicators include the Financial Times All-Share Index (London); CAC Index (Paris); Frankfurter Allgemeine Zeitung Index (Frankfurt); Nikkei Dow Jones Average (Tokyo); Hang Seng Index (Hong Kong); Gold Stock Index (Johannesburg); and the Toronto Stock Exchange Index (Toronto). There is also a World Index prepared by Capital International Perspective.[1]

Before examining the Dow average, let us look briefly at the composition of several other popular U.S. indicators. Standard & Poor's composite index, for example, has a much broader base than the Dow. S&P comprises 500 issues (400 industrials, 20 transportations, 40 utilities, and 40 financial institutions). Its companies appear on the various exchanges, with a few traded over the counter. In contrast to the Dow's sole reliance on the daily price of individual stocks (unweighted average), Standard & Poor's is weighed by taking into consideration the number of shares outstanding of each corporation. The daily market price of each issue is multiplied by the number of shares to obtain the total value of all 500 issues. This figure is divided by the market value of all S&P stocks during the period from 1941 to 1943. The answer is then multiplied by 10.[2]

The New York Stock Exchange Composite Index comprises all the stocks on that exchange and is computed daily. The index is based on a value of 50, which was the approximate price of NYSE issues on December 31, 1965. The NYSE has four other indexes: industrials, utilities, transportation, and finance. The Wilshire 5000 Equity Index is the total market value of all stocks listed on the New York and American Stock Exchanges as well as those actively traded over the counter.

The over-the-counter (OTC) market has seven indexes to reflect daily price movements. They include the following: composite, industrials, banks, insurance, other finance, transportation, and utilities. The composite index of NASDAQ (National Association of Security Dealers Automated Quotations) comprises about 2,400 OTC companies. The index is based on a value of 100, which was the approximate price of the selected OTC issues on February 5, 1971.

FIGURE 5-1   Stocks Used in The Current Dow Jones Averages

Industrial (30)

Allied-Signal	General Electric	Owens-Illinois
Aluminum Company of America	General Motors	Philip Morris
American Can	Goodyear	Procter & Gamble
American Express	Inco	Sears Roebuck & Co.
American Telephone &	International	Texaco
Telegraph	Business Machines	Union Carbide
Bethlehem Steel	International Harvester*	United Technologies
Chevron	International Paper	U.S. Steel
Du Pont	McDonald's	Westinghouse Electric
Eastman Kodak	Merck	Woolworth
Exxon	Minnesota Mining &	
	Manufacturing	

Transportation (20)

AMR Corporation	Delta Air Lines	Santa Fe
American President	Eastern Air Lines	Southern Pacific
Burlington North	Federal Express	Transway
Canadian Pacific	Norfolk Southern	International
Carolina Freight	NWA Inc.	Trans World Airlines
Consolidated Freight	Overnite Transportation	UAL Inc.
CSX Corporation	Pan Am Corporation	Union Pacific
		U.S. Air Group

Utilities (15)

American Electric Power	Detroit Edison	Philadelphia
Cleveland Electric Ill.	Houston Industrial	Electric
Columbia Gas System	Niagara Mohawk	Public Service
Commonwealth Edison	Power	Electricity & Gas
Consolidated Edison	Pacific Gas & Electric	Southern California
Consolidated Natural	Panhandle Eastern	Edison
Gas	Peoples Energy	

*Name to be changed in 1986.

The four Dow Jones Stock Averages are the best known of these market computations.[3] The composite average consists of all the stocks in the three individual averages—industrials, transportation, and utilities—each comprising large and well-established companies.[4] Figure 5-1 lists the 65 "blue-chip" giants of American industry currently comprising the Dow Jones Stock Averages (DJA). The most popular of the four averages is the industrial category, which may be plotted back to 1896.

COMPUTING THE DJIA

The daily Dow Jones Industrial Average (DJIA) was at first computed by adding up the current market prices of all of the stocks and dividing the aggregate by the number of corporations. A look back at Figure 2–1 points out how Dow determined his initial 12-stock industrial average. At the close of the NYSE on May 26, 1896, the share values totaled 491.28. This figure was divided by 12 (the number of companies in the Dow Jones Industrial Average at that time). It resulted in an average market price of approximately $41. If this figure had been $42 the day after, it could be said the market was up for the day.

In order to permit appropriate comparison of the DJIA over the years, it has been essential to make frequent adjustments in the divisor as the result of stock splits, stock dividends, and changes in the composition of the DJIA. Let me illustrate why it has been essential to make adjustments over the years in order to make valid comparisons. For simplicity, assume that only three stocks comprise an average. If the closing prices of these three issues on Thursday, February 20, 1986, totaled $360 ($180 + $120 + $60), then the average for the day would have been $120 (360 ÷ 3). If the $180 stock had a 2 for 1 split effective the next day, then an adjustment would have to be made. Otherwise the continuity of the average, for comparative purposes, would be destroyed. Assume no change in the closing price of these three issues on Friday, February 21, 1986. If the divisor remained at 3, it would produce the following distortion in comparing it with the previous day's close:

$$\begin{array}{r} \$\ 90 \\ 120 \\ \underline{60} \\ \$270 \div 3 = \$90 \end{array}$$

If no change were made, the new figure would indicate that the three-stock average declined markedly ($30). In order to avoid this distortion, a modification could be made in the dividend or divisor as follows:

Dividend correction:	Divisor correction:
$ 90*	$ 90
90*	120
120	$\underline{60}$
$\underline{60}$	$270 ÷ 2.25 = $120
$360 ÷ 3 = $120	

*Double weight is given to the stock that split 2 for 1.

The *Journal* editors decided to reduce the divisor. In order to obtain the updated divisor each time a stock split or other change occurs, the following formula may be used:

$$\frac{PV}{PD} = \frac{CV}{X}$$

where

PV = previous value of the DJI
PD = previous divisor
CV = current value of the DJI
X = updated divisor.

If we apply this formula to the example above it works out as follows:

$$\frac{360}{3} = \frac{270}{X}$$
$$360X = 810$$
$$X = 2.25$$

The DJIA is actually an unweighted arithmetic mean. The formula utilized to compute the daily average is as follows:

$$\frac{\text{Sum of the current market prices of 30 issues}}{\text{Current divisor}}$$

or $\dfrac{\Sigma P}{D}$ = DJIA

where

Σ = sum
P = price of each stock comprising the DJIA
D = current DJIA divisor.

If we apply the formula over different time frames, it would provide the following answers:

October 7, 1896 (12 stock series)	:	$\dfrac{423.60}{12}$ = 35.30
October 2, 1916 (20 stock series)	:	$\dfrac{2260.20}{20}$ = 103.01

October 7, 1896 (12 stock series)	:	$\dfrac{423.60}{12} = 35.30$
October 2, 1916 (20 stock series)	:	$\dfrac{2260.20}{20} = 103.01$
October 1, 1928 (30 stock series)	:	$\dfrac{4000.9667}{16.67} = 240.01$
May 27, 1977* (30 stock series)	:	$\dfrac{1324.87542}{1.474} = 898.83$
November 23, 1985 (30 stock series)	:	$\dfrac{1604.6217}{1.090} = 1472.13$

*See Figure 5–2 for details on computing the DJIA for May 27, 1977.

Note the changes in the composition of the Dow Jones Industrial Average between 1977 (Figure 5–2) and 1985 (Figure 5–1). Allied merged with Signal to become Allied-Signal. Standard Oil of California changed its name to Chevron. New members included International Business Machines, American Express, Merck, McDonald's and Philip Morris. The five eliminated were Johns-Manville, Esmark, Chrysler, American Brands, and General Foods. In addition, American Telephone & Telegraph had a marked change in its corporate responsibilities (and market price) after the divestiture of major holdings in 1984.

It is apparent from a look at the makeup of the DJIA since 1896 that change has been the name of the game. The modifications have been pointed out in Chapters 2, 3, and 4. Factors that have resulted in corporations being deleted from the DJIA include: massive law suits, poor management, increased competition, new products and services, government regulations, court decisions, and economic hard times.

PROBLEMS WITH THE DJIA

Unweighted. The unweighted approach results in more importance being given to higher-priced issues in the DJIA. Likewise, a stock with the greatest market value (current price times number of shares outstanding) is given the same weight as one with the smallest number of shares in the DJIA.

FIGURE 5-2 An Example of How to Compute the DJIA (Dow Jones Industrials on May 27, 1977)

Corporation	Market Price
Allied-Signal	$ 46.500
Aluminum Company of America	56.000
American Brands	46.000
American Can	40.000
American Telephone & Telegraph	63.000
Bethlehem Steel	32.875
Chrysler	16.625
Du Pont	119.000
Eastman Kodak	56.000
Esmark Inc.	51.125
Exxon	54.500
General Electric	32.375
General Foods	66.625
General Motors	19.375
Goodyear	27.125
Inco	36.750
International Harvester	51.250
International Paper	34.500
Johns-Manville	47.500
Minnesota Mining & Manufacturing	27.625
Owens-Illinois	31.500
Procter & Gamble	74.500
Sears Roebuck & Co.	55.250
Standard Oil of California	41.375
Texaco	26.250
Union Carbide	50.375
United Technologies	37.500
U.S. Steel	41.875
Westinghouse Electric	19.750
Woolworth	21.750
Total	$1,324.875

Dow Average (May 27, 1977)

$$\frac{1,324.875}{1.474} = 898.83$$

Distortion. A slight change in actual prices of its 30 stocks results in a large change in the DJIA. This is due to the fact that the divisor continues to be reduced in size with each stock split and stock dividend. Thus, a 25-cent rise (¼ point) in the price of its stocks would be currently reflected in a movement approaching seven points in the DJIA. It is important to remember that the

FIGURE 5–3 Dow Jones Industrials as of November 1985 (by industry)

Aerospace
  United Technologies
Automobile, truck and related
  General Motors
  Goodyear
  International Harvester
Chemicals and other
  Allied-Signal
  Du Pont
  Union Carbide
Electrical
  General Electric
  Westinghouse Electric
Electronic
  International Business
    Machines

Financial
  American Express
Health care
  Merck
Manufacturing—steel, aluminum, nickel, and copper
  Aluminum Company of America
  Bethlehem Steel
  Inco
  U.S. Steel
Manufacturing—containers, and tapes
  American Can
  Minnesota Mining & Manufacturing
  Owens-Illinois
Paper and paper products
  International Paper

Petroleum
  Chevron
  Exxon
  Texaco
Photography
  Eastman Kodak
Restaurant, food, tobacco, and soap
  McDonald's
  Philip Morris
  Procter & Gamble
Retail stores and other
  Sears Roebuck & Co.
  Woolworth
Utility
  American Telephone & Telegraph

DJIA presents an overview of how the market is doing as measured by daily trading. It does *not* reflect either the true dollar value of corporate stocks or the actual dollar increase or decrease.

Limited size. The DJIA consists of only 30 issues that may be divided into 15 categories (see Figure 5–3). A review of these stocks indicates that several significant categories are missing: these include major U.S. banks; hotel, and entertainment; media; and transportation (appears in the 20 Stock Transportation Average). There is also too limited representation in electronics and health care.

ATTRIBUTES OF THE DJIA

Continuity. The Dow Jones Industrial Average is the dean of stock market indicators. As pointed out in Chapter 2, it first appeared in *The Wall Street Journal* in 1896. The only interruption occurred when the New York Stock Exchange was closed in 1914 because of World War I (see Figure 2–5). The ability to analyze the Dow movement over an 89-year period is a valuable tool for students of the stock market. Dow deserves much credit for devising an industrial average as early as 1896. There were few actively traded industrials available at that time. But he had the foresight to recognize the potential growth in such corporations. Keep in mind that he lived only six years after the 12-stock average was published.

Availability of information. There is an abundance of daily information available on the Dow Jones Industrial Average. The major TV networks report its daily close on prime news time. "Wall $treet Week" highlights the daily movement of the DJIA in its weekly program, and the "Nightly Business Report" looks to the 30 industrials first in reporting what market action took place in the financial community.

Radio stations nationwide provide coverage each half hour on the Dow Industrials.[5] Today a CBS affiliate said, "On Wall Street at noon the Dow is down a little over five points on a volume of 89 million shares."

The financial sections of newspapers throughout the country normally give the DJIA top billing. In New Orleans the business section, for example, of the *Times Picayune/States Item* features a chart titled "Dow Jones Industrial Average." It includes the *daily* high, low, and close for a two-month period.

The year 1985 was an exceptional one for the DJIA. Between January and mid-December the DJIA established new highs on 36 occasions. The record-breaking highs received excellent media coverage. *USA Today* reported, on November 25, 1985, that "Last week, the Dow jumped 29.24 points to close at a record 1464.33."[6]

As to be expected, the most comprehensive coverage of the Industrials (and other Dow stock averages) appears in *The Wall Street Journal*. In addition to a chart plotting its daily movement (Figure 5–4), there is ample material for technical analysis. The information available includes:

- Hourly movement.
- Daily shares sold.
- Divisor.
- Yearly range for five years (listed each Monday).
- Current and previous year P/E ratios and dividend yields (listed each Monday).
- Thirty industrials currently comprising the DJIA (listed each Monday).
- Current closing average compared to a year ago and since the previous December 31. This closing average is provided both in points and on a percentage basis. The percentage material on the DJIA provides a picture of the true movement of this average.

Barron's also provides helpful material as follows:

- Weekly high, low, and close of the DJIA.
- Chart on the DJIA indicating the high, low, and close for the most recent five-month period.
- Table titled "Return on Dow Jones Industrial Stock Average." This one-page table covers a period from 1897 to 1985. It provides a wealth of statistical information that includes: yearly high, low, and close; return on equity (actual and percent change from the previous year); book value; earnings; P/E; dividends; and yield.

TIME FOR A MAJOR CHANGE IN THE DJIA?

The selling of the Dow has been superb since its inception in 1896. Dow not only created the DJIA but also provided a vehicle to market it. As a founder-owner of *The Wall Street Journal*, he ensured his brainchild ongoing free publicity. Shortly before his death,

FIGURE 5-4 Information on the Dow Jones Averages

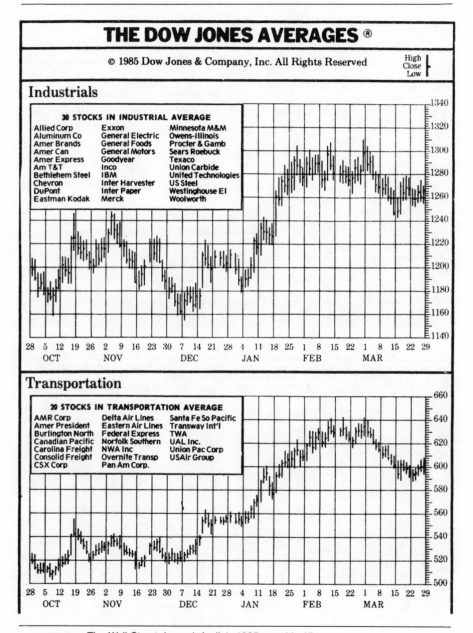

THE DOW JONES AVERAGES ®

© 1985 Dow Jones & Company, Inc. All Rights Reserved

High
Close
Low

Industrials

30 STOCKS IN INDUSTRIAL AVERAGE

Allied Corp	Exxon	Minnesota M&M
Aluminum Co	General Electric	Owens-Illinois
Amer Brands	General Foods	Procter & Gamb
Amer Can	General Motors	Sears Roebuck
Amer Express	Goodyear	Texaco
Am T&T	Inco	Union Carbide
Bethlehem Steel	IBM	United Technologies
Chevron	Inter Harvester	US Steel
DuPont	Inter Paper	Westinghouse El
Eastman Kodak	Merck	Woolworth

28 5 12 19 26 2 9 16 23 30 7 14 21 28 4 11 18 25 1 8 15 22 1 8 15 22 29
  OCT   NOV   DEC   JAN   FEB   MAR

Transportation

20 STOCKS IN TRANSPORTATION AVERAGE

AMR Corp	Delta Air Lines	Santa Fe So Pacific
Amer President	Eastern Air Lines	Transway Int'l
Burlington North	Federal Express	TWA
Canadian Pacific	Norfolk Southern	UAL Inc.
Carolina Freight	NWA Inc	Union Pac Corp
Consolid Freight	Overnite Transp	USAir Group
CSX Corp	Pan Am Corp.	

28 5 12 19 26 2 9 16 23 30 7 14 21 28 4 11 18 25 1 8 15 22 1 8 15 22 29
  OCT   NOV   DEC   JAN   FEB   MAR

SOURCE *The Wall Street Journal*, April 1, 1985, pp. 44-45.

FIGURE 5-4 *(continued)*

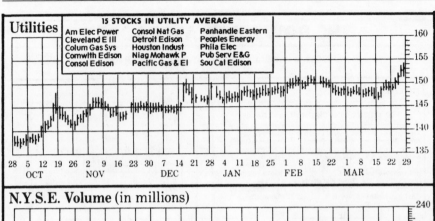

Utilities — 15 STOCKS IN UTILITY AVERAGE
Am Elec Power, Cleveland E Ill, Colum Gas Sys, Comwlth Edison, Consol Edison, Consol Nat Gas, Detroit Edison, Houston Indust, Niag Mohawk P, Pacific Gas & El, Panhandle Eastern, Peoples Energy, Phila Elec, Pub Serv E&G, Sou Cal Edison

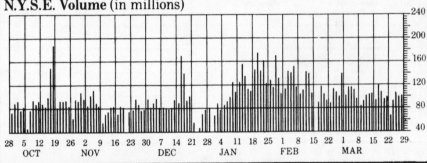

N.Y.S.E. Volume (in millions)

Following are the Dow Jones averages of INDUSTRIAL, TRANSPORTATION and UTILITY stocks with the total sales of each group for the period indicated.

DATE	OPEN	11 AM	12 NOON	1 PM	2 PM	3 PM	CLOSE	CH	%	HIGH*	LOW*	VOLUME
30 INDUSTRIALS												
Mar. 29	1263.47	1260.71	1261.70	1264.02	1265.68	1263.36	1266.78	+ 6.07	+ 0.48	1270.65	1255.85	9,805,600
Mar. 28	1265.90	1270.98	1270.32	1268.55	1267.23	1266.45	1260.71	− 4.20	− 0.33	1275.51	1256.63	8,701,200
Mar. 27	1260.16	1263.91	1264.02	1266.78	1265.24	1264.36	1264.91	+ 5.19	+ 0.41	1270.87	1255.96	8,962,800
Mar. 26	1257.07	1260.05	1258.94	1256.96	1259.05	1263.25	1259.72	− 0.22	− 0.02	1267.56	1252.10	9,523,800
Mar. 25	1261.70	1261.59	1260.38	1262.26	1263.25	1261.48	1259.94	− 7.51	− 0.59	1268.33	1252.87	7,933,480
20 TRANSPORTATION COS.												
Mar. 29	597.43	597.43	598.76	602.19	603.63	601.86	603.08	+ 2.99	+ 0.50	608.17	594.11	4,921,200
Mar. 28	600.64	603.52	602.64	603.30	603.74	603.74	600.09	+ 0.56	+ 0.09	606.40	596.21	3,378,800
Mar. 27	595.22	598.32	597.98	598.98	598.65	599.20	599.53	+ 3.87	+ 0.65	602.30	592.45	2,430,100
Mar. 26	592.89	594.11	593.00	592.12	594.00	596.32	595.66	+ 2.66	+ 0.45	599.42	589.24	2,871,600
Mar. 25	594.22	592.56	592.23	592.67	592.89	592.67	593.00	− 1.88	− 0.32	598.10	587.80	1,946,800
15 UTILITIES												
Mar. 29	152.44	152.24	152.19	151.98	152.60	152.44	153.01	+ 0.16	+ 0.10	154.08	151.06	3,601,900
Mar. 28	151.67	152.65	152.60	152.95	153.06	153.11	152.85	+ 1.49	+ 0.98	153.88	151.06	2,080,900
Mar. 27	149.98	150.70	150.65	150.85	151.01	150.95	151.36	+ 1.18	+ 0.79	152.13	149.52	2,384,700
Mar. 26	149.31	149.47	149.83	149.93	150.29	150.34	150.18	+ 1.02	+ 0.68	151.01	148.65	1,724,300
Mar. 25	148.75	148,80	148.85	148.70	149.16	149.31	149.16	− 0.10	− 0.07	149.93	148.13	1,433,800
65 STOCKS COMPOSITE AVERAGE												
Mar. 29	512.68	511.93	512.45	513.69	514.73	513.69	515.06	+ 2.20	+ 0.43	517.70	509.42	18,328,700
Mar. 28	513.61	515.97	515.58	515.50	515.35	515.19	512.86	− 0.11	− 0.02	518.32	510.09	14,160,900
Mar. 27	510.14	512.11	512.03	513.02	512.66	512.55	512.97	+ 2.72	+ 0.53	515.40	508.28	13,777,600
Mar. 26	508.54	509.60	509.27	508.64	509.76	511.31	510.25	+ 1.09	+ 0.21	513.38	506.19	14,119,700
Mar. 25	509.65	509.27	508.93	509.39	509.91	509.52	509.16	− 2.25	− 0.44	512.71	505.77	11,314,000

Averages are compiled daily by using the following divisors: Industrials, 1.132; Transportation, 1.129; Utilities, 2.437; 65 Stocks, 4.830.

*Averages of the highs and lows reached at any time during the day on the New York Stock Exchange by the individual stocks.

FIGURE 5-4 *(concluded)*

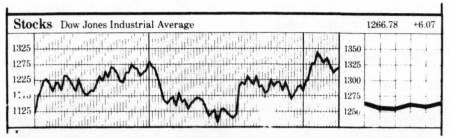

Stocks Dow Jones Industrial Average   1266.78   +6.07

HIGH	LOW	(12 MOS)	CLOSE	NET CH	% CH	12 MO CH	%	FROM 12/31	%
DOW JONES AVERAGES									
1299.36	1086.57	30 Industrials	x1266.78	+ 6.07	+ 0.48	+ 101.89	+ 8.75	+ 55.21	+ 4.56
635.30	444.03	20 Transportations	603.08	+ 2.99	+ 0.50	+ 92.89	+18.21	+ 44.95	+ 8.05
153.01	122.25	15 Utilities	x153.01	+ 0.16	+ 0.10	+ 26.18	+20.64	+ 3.49	+ 2.33
528.78	421.36	65 Composite	x515.06	+ 2.20	+ 0.43	+ 58.41	+12.79	+ 25.20	+ 5.14

DOW JONES 65 COMPONENTS

	--P/E Ratios--		Dividend Yields	
	March 29, 1985	Yr. Ago	March 29, 1985	Yr Ago
Industrials	11.2	16.1	4.82%	4.74%
Transportation	9.7	13.1	2.42%	2.61%
Utilities	7.3	6.4	9.00%	10.30%

Price earnings ratios are based on per share earnings for the 12 months ended December 31, 1984 of $113.58 for the 30 Industrials; $62.37 for the 20 transportation issues; $21.02 for the 15 utilities.

DOW JONES YEARLY RANGE

	Industrials		Transport		Utilities		Composite	
	High	Low	High	Low	High	Low	High	Low
1985	1299.36	1184.96	635.30	553.03	153.01	146.54	528.78	480.93
1984	1286.64	1086.57	612.63	444.03	149.93	122.25	514.02	421.86
1983	1287.20	1027.04	612.57	434.24	140.70	119.51	515.11	401.03
1982	1070.55	776.92	464.55	292.12	122.83	103.22	416.33	299.44
1981	1024.05	824.01	447.38	335.48	117.81	101.28	394.56	320.59

in 1902, he sold Dow, Jones & Company to Clarence W. Barron (see Chapter 1). This sale provided financial strength, competent leadership, and eventually another national business and financial newspaper, *Barron's*, to highlight the DJIA. Over the years, Dow, Jones & Company (thanks to its editors and owners) has made Dow's list of 30 the preeminent average. But is it time for a facelift?

The Dow Jones Industrial Average provides an indication of the daily movement of the stock market. Today, however, the wide fluctuations badly distort the size of the movement. There is also a lack of balanced industry representation in the list of 30 stocks. Keep in mind that the present list has been in existence for 57 years. The initial 12-stock average lasted only 20 years before the number was increased to 20. Twelve years later the 20 stock series was increased to 30. On both occasions the editors of the *Journal* recognized the need for expanding the list as the number of actively traded corporations increased. However, in spite of the continued expansion of large publicly held corporations, there has been no increase in the number of companies in the DJIA since 1928.

Recommendations

The small size and lack of representation by certain industries should be corrected. This can be accomplished by expanding the list to 40 corporations. However, this still leaves the problem of the divisor that distorts the magnitude of the daily change. If we look far enough ahead, the Dow divisor will approach zero. Consequently, daily changes will be absurdly wide in comparison to actual fluctuations. At some point the *Journal* editors must face the necessity of providing a more realistic reflection of the daily movement of the stocks comprising the DJIA. My recommendation is to increase the corporate issues to 40 and modify the divisor. This will present the *Journal* editors with problems, but major changes were made successfully in the DJIA in 1916 and 1928.

The Wall Street Journal on October 2, 1928, pointed out the reasons for enlarging and modifying membership in the DJIA:

> The purposes of these changes are obvious: To make the averages more representative of a greatly expanded market; to substitute for inactive or unrepresentative issues, stocks of greater activity and significance, not only market wise, but as indexes of the country's business; and to minimize the possibility of unusual fluctuations in any one stock distorting the averages on any given day.[7]

The article also points out that "the historical continuity" of the Dow will not be affected by this change in view of the constancy of the divisor (see Figure 5–5).

In addition to expanding membership in the Dow Industrials, on two occasions *The Journal* editors also have made numerous substitutions since 1896. The list of 30 industrials, for example, has been modified on 15 occasions between 1928 and present (see Figure 4–2). The most recent substitutions occurred on October 30, 1985 when McDonald's and Philip Morris replaced Allied Brands and General Foods. The majority of modifications were made during the 1930s. A review of all the DJIA changes over the past 89 years indicates that troubled economic times produce more frequent replacements. In addition, the editor designated as Keeper of the Dow influences the frequency of change as well as its com-

FIGURE 5-5 Announcement of New List of 30 Stocks in the DJIA

DOW-JONES STOCK AVERAGE ENLARGED

Composed of 30 Instead of 20 Stocks to Reflect Better the Broader Market

Beginning with Monday, October 1, the Dow-Jones industrial averages are being increased to 30 from 20 stocks. At the same time a few substitutions are being made in the old list of 20 stocks. The purposes of these changes are obvious: To make the averages more representative of a greatly expanded market; to substitute for inactive or unrepresentative issues stocks of greater activity and significance, not only marketwise, but as indices of the country's business; and tó minimize the possibility of unusual fluctuations in any one stock distorting the averages on any given day.

The new list of 30 stocks follows, with those issues starred which were in the former average of 20 stocks:

* Allied Chemical
* American Can
* Americaŋ Smelting
* American Sugar
† Amⁿrican Tobacco B
Atlantic Refining
Bethlehem Steel
Chrysler
* General Electric
* Generaꞏ Motors
General Railway Signal
Goodrich
* International Harvester
International Nickel
* Mack Trucks

Nash Motors
North American
* Paramount-Famous (new)
Postum
Radio Corp.
* Sears Roebuck
Stand. Oil of N. J.
* Texas Corp.
Texas Gulf Sulphur
Union Carbide
* U. S. Steel
Victor Talking Machine
Westinghouse Electric
* Woolworth
Wright Aero

† American Tobacco "B" substituted for "A" stock.

The aboye list includes 20 of the 25 stocks that have not failed to be among the 50 most active leaders in 75% or more of the weeks so far this year. A few substitutions have been made in eliminating stocks used in the old list of 20 stocks; General Railway Signal was substituted as an equipment stock for American Car & Foundry and American Locomotive; American Tobacco 'B' was substituted for 'A' because of its greater activity; American Telephone and Western Union were dropped because they represented industries whose profits were directly under public regulation, and in their place North American was, substituted, representing a large utility holding company and one whose profits are only indi-

Clarence W. Barron, longtime president and owner Dow Jones Company, Inc., died at the Battle Creek Sanatorium (Battle Creek, Michigan) the day this announcement of the new list of 30 stocks appeared in the Journal. *William Peter Hamilton, editor at the time, was responsbile for implementing the change.*

SOURCE *The Wall Street Journal*, October 2, 1928, p.21.

FIGURE 5–5 *(concluded)*

---

rectly subject to regulation: Goodrich was substituted for
U. S. Rubber; *.* *. .* Kodak was dropped because of its
inactivity, while another luxury stock, Victor, was substituted; National Biscuit was displaced in favor of another food stock, Postum.

As constituted at present, the new Dow-Jones averages of industrial stocks represent a fair cross-section of American business. Roughly, the total of the 30 stocks is composed as follows: Motors, 13%; chemicals, 9%; steel and equipments, 8%; oils, 7%; mining, etc., 11%; electrical equipment, 7%; food products, 4%; stores, 8%; farm equipments 7%; amusements, luxuries and miscellaneous, 26%.

As explained in The Wall Street Journal of September 11, the historical continuity of the Dow-Jones averages will not be affected by changes of this nature. The total of the 30 stocks is merely divided by a constant figure which on a given day gives the same resulting average as resulted from the old method. In this case the constant divisor is based upon Saturday's closing prices, and the figure is 16.67. This constant will be used indefinitely until there is some further change in the averages: either by stock split-ups, large stock dividends, or actual substitutions.

---

position. Dow, for instance, in six years (1896 to 1902) made 15 substitutions. Three succeeding editors made five changes in 14 years (1902 to 1916). There have been only six changes in the past 26 years.

In 1970 the Railroad Average (originated in 1896) became the Transportation Average. This significant 1970 modification resulted in the replacement of nine railroad issues by nine airline and trucking companies. As pointed out in *The Wall Street Journal* (see Figure 5–6), this revision required a change in the divisor. The *Journal* article also indicated the reason for this action: "Dictating the change in the average is the drastically altered pattern of commercial transportation itself. When the railroad average was begun toward the end of the 19th century, the rails were the giant movers of both freight and people. Automobiles, trucks, buses, and airplanes hadn't even arrived on the scene."[8]

It is apparent there is precedent for making a major revision in the DJIA—and now is the time. We are witnessing a drastic change in our economy. The United States is moving from primary emphasis on basic industries and manufacturing to a nation providing an abundance of consumer services and products. In order for the Dow Industrials to reflect a broader cross section of our economy, I recommend the following modifications:

Delete:
American Telephone &
   Telegraph
International Harvester

Add:
American Broadcasting
CBS Inc.
Citicorp
Hewlett-Packard
Hilton
Holiday Inns
Honeywell, Inc.
Hospital Corporation of
   America
Merrill Lynch
Pillsbury
Schering Plough
Wells Fargo

My *proposed* list of 40 Dow Jones Industrials may be divided into 16 categories, as shown in Figure 5–7.

In addition to the problem of the composition of the DJIA, there is also the divisor difficulty. The lower the divisor goes, the wider the fluctuation. This can be remedied by weighting the stock being split. The result would be to stabilize the divisor. This concept would also be used to make substitutions[9] in the Dow and to allow for stock dividends. There is precedence for using this method. During the life of the 20-stock average (1916 to 1928), for example, the divisor remained at 20. This was accomplished by weighting each stock split based on the size of the split. A 2 for 1 split would require double weighting. The following companies split their stock between 1916 and 1928:

Company	Multiplier
American Can	6
American Car & Foundry	2
American Tobacco	2
General Electric*	4
Sears Roebuck*	4

*What a buy Sears and GE would have been in 1928. Since that date Sears has split 4 for 1; 3 for 1; 2 for 1; and 2 for 1. As a result 100 shares would have increased to 4800 shares. Between 1928 and 1983 GE split 4 for 1; 3 for 1; 2 for 1; and 2 for 1. The 100 shares of GE (cost—$16,400) would have grown to 4,800 shares and be worth $290,400 at this writing.

FIGURE 5-6   Announcement of New List of 20 Stocks in the Dow Jones
Transportation Average

'Dow-Jones 20 Rails' Gets 9 Non Rail Stocks And a New Designation

'Transportation Average' Is Name, As of Last Friday; Securities Of 9 Roads Have Been Deleted

By a WALL STREET JOURNAL *Staff Reporter*

NEW YORK — Starting with the market prices of last Friday, the Dow-Jones average of 20 railroad stocks was modified to include other forms of transportation.

The transportation average, as it will be known henceforth, is a continuation of the railroad average, except that nine railroad stocks have been deleted and replaced by nine other transportation securities.

Thus the number of stocks in the average remains at 20, and the total in the Dow-Jones composite average continues unchanged at 65.

Transition to the revised average has been effected smoothly through adjustment of divisors for the transportation average and the average of 65 stocks.

Continued in the transportation average from the railroad average are the stocks of the following 11 railroads: Canadian Pacific Railway, Great Northern Railway, Louisville & Nashville Railroad, Norfolk & Western Railway, Penn Central, St. Louis-San Francisco Railway, Santa Fe Industries Inc., Seaboard Coast Line Industries Inc., Southern Pacific Co., Southern Railway and Union Pacific Corp.

To these have been added the stocks of the following nine companies: American Airlines, Consolidated Freightways Inc., Eastern Air Lines, Northwest Airlines, Pacific Intermountain Express Co., Pan American World Airways, Trans World Airlines, UAL Inc. (holding company for United Air Lines) and U.S. Freight Co.

SOURCE   *The Wall Street Journal,* January 5, 1970, p.19.

FIGURE 5–6   *(concluded)*

Stocks of the following nine concerns, which were in the railroad average, have been deleted from the transportation average: Chesapeake & Ohio Railway, Florida East Coast Ry., Gulf, Mobile & Ohio Railroad, Illinois Central Industries Inc., Kansas City Southern Industries Inc., Missouri Pacific Railroad, Northwest Industries Inc., Rio Grande Industries Inc. and Western Pacific Railroad.

The additions and deletions created a divisor for the Dow-Jones transportation average of 4.084, compared with the old rail average divisor of 4.721, and changed the divisor for the 65 stocks to 10.141 from 10.568.

Dictating the change in the average is the drastically altered pattern of commercial transportation itself. When the railroad average was begun toward the end of the 19th Century, the rails were the giant movers of both freight and people. Automobiles, trucks, buses and airplanes hadn't even arrived on the scene.

As recently as 20 years ago, the rails still carried 62% of all intercity freight on a ton-mileage basis. By last year, though, that share had shrunk to 41%. And, over the same 20 years, the share carried by commercial truckers nearly doubled, rising from 11% to 21%. The rest of the load is moved by pipelines, water transport and airplanes.

By last year the railroad movement of intercity passengers had shrunk to a thin 1.2% of the total, on a passenger-mile basis, from nearly 10% two decades earlier. Private autos carried a huge 86% of the intercity passenger load last year, airlines had 9.4% of the traffic and buses 2.5%.

Also considered in revision of the average was the contraction through merger of the number of leading railroads and the diversification of some railroad companies into non-transportation business.

FIGURE 5–7 Stillman's Proposed List of 40 Dow Jones Industrials

Aerospace
United Technologies
Automobile, truck and related
General Motors
Goodyear
Chemicals and other
Allied-Signal
Du Pont
Union Carbide
Electrical
General Electric
Westinghouse Electric
Electronic
Hewlett-Packard
Honeywell, Inc.
International Business
Machines
Financial
American Express
Citicorp
Merrill Lynch
Wells Fargo

Health care
Hospital Corporation of America
Merck
Schering Plough
Hotel and entertainment
Hilton
Holiday Inns
McDonald's
Manufacturing—steel, aluminum, nickel and copper
Aluminum Company of America
Bethlehem Steel
Inco
U.S. Steel
Manufacturing—containers, and tapes
American Can
Minnesota Mining & Manufacturing
Owens-Illinois
Media
American Broadcasting
CBS Inc.

Paper and paper products
International Paper
Petroleum
Chevron
Exxon
Texaco
Photography
Eastman Kodak
Restaurant, food, tobacco, and soap
Philip Morris
Pillsbury
Procter & Gamble
Retail stores and other
Sears Roebuck & Co.
Woolworth

Summary of Recommendations.

1. *Stabilize the divisor.* It is apparent that eventually the Dow editors must face up to the problem of a shrinking divisor. This problem could be resolved as outlined in the paragraph above and not harm the continuity of the DJIA.

2. *Expand and modify the membership.* It would be desirable to increase the number of stocks in the Industrial Average to 40 and to replace two stocks currently in the list. Such action would provide better representation of the stock market.

3. *Remove "weak sisters."* The current Keeper of the Dow should respond more rapidly to changing company fortunes by making prompt substitutions. The significant DJIA switch on October 30, 1985 was a step in the right direction. (See p. 62.)

NOTES

[1]Capital International, S.A., Geneva, Switzerland, compiles a market value weighted index composed of stocks from many nations.

[2]Standard & Poor's averages are weighted arithmetic means. In contrast, the Dow averages are unweighted arithmetic means. A further refinement is Value Line's (VI) unweighted geometric mean, which is used to determine its seven averages. Price fluctuations are weighted equally in the VLA by use of ratios.

[3]In addition to the four stock averages, Dow Jones has six bond averages and an average of yields on a group of bonds.

[4]The first average (20 stocks), composed exclusively of railroads, was published by Dow in *The Wall Street Journal* on October 26, 1896. The Railroad Average was modified and renamed the Transportation Average effective January 2, 1970. The Utility Average (15 stocks) was not published in the *Journal* until January 2, 1929.

[5]The Dow Jones News Service makes this information available worldwide momentarily after it is computed.

[6]*USA Today*, November 25, Section B, p. 1.

[7]*The Wall Street Journal*, October 2, 1928, p. 21.

[8]*The Wall Street Journal*, January 5, 1970, p. 19.

[9]Substitutions currently require a change in the divisor unless the stock replaced is selling at exactly the same price. If the replacement is selling at a higher price, then the divisor will rise. Conversely, it will be lower if the old issue sells at a higher price.

6

The Dow Theory

Charles H. Dow never intended his theory of price movements to be construed as being a method whereby the royal road to riches could be found.
— *Robert Rhea*

What has come to be spoken of as the Dow Theory is in effect the combined wisdom of the late Charles H. Dow and William Peter Hamilton.
— *Hugh Bancroft*

DEFINITION

The Dow Theory may be defined as a technique for predicting the movement of stock prices. The tools used over the years to forecast the movement are the Dow Jones Industrial Average (DJIA) and the Dow Jones Transportation Average (DJTA).[1]

According to Dow, fluctuations in the stock market can be divided into three categories of movement which all occur at the same time:

1. Main movement (four or more years).[2]
2. Short swing (two weeks to a month or more).
3. Narrow movement (daily change).

Future trends (up or down), according to Dow theorists, can be determined if the preceeding secondary high or low trend is exceeded by both the industrial and transportation averages.[3] If the trend is up, this would signal a bullish move ahead, whereas a downward penetration would indicate a downward or bearish direction. In addition to the movement of the DJIA and DJTA, Dow theorists take into consideration the number of shares traded—the greater the volume, the stronger the trend confirmation.

DOW THEORY CONTRIBUTORS

There are five writers who made significant contributions to the Dow Theory body of knowledge. Let us look briefly at the following individuals:

Name	Born	Died	Principal Occupation
Charles Henry Dow	November 6, 1851	December 4, 1902	journalist–entrepreneur
Samuel Armstrong Nelson*	1877	October 28, 1907	writer–publisher
William Peter Hamilton	January 20, 1867	December 9, 1929	journalist
Robert Rhea	October 26, 1896	November 6, 1939	writer–publisher
George Wesley Bishop, Jr.	January 13, 1910	August 14, 1974	writer–professor

*The *New York Times* obituary section of Thursday, October 31, 1907, said, "Mr. Nelson was born on Staten Island 30 years ago." If correct, this meant that Nelson published his first book at age 21. It was titled *How To Gain Admission To Annapolis, West Point, The Navy Or The Schoolship St. Mary's* (New York 1898).

Charles Henry Dow

A look at Figure 1–11 (The Life and Times of Charles H. Dow) indicates that Dow lived little more than six years after devising his industrial and railroad averages. Yet during this time he evolved his theory on forecasting the movement of the market. He stated his views in articles appearing in *The Wall Street Journal* between 1899 and 1902.

However, Dow never signed his name to any of the *Journal* articles since it was not the custom to do so at that time. Nor did he leave any handwritten records providing positive evidence that his theory or the averages were his sole creation. But William P. Hamilton, the fourth editor of *the Journal* (1908 to 1929), wrote in his book *The Stock Market Barometer*:

> Knowing and liking Dow, with whom I worked in the last years of his life, I was often, with many of his friends, exasperated by his overconservatism. It showed itself particularly in his editorials in *The Wall Street Journal*, to which it is now necessary to allude because

they are the only written record of Dow's theory of the price movement.[4]

Samuel A. Nelson was also a firsthand observer of Dow's work. Writing in 1902 he said:

Following the publication of *The ABC of Wall Street* there were many requests for a book dealing with the principles governing stock speculation. If there is one man better qualified than another to produce such a book that man is Charles H. Dow. Several attempts were made to have him write the desired volume but they were unavailing. From time to time in his Wall Street career, extending over a quarter of a century, Mr. Dow has carefully evolved his theories of successful stock speculation.[5]

Thomas F. Woodlock succeeded Dow as editor of *The Wall Street Journal* in 1902. He had been working with the firm since 1892. He pointed out that "Dow attended to the stock market end of the news and wrote the stock market gossip."[6] In the same article he stated that it was "Dow who wrote the 'Review and Outlook' " editorial column. This column first appeared in the *Journal* in 1899. It was in the "Review and Outlook" that Dow presented his stock market theories.

The writings of Nelson, Hamilton, and Woodlock provide sufficient evidence that Dow is author of the material on market movements. In the beginning of this chapter the definition of the Dow Theory was presented as including three movements. Dow, in 1900, wrote about these movements as follows:

We have spoken in a preceeding article of the fact that the experience of great interests in the market seems to have crystalized into three general lines of reasoning.

The first is that the surface appearance of the market is apt to be deceptive. The second is that it is well in trading to cut losses short and let profits run. The third is that correctly discounting the future is a sure and easy road to wealth. The problem is how these rules, which are undoubtedly sound, can be operated in a practical way.

Let us take first the notion of the general market with reference to the time to buy. The market is always to be considered as having three movements, all going on at the same time. The first is the narrow movement from day to day. The second is the short swing, running from two weeks to a month or more; the third is the main movement covering at least four years in its duration.

The day to day movement should be disregarded by everybody, except traders who pay no commissions. The medium swing is the one for ordinary consideration. The outside trader should not attempt to deal in more than two or three stocks at a time. He should keep a chart of the price movements of these stocks so as to know their swings for months or years, and thus be able to tell readily where in the general swing his particular stocks appear to be.

He should keep with his price movement a record of the volume of transactions and notes of any special facts bearing on that property, such as increases or decreases in earnings, increases in fixed charges, development of floating debt, and above all the actual dividend earnings as shown from month to month. He should observe the movement of the general market as indicated by the averages given daily in the Journal as this shows the market more clearly than it is shown by any one stock.

The main purpose of this study is to enable the trader to determine, first, the value of the stock he is in; whether it is increasing or decreasing and, second, when the time to buy seems opportune. Assuming the thirty day swing to be about 5 points, it is in the highest degree desirable not to buy when three of these have passed, as such a purchase limits the probable profits to about two points.

It is therefore generally wise to look for a low point on a decline. Suppose, for instance, that Union Pacific was the stock under consideration; that it was clearly selling below its value, and that a bull market for the four-year period was under way. Assume further that in a period of reaction Union Pacific had fallen four points from the previous highest. Assume earnings and prospects to be favorable and the outlook for the general market to be about normal.

This would be the time to begin to buy Union Pacifics. The prudent trader, however, would take only part of his line. He would buy perhaps one-half of the stock he wanted and then give an order to buy the remainder as the price declined. The fall might go much further than he anticipated. It might be necessary to wait a long time for profit. There might even be developments which would make it wise to throw over the stock bought with the hope of replacing it materially lower.

These, however, are all exceptions. In a majority of cases this method of choosing the time to buy, founded upon clear perception of value in the stock chosen and close observation of the market swings under way will enable an operator to secure stock at a time and at a price which will give fair profits on the investment.

The comparative advantages of trading with stop orders and of trading with reference to the future will be made the subject of another article.

Note that Dow refers to the various market movements as "three general lines of reasoning." He goes on to point out how these "swings" may be utilized. Dow states that "The day-to-day movement should be disregarded by everybody, except traders, who pay no commissions." It is apparent that he recognized such traders both had the time to monitor the market closely and were able to buy/sell with no brokerage fee. The medium swings (two weeks to a month or more) he suggests are for the outsider who "should not attempt to deal in "more than two or three stocks at one time."

Dow uses the article to offer advice to both the technical analyst and the fundamentalist:[7]

> He should keep a chart of the price movements of these stocks so as to know their swings for months or years, and thus be able to tell readily where in the general swing his particular stocks appear to be.
>
> He should keep with his price movement a record of the volume of transactions and notes of any special facts bearing on that property, such as increases or decreases in earnings, increases in fixed charges, development of floating debt, and, above all, the actual dividend earnings as shown from month to month.

Dow gives both his newspaper and his averages a plug in this editorial by advising the outside trader to "observe the movement of the general market as indicated by the averages given daily in the *Journal* as this shows the market more clearly than it is shown by any one stock."

In the final two paragraphs Dow hedges in his advice to readers:

> This would be the time to begin to buy Union Pacifics. The prudent trader, however, would take only part of his line. He would buy perhaps one half of the stock he wanted and then give an order to buy the remainder as the price declined. The fall might go much further than he anticipated. It might be necessary to wait a long time for profit. There might even be developments which would make it wise to throw over the stock bought with the hope of replacing it materially lower.
>
> These, however, are all exceptions. In a majority of cases this method of choosing the time to buy, founded upon clear perception of value in the stock chosen and close observation of the market swings under way, will enable an operator to secure stock at a time and at a price which will give fair profits on the investment.

It is apparent from a study of Dow's article that he considered both technical factors and fundamental data in arriving at his recommendations. He was prudent in advising readers. His other writings in the *Journal* between 1899 and 1902 support this approach.

It is quite remarkable that Dow developed his concept after relatively limited experience with his averages. Remember that the DJIA and the DJRA were born in 1896 and that Dow died in 1902. Dow himself never referred to his concept as the Dow Theory. And he intermingled his "Review and Outlook" articles on the stock movements with other information.

Samuel Armstrong Nelson

S. A. Nelson was the first person to use the actual term *Dow's Theory*. Nelson used it to describe a number of articles written by Dow which were published in Nelson's 1902 book titled *The ABC of Stock Speculation*. Of the 35 chapters in the book (232 pages), *Dow's Theory* comprises Chapters V through XX (a total of 72 pages) which are titled as follows:

Chapters	Title
V	Scientific Speculation
VI	The Two General Methods of Trading
VII	Three General Lines of Reasoning
VIII	Swings within Swings
IX	Methods of Reading the Market
X	The Operation of Stop Orders
XI	Cutting Losses Short
XII	The Danger in Overtrading
XIII	Methods of Trading
XIV	The Out of Town Trader
XV	The Short Side of the Market
XVI	Speculation for the Decline
XVII	Concerning Discretionary Accounts
XVIII	The Liability for Loss
XIX	The Recurrence of Crises
XX	Financial Criticism

The term *Dow's Theory* appears as a footnote at the beginning of Chapters V through XX (see Figure 6–1). Nelson states in his preface that "From time to time in his Wall Street career, extending over a quarter of a century, Mr. Dow has carefully evolved his theories of successful stock speculation," and he also states, "In the preparation of this little volume, thanks are also due to *The Wall Street Journal* . . . Dow, Jones & Co.'s News Agency."[11] It must be assumed that Dow authorized use of this material as he did not die until December 4, 1902, and the book was published that year.

FIGURE 6–1 Nelson Names Dow's Theory

28   THE A B C OF STOCK SPECULATION.

CHAPTER V.

*SCIENTIFIC SPECULATION.

The question whether there is such a thing as scientific speculation is often asked. Various answers of a somewhat affirmative character have been given but they have generally been hedged about with so many qualifications as to be nearly useless for practical purposes. The experiences of operators have, however, crystallized into some general rules worth heeding.

The maxim "buy cheap and sell dear" is as old as speculation itself, but it leaves unsolved the question of when a security or a commodity is cheap and when it is dear, and this is the vital point.

The elder Rothschilds are said to have acted on the principle that it was well to buy a property of known value when others wanted to sell and to sell when others wanted to buy. There is a great deal of sound wisdom in this. The public, as a whole, buys at the wrong time and sells at the wrong time. The reason is that markets are made in part by manipulation and the public buys on manipulated advances and after they are well along. Hence it buys at the time when manipulators wish to sell and sells when manipulators wish to buy.

In some commission offices, there are traders who, as a rule, go against whatever the outside customers of the

_____
*Dow's Theory.

The term Dow's Theory *is named by S. A. Nelson for the first time as a footnote in Chapter V.*

Nelson covered a number of other subjects in the remaining chapters of his book. Topics included "The Bucket Shop," "The Tipster," "Methods of Trading," and 16 others related to the stock market. *However, Nelson, made no attempt to analyze Dow's work.* He took only selected *Journal* editorials (16) and, with minor modifications, gave them chapter heading titles.

The only changes Nelson made in Dow's December 14, 1900, article, for example, were to title it "Scientific Speculation" (see Figure 6–1) and to delete the last paragraph, which states, "The application of these methods of trading will be made the subject of future articles." You may wish to read Dow's article as it appeared in the *Journal* (see Figure 6–2). It is interesting to note that in this writing Dow presents general trading guidelines worth heeding today:

1. Buy cheap and sell dear. Dow cautioned, however, that the vital point is determining when it is cheap or dear. He believed that the public as a whole bought and sold at the wrong time. Dow said "that markets are made in part by manipulation." I wonder what his reaction would be to the "greenmail" artists today who threaten corporate takeovers and make millions doing it.
2. Buy a property of known value when the public is generally disposed to sell and sell it when the general public thinks it is time to buy (Rothchild Principle).
3. Cut your losses short and let your profits run (Daniel Drew Principle).
4. Endeavor to foresee future conditions in a property and then exercise great patience in awaiting results (Jay Gould Principle). Dow believed that "within limits the future can be foreseen. The present is always tending toward the future and there are always in existing conditions signals of danger or encouragement for those who read with care." It would appear that he meant to imply that Dow's Theory provided appropriate signals regarding future conditions.

Nelson's contribution is significant because he recognized the importance of Dow's concept, gave it a name, and made it available to the public.

Dow theorist Richard Russell applauded Nelson's book in the Introduction to a republished 1964 edition:

Study this little book, "The ABC of Stock Speculation." You will probably be amazed at how modern most of Dow's observations seem

FIGURE 6-2 Dow's Article on Stock Market Concepts

REVIEW AND OUTLOOK.

The question whether there is such a thing as scientific speculation is often asked. Various answers of a somewhat affirmative character have been given but, they have generally been hedged about with so many qualifications as to be nearly useless for practical purposes. The experiences of operators have, however, crystalized into some general rules worth heeding.

The maxim "buy cheap and sell dear", is as old as speculation itself, but it leaves unsolved the question of when a security of a commodity is cheap and when it is dear, and this is the vital point.

The elder Rothschilds are said to have acted on the principle that it was well to buy a property of known value when others wanted to sell and to sell when others wanted to buy. There is a great deal of sound wisdom in this. The public, as a whole, buys at the wrong time and sells at the wrong time. The reason is that markets are made in part by manipulation and the public buys on manipulated advances and after they are well along. Hence it buys at the time when manipulators wish to sell and sells when manipulators wish to buy.

In some commission offices, there are traders who, as a rule, go against whatever the outside customers of the house are doing. When members of the firm say, "all our customers are getting long of stocks," these traders sell out; but they buy when the firm says, "the customers are all short." There are of course, exceptions to this rule. If there were no exceptions, the keepers of bucket shops would all get rich. When the market has an extraordinary rise, the public makes money, in spite of beginning its purchases at what would ordinarily be the wrong time, and this is when the bucket shops either lose their money or close out in order to keep such money of customers as they have in hand.

All this points to the soundness of the Rothschild principle of buying a property of known value when the public generally is disposed to sell; or of selling it when the general public thinks it a time to buy.

Daniel Drew used to say, "cut your losses short, but let your profits run." This was good preaching, but "Uncle Dan" did not, in his later years, practice his rule, when it would have been better for him if he had. The thought here is unquestionably one of the sound principles in trading. It means that if a stock has been purchased and it goes up, it is well to wait; but if it goes down, it is well to stop the loss quickly on the ground that the theory on which the purchase was made was wrong.

SOURCE *The Wall Street Journal,* December 14, 1900, p.1.

FIGURE 6–2 *(concluded)*

The public, as a whole, exactly reverses this rule. The average operator, when he sees two or three points profit, takes it; but, if a stock goes against him two or three points, he holds on waiting for the price to recover, with, oftentimes, the result of seeing a loss of two or three points run into a loss of ten points. He then becomes discouraged and sells out near the bottom to protect the margin in which he has left.

How many operators in looking over their books find a considerable number of small profits swept away by one large loss? When a trader finds by his accounts that his profits have been relatively large and his losses relatively small, he can make up his mind that he is learning how to trade.

The trouble with carrying out this plan is that a series of losses of from 1½ to 2 points are very discouraging. A trader who sees that he has taken twice or three times a loss of two points when, if he had waited a few days he need not have taken any loss, is very apt to decide that he will not cut his losses short any more, but will wait, and this is the time when the recovery does not come.

Mr. Jay Gould said his policy was to endeavor to foresee future conditions in a property and then, having made his commitments carefully, to exercise great patience in awaiting results. This also is sound doctrine, but proceeds along very different lines. Assuming the ability to foresee the future, it is the wisest of all courses; but many who have tried this method have found that the omission of essential factors made their forecast valueless, and both their courage and their patience of little avail. Nevertheless, this method should not be discarded on account of the difficulties involved. Within limitations, the future can be foreseen. The present is always tending toward the future and there are always in existing conditions signals of danger or encouragement for those who read with care.

The application of some of these methods of trading will be made the subject of future articles.

and sound. And be glad you own this book. Had I been fortunate enough to own it many years ago, I probably would have saved most of my first and only inheritance.[9]

Russell succinctly discusses Dow's contribution to Nelson's book.

Dow wrote for his *Wall Street Journal*. All his market observations, observations so penetrating and universal that they form the basis of modern technical analysis, were written in the form of editorials for the *Journal* around the turn of the century. At that time a man named S. A. Nelson was publishing a library of books about Wall Street. Nelson was a great admirer of Dow's and to his everlasting credit, Nelson recognized the historic value of Dow's work. Nelson begged Dow to write a special book on his unique theories of the stock market. But Dow was a reticent man. Finally, Nelson did get permission to include a number of Dow's *Wall Street Journal* editorials.[10]

Russell is right: Nelson produced a splendid little book that is worth reading today.

William Peter Hamilton

The fourth editor of *The Wall Street Journal* was W. P. Hamilton. He assumed that position in 1908 and retained it until his death on December 9, 1929. He was 32 years old when he began working for the *Journal* and had an opportunity to work closely with Dow between 1899 and 1902.

There was a long hiatus after Nelson's 1902 book on Dow's Theory. Although Hamilton had written articles in *The Wall Street Journal* and *Barron's* on the Dow Theory, the topic did not receive considerable publicity until after publication of his book, *The Stock Market Barometer*, in 1922.[11] The subtitle highlighted Hamilton's contribution: *A Study of Its Forecast Value Based on Charles H. Dow's Theory of the Price Movement with an Analysis of The Market and Its History Since 1897.*

Hamilton's 278-page text covered 22 topics (chapters) as follows:

Cycles and Stock Market Records

Wall Street of the Movies

Charles H. Dow, and his Theory

Dow's Theory, Applied to Speculation

Major Market Swings

A Unique Quality of Forecast

Manipulation and Professional Trading

Mechanics of the Market

"Water" in the Barometer

"A Little Cloud Out of the Sea, Like A Man's Hand"—1906

The Unpunctured Cycle

Forecasting a Bull Market—1908–09

Nature and Uses of Secondary Swings

1909 and Some Defects of History

A "Line" and an Example—1914

An Exception to Prove the Rule

Its Greatest Vindication—1917

What Regulation Did to Our Railroads

A Study in Manipulation 1900–1901

Some Conclusions—1910–4

Running True to Form—1922–1925

Some Thoughts for Speculators

Material from Hamilton's book appeared initially in *Barron's*. He points out that it was not his plan to publish a book on Dow's Theory:

> When *The Stock Market Barometer* first appeared serially in the columns of *Barron's*, mostly in the latter part of 1921, the order of the chapters adopted in the subsequent publication of the book was not used. Indeed, this study of Dow's theory of the price movement did not start out with the intention of making a book of itself. It was what an incurable newspaper man like myself would call a newspaper assignment.[12]

Hamilton's work gave the Dow Theory a solid foundation upon which others might build. Hugh Bancroft (president of Dow, Jones & Company from 1928 to 1933) put it well when he said, "What has come to be spoken of as the Dow Theory is in effect the combined wisdom of the late Charles H. Dow and William Peter Hamilton."[13]

Robert Rhea

Rhea was badly injured in an airplane accident during World War I, but like Franklin D. Roosevelt, he overcame his handicap. Despite being bedridden he made an important contribution to the body of Dow Theory knowledge. In his book, Rhea wrote about his handicap and how he turned a hobby into a success story:

> For more than 10 years my business affairs have been conducted from my bed and my only recreation has been the study of business economics—particularly the trends of business and of the stock market; and either the Dow theory or just plain luck caused me to buy a few stocks at the proper time in 1921 and prevented my owning any during the final stages of the 1929 uprush. Moreover, either the Dow theory or luck caused me to carry a short account of small proportions during the two years after the crash. Thus my study has paid dividends, and if I can explain the theory as I try to practice it, others may be helped. I hope so, anyhow.[14]

Rhea wrote his first book about Dow's work in 1932, titled *The Dow Theory: An Explanation of Its Development and an Attempt to Define its Usefulness as an Aid in Speculation*. It was first published in 1932 and republished in 1959 by Rhea, Greiner & Co. (executors of Robert Rhea), Colorado Springs, Colorado. His dedication read "To William Peter Hamilton, late editor of *The Wall Street Journal*, whose editorial comment on the stock price movement aided many of his readers to become successful traders." Rhea also hoped his book would be helpful to traders:

> Many will perhaps disagree with the conclusions drawn and definitions chosen, but it is possible that some of those reading this book with a sympathetic understanding of my limitations as a writer may find things in it that will prove helpful in their trading. It is for them that this study is written.[15]

Prior to *The Dow Theory* text Rhea published *Graphic Charts*, a set of charts showing the daily movement of the Dow Jones Averages (industrials and railroads) along with daily total sales on the New York Stock Exchange. About his chart venture Rhea said in the preface to *The Dow Theory*:

> A satisfactory demand developed at once, with a few remarks on the introductory sheet concerning the Dow theory and the writings of the late William Peter Hamilton, editor of *The Wall Street Journal*, bringing in an unexpected by-product in the shape of more than 500 letters of inquiry. So this book is being written as a means of offering those

correspondents, many of whom I now call friends, the benefit of my study of the theory.[16]

Robert Rhea wrote two other books and they were both on the Dow Theory. They were *The Story of the Averages: A Retrospective Study of the Forecasting Value of Dow's Theory as Applied to the Daily Movements of The Dow-Jones Industrial and Railroad Stock Averages* and *Dow's Theory Applied to Business and Banking.* The contributions of Rhea might be categorized as follows:

1. He provided students of the Dow Theory with loose-leaf charts in a binder to assist them in their technical analysis. He prepared 35 plates charting the daily movement of the industrial and railroad averages from 1897. This material permitted buyers to examine all lines made by the DJIA and DJRA over the years and observe the resultant action that occurred when lines were penetrated or the trading range broken.

2. *The Dow Theory* book contained William Peter Hamilton's 252 editorials in the *Journal* and *Barron's* pertinent to the averages and the Dow Theory between December 5, 1903 and December 8, 1929 (p. 115–252).

George Wesley Bishop, Jr.

The most scholarly work on the Dow Theory was written by Professor Bishop. He first submitted his material as a doctoral dissertation at New York University. He received his Ph.D. in 1959 and *Charles H. Dow and The Dow Theory* was published the following year.[17]

In his book Bishop cites the two reasons for his publication— lack of an adequate study of Dow's material and lack of a truly objective study.

There have been many attempts to interpret the fluctuations that occur in the stock market, and William Armstrong, as early as 1848, noted that although "intrinsic value" is the principal determinant in setting the market prices of securities, it is not the only factor involved. Since that time much has been written about intrinsic value, and the other market factors, and although the work of Charles H. Dow is often cited in this respect, an adequate study of Dow's writings has never been undertaken. Likewise, a truly objective study of the Dow Theory remains to be published. This book . . . is an attempt to fill this gap.[18]

Bishop's book does fill a major void in the Dow Theory literature. His first 247 pages cover the following subjects:[19]

The Early Life of Charles H. Dow

A Newspaper in Providence

Letters From the Magic City

Dow in New York City

The S. A. Nelson Version of the Dow Theory

The Editorials of Charles H. Dow

The Interpretation of William Peter Hamilton

The Work of Robert Rhea

The Evolution of the Dow Theory

Bishop met his two Dow Theory goals. He was objective and thorough. His background prepared him well to undertake such a project: he had a first rate education and excellent experience prior to undertaking the project: and he had attended school in New York City thereby having easy access to the *Journal* and other highly qualified sources. He also did not allow himself to be influenced by the Dow aura. Both Hamilton and Nelson knew Dow personally and Rhea had great admiration for Hamilton. Finally, Bishop was able to capitalize on the excellent contributions of his predecessors.

Bishop graduated with an A.B. from William and Mary in 1935. He then worked in New York City for U.S. Gypsum (1935 to 1936) and Union Carbide (1936 to 1942). In World War II (1942 to 1946) and the Korean Conflict (1950 to 1954) he served in the Navy. He retired as a Captain, USNR, and is buried in Arlington National Cemetery.

After both World War II and the Korean conflict he was employed by Merrill Lynch (1947 to 1950, 1954 to 1956, and 1957 to 1959). Bishop gained excellent financial experience at the brokerage firm as an account executive and portfolio analyst. He took advantage of the GI educational benefits and obtained both an M.B.A. (1955) and Ph.D. (1959). At age 49 he decided to seek a third career. He taught initially at the University of Tennessee (1959 to 1965) and later at Northern Illinois University (1965 until his death in 1974). In 1967, while at Northern Illinois, he edited *Charles H. Dow Economist: A Selection of His Writings on Business Systems*.

It is apparent that Bishop was well equipped to write about the Dow Theory. Each of the men presented in this section were well

THE DOW THEORY / 115

FIGURE 6–3   The House of Dow Theory

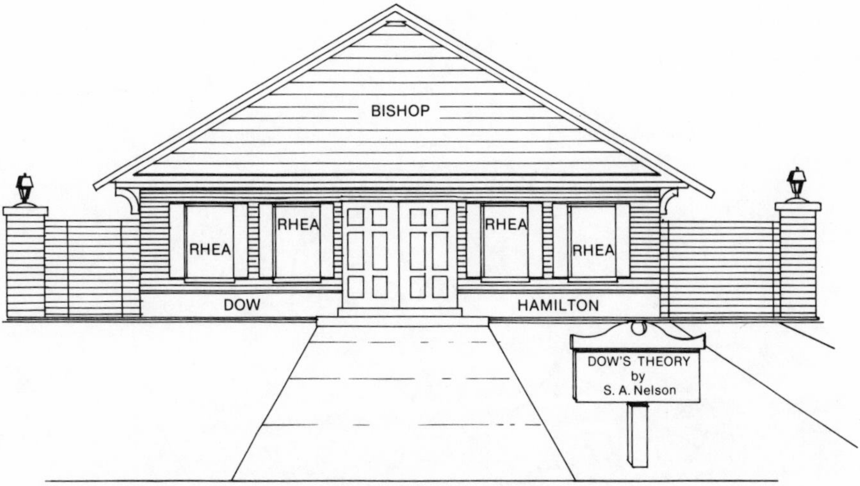

A graphic presentation of individual contributions to the Dow Theory body of knowledge by Dow, Nelson, Hamilton, Rhea, and Bishop.

© Copyright 1986, Richard J. Stillman. All Rights Reserved.

equipped to add to Dow's theory. I like to compare the five contributors to skilled subcontractors who built a custom home. Each provided part of the essential ingredients (see Figure 6–3). Dow and Hamilton furnished the architectural plans and solid foundation; Nelson prepared the framework and determined the name; Rhea did the custom interior with such rooms as charting, banking, primary movements, lines, double tops, and double bottoms; and Bishop completed the project (roof, exterior bricks, and landscaping) with his overview and analysis.

THREE CONVENTIONAL APPROACHES TO ANALYZING SECURITIES

We spoke earlier about Dow offering advice to both the technical analyst and the fundamentalist. Let us look briefly at the three conventional approaches that may be utilized in developing a securities program as shown in Figure 6–4. In the next chapter we

FIGURE 6–4   Three Approaches to Investment Analysis

These three approaches to investment analysis may be used to help you achieve your investment goals.

will examine an investment strategy that makes use of these three methods.

Chartist

The approach of technical analysis is primarily through the use of charts. By plotting daily price movements chartists observe trends in their issues. These patterns made by movements determine whether to buy, sell, or hold a particular stock. There is much work involved in plotting the daily changes, but there are firms that will provide this service for a fee.

The interpretation of charts varies with individuals. When a chart breaks out of a range, it is an indication of a buy or sell signal. Chartists rely on a variety of chart formations, such as head and shoulders, rectangles, flags, and triangles. The buy, sell, and hold indicators vary among chartists, for this is far from an exact science.

An excellent synopsis of market analysis techniques, written from a European perspective, appeared in R. J. Briston's 1973 book:

The first significant attempt to formulate a theory for the prediction of future levels of share prices based upon charts and index numbers was the Dow Theory. This was based upon the work of Charles H. Dow, the first editor of *The Wall Street Journal*, who began the compilation of daily averages of stock prices in order to obtain a pattern of price movements. On January 1, 1897, he first published two averages—the index of industrial stocks and the index of rail stocks.

From his studies he pioneered chartist terminology, distinguishing between primary, secondary, and tertiary trends. He also recognized the basic chartist tenet that an index of stock prices reflects all that is generally known about the overall prospects of business and expresses all the hopes and fears for the prospects of the individual companies of which it is comprised. Although he did not formally develop a theory based upon his indices his ideas were extended and formulated by W. P. Hamilton.

Movements of Dow's indices were analysed over a period of years and it was found that certain patterns tended to repeat themselves so that it was possible to predict future movements of the indices with some degree of success. The basic feature of the Dow Theory, which was based upon this analysis, was that a movement of one of the indices should not be acted upon unless it was confirmed by a movement in the same direction of the other index. Proponents of the theory argued that confirmed movements of this sort generally preceded a turn in the state of the economy by about six months and they claimed to have predicted successfully the market break of 1929 though their record at other times was inconsistent.

Since its formulation the theory has been adapted to include other confirmatory indices such as the breadth index, which is computed by dividing the figure of net advances or declines by the total number of issues which were dealt in, and the activity index. Despite the serious theoretical arguments against the theory, and, indeed, against all technical analysis, it has many adherents and as such constitutes an important factor on Wall Street.

Although the pure form of the Dow Theory is not applicable to the London Stock Exchange due to the absence of an index of rail stocks, there are nevertheless many similar theories.[20]

Fundamentalist

The fundamentalist takes a hard look at statistical data and other relevant facts in analyzing the investment merits of corporations. For example, the following areas are considered important in deciding which growth securities to select.

Earnings. In order to survive and expand in our economic system, a corporation must make a profit. Ideally, from an investor's viewpoint, these earnings should increase yearly and at a faster rate than the Dow Jones Industrial Average, thus permitting the growth-minded company to plow back much of its profits for such undertakings as plant expansion, research and development, and long-range planning. These actions should result in greater profits in the long run.

Dividends and price. As a potential stockholder, you should be concerned with dividend payments. Normally, growth companies pay out little in the way of cash dividends. However, in the long run the dividend payments may be larger, based on your original investment, than if you had placed your money in income-producing issues. The primary purpose of going into growth issues is the capital gains potential; that is, you expect the price to appreciate at a faster rate than the stock market averages.

Other quantitative data. In order to make valid comparisons, it helps to look at important ratios, including liquidity ratios that reflect on a corporation's ability to meet its short-term obligations. Two of these are the current ratio and the acid-test ratio. Stock ratios of interest are price/earnings, earnings per share, and yield. Profitability ratios indicate earnings in relation to sources that generate them, such as profit margin to total sales, net profit to total assets, and net worth to net profit. It is also desirable to look at the cash flow, because without adequate money to meet its expansion and debt needs, a company can be in deep trouble. Other useful information may be book value, long-term debt, and capital expenditures.

Management. First-class leadership has a favorable influence on the success of any organization. Make every effort, prior to investment, to get information about the top managers. A factor such as rapid turnover of senior officers is not a healthy situation.

In this era of social awareness, it is also important for the company leadership to be in the hands of people who demonstrate a sense of responsibility concerning the key issues of our time. There is much that industry can do in seeking solutions to such problems as hard-core unemployment, pollution, poor race relations, inadequate education, ecological imbalance, overpopulation, urban decay, alienation of youth, drug addiction, and improper allocation of resources.

Formulator

A formulator is one who reduces things to a formula. In the stock market there are several formulas that may be utilized. This approach may be combined with the fundamentalist view to trigger certain buy or sell actions. For example, you may wish to keep a balance in your portfolio of 80 percent stock and 20 percent cash reserves. In a market advance, your formula may call for a portfolio to double before you would sell stock and buy bonds to keep the same ratio. Suppose you initially had $2,000 in cash reserves and $8,000 in stocks. If the value of your stock moved from $8,000 to $18,000, you would sell $2,000 in securities and increase cash reserves by the same amount.

Another formula approach is based on the Dow Jones Industrial Average. The higher it goes, the more stock you would sell and convert the proceeds into bonds. Conversely, when the average goes down, you increase stock purchases and sell bonds.

In a sense, dollar averaging can be considered a formula approach. This is a systematic stock-purchase plan that involves investing the same number of dollars each month (or in whatever period you may select) in order to purchase shares of a corporation, thus buying more shares in periods of lower prices than in the higher range. In the long run this dollar averaging gives you a lower cost basis than if you bought the same number of shares periodically. The secret, of course, is to find a stock that has a healthy growth in spite of fluctuations. If your stock should have a marked decline over a period of years, dollar averaging or not, you will lose money.

Although dollar averaging sounds great on paper, many people may not have the same amount of money available at regular intervals. Therefore, it is sounder to invest on a dollar-availability basis. If a raise or bonus comes your way, put the increased dollars to work at once. Within the dollar-availability concept, it is possible to use a portion for dollar-averaging purposes and yet keep all your funds working. If the market appears over-priced at the time you receive a healthy bonus, it would be wise to place the money temporarily in a cash-reserve investment.

FIGURE 6–5 Stillman's Totalistic Approach to Investment Analysis

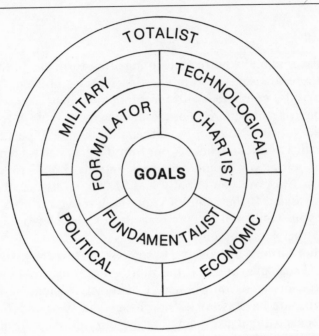

Stillman's totalistic approach to investment analysis may be used to help you achieve your investment goals.

STILLMAN'S TOTALISTIC APPROACH TO INVESTMENT ANALYSIS

I would like to present what I call a totalistic approach to investment analysis. Figure 6–5 indicates that in order to achieve your goals (inner ring) you should consider appropriate input derived from charts, formulas, and fundamentals (second ring).

PEMT and Vulnerability Indexes

But there is more to investment analysis than this. The impact of significant political, economic, military, and technological events (third ring) should also be considered in arriving at a total evaluation (outer ring). In the first four chapters I have presented graphically my significant PEMT events. One approach to weighing the impact of PEMT on the stock market is to use my PEMT index shown below.

PEMT Index

Factors	Your Rating as of_____
Political	
Economic	
Military	
Technological	

Ratings Scale	
Outstanding	4
Good	3
Fair	2
Poor	1

You can determine from your own analysis how good or bad the situation is at a particular time. The abundance of information available should enable you to perform this task *if you have the time*. Reading publications like the *New York Times* and *The Wall Street Journal* can help you in your evaluation. The lower (higher) the PEMT index rating, the stronger the buy (sell) signal. The PEMT Index should be used in conjunction with my Vulnerability Index. The Vulnerability Index indicates that the higher (or lower) the Dow (or a particular stock) rating, the greater the chance of a correction.[21]

Vulnerability Index

Rating Scale		Your Rating as of_____
New high	5	
Above normal	4	
Normal range	3	
Below normal	2	
New low (last 10 years)	1	

Now let us look at a specific time and apply the PEMT and Vulnerability indexes, first PEMT. A study of Figure 4–4 indicates that in the summer of 1974, Richard M. Nixon, as an aftermath of Watergate, resigned as president. It was a year of double-digit inflation, and the U.S. military was reeling from the impact of our nation's first war loss in history. The presidency was in a shambles and no major technological developments occurred. In regard to Vulnerability Index data we find that the DJIA closed at 777.30 on August 9, 1974, and by December 6, 1974, bottomed at 577.60.

Based on the information above, here are my PEMT and Vulnerability ratings.

PEMT Index

Factors	My Rating as of August 9, 1974
Political	1
Economic	1
Military	1
Technological	2
Total	5

Vulnerability Index

DJIA	
Below normal	2*
Grand total	7

---

*Later in 1974 this rating would drop to 1.

It is apparent that this 7 rating indicates a strong buy signal. The best buy signal would be a 5 and the best sell a 21. In the next chapter we will examine an investment strategy that uses my total approach to money management.

Why is only the DJIA included in the Vulnerability Index? Charles Henry Dow, in his significant "Watching the Tide" editorial of January 31, 1901 (see Figure 6–6), used only *one* average (the railroads) to explain his theory. The rails were the dominant average at that time. In his "Watching the Tide" article Dow compares the 20 Railway Stock Average to the tide as follows:

> A person watching the tide coming in and who wishes to know the spot which marks the high tide, sets a stick in the sand at the points

FIGURE 6–6   Dow's "Watching the Tide" Editorial

WATCHING THE TIDE.

A person watching the tide coming in and who wishes to know the spot which marks the high tide, sets a stick in the sand at the points reached by the incoming waves until the stick reaches a position where the waves do not come up to it, and finally recede enough to show that the tide has turned.

This method holds good in watching and determining the flood tide of the stock market. The average of twenty stocks is the peg which marks the height of the waves. The prices-waves, like those of the sea, do not recede all at once from the top. The force which moves them checks the inflow gradually and time elapses before it can be told with certainty whether high tide has been seen or not.

Take the market in the last few weeks, as shown by the table following:

20 railway stocks Saturday, Jan. 12 ....,. 97.85
20 railway stocks Saturday, Jan. 19. .. .. .. 93.56
20 railway stocks Wednesday, Jan. 23 .. .. 95.00
20 railway stocks Thursday, Jan. 24 ...... 93.90
20 railway stocks Wednesday, Jan. 30 .. . . 96.08

Here are the waves as they have come in. The high point January 12, the recession on the 19th, the next wave on the 23d, another recession on the 24th, and now another high point, crossing that on the 23d, but lacking more than a point of reaching the high level on the 12th.

Nobody can say with any certainty whether high tide has been seen or not. If the average rises above the level on the 12th, it will increase the probability of a new high level in the near future. If this does not occur the chances will favor a receding tide and a level lower than that on the 19th.

The market shows great strength in view of the unquestioned fact that quite a proportion of the strong interests are not participating in the advance, and, as far as their influence goes, are turning from rather than toward higher prices. The advance in St. Paul has destroyed the probability of an early deal in that stock. The advance in other stocks has led cliques to realize and induced prominent and successful houses to advise caution instead of confidence.

It has, on the other hand, led some operators to extend themselves with the idea of taking advantage of favorable conditions. If these operators obtain public support they will succeed, yet commission houses are not very bullish, and the public has not shown a great disposition to follow leads given by strong stocks.

There are indications that somebody long of the market is making advances in one stock after another for the purpose of drawing attention to them while he sells elsewhere. This is the generally accepted explanation of some of the recent moves in St. Paul and of the advance which occurred yesterday in Rock Island. It takes a large operator a good while to turn round. It is necessary some times to do a good deal of manipulation in order to market a moderate amount of stock, and something of this kind may be going on.

Six months ago, we occasionally pointed out that leading roads had increased earnings very materially in the course of six or eight months, while prices had actually declined. This was abnormal, and certain to result either in large loss of railway earnings or advance in stock prices. Whoever will look over the record of net earnings during the last six months will see only moderate gains except in special cases. Nevertheless, prices have gone up from 20 to 40 points. This has been partly a response to improved conditions early in the year, but it is a question whether the advance in prices has not discounted in most cases the improvement which has occurred.

There remains the advantage to be derived in the future from community of ownership. This is a fact of real importance and will have weight, but the rise in the market has interfered with these plans to such an extent that it is a question whether all that is involved in community of ownership will not be promoted more by receding prices than by advancing.

The market may be going up a great deal more, but there is no escape from the fact that it has risen a great deal in the last few months, and is at a level where prices occupy no such relation to values as they did six months ago.

reached by the incoming waves until the stick reaches a position where the waves do not come up to it, and finally recede enough to show that the tide has turned.

This method holds good in watching and determining the flood tide of the stock market. The average of 20 stocks is the peg which marks the height of the waves. The prices-waves, like those of the sea, do not recede all at once from the top. The force which moves them checks the inflow gradually and time elapses before it can be told with certainty whether high tide has been seen or not.

Take the market in the last few weeks, as shown by the table following:

20 railway stocks Saturday, Jan. 12	97.85
20 railway stocks Saturday, Jan. 19	93.56
20 railway stocks Wednesday, Jan. 23	95.00
20 railway stocks Thursday, Jan. 24	93.90
20 railway stocks Wednesday, Jan. 30	96.08

Here are the waves as they have come in. The high point January 12, the recession on the 19th, the next wave on the 23rd, another recession on the 24th and now another high point, crossing that on the 23rd but lacking more than a point of reaching the high level on the 12th.

Nobody can say with any certainty whether high tide has been seen or not. If the average rises above the level on the 12th, it will increase the probability of a new high level in the near future. If this does not occur the chances will favor a receding tide and a level lower than that on the 19th.[22]

Today Dow could apply his concept to the Industrial Average as it is now the dominant index. It is apparent that the higher (or lower) the DJIA goes the more vulnerable it becomes to a correction. Likewise, a penetration of the previous high (or low), on volume, could signal a continuation of a bull or bear market. In my view the Vulnerability Index should only be considered as one factor in making your investment analysis.

I recommend that you take the time to read Dow's entire editorial (Figure 6–6). Note how cautious he is about his forecast. The last paragraph sums it up well:

The market may be going up a great deal more, but there is no escape from the fact that it has risen a great deal in the last few months and is at a level where prices occupy no such relation to values as they did six months ago.[23]

DEVOTING TIME TO ANALYSIS

Note in Figures 6–4 and 6–5 that *goals* occupies the center ring. Part of the goal-setting exercise is to determine how much time you can devote to your stock program. You can make the study as simple or complex as you desire based on the available time you can devote to it.

Martin Zweig has prepared a helpful pamphlet titled *The ABC's of Market Forecasting*. It points out how to use the abundance of material in *Barron's* Market Laboratory pages published by Dow, Jones & Company. Zweig said that "Many investors believe that technical forecasting—using a variety of indicators to anticipate future market moves—is complicated and mysterious. It needn't be. In this booklet, you'll find that understanding technical forecasting can be easy and fascinating . . . as well as rewarding."

The fundamentalist can find ample information by selecting publications listed in Appendixes C and D.

One aid that can increase your time for analysis is a computer. Can you imagine how valuable this tool would have been to Dow?

PERSONAL COMPUTERS

Computers will play an ever-increasing role in managing your investments. This facility, because of its speed and accuracy, permits you to analyze a far greater amount of statistical data than would otherwise have been possible. You will find it helpful to have a home computer assist you in your own program. Time is money, and the less time you devote to investments, the more you will have available for other activities. Its capabilities in this area are fairly broad. Take time to learn about computers. Small computers are now reasonably priced so many families are able to buy them for home use. Therefore, acquiring a basic understanding of their capabilities will make it easier to select the home computer appropriate for your needs. However, I recommend that a purchase not be made at this time unless you have a real requirement for it. Major changes are rapid, and computer costs will be reduced in the future.

Take time to go to stores like Radio Shack (Tandy Corporation models) as well as firms selling IBM, Commodore, and Apple models. Have a demonstration of the current capabilities of the personal computer in regard to investments. This should include the use of disks and tapes already programmed for investment purposes. Ask to see the state of the art in such software programs as investments and portfolio analysis. It is also desirable to discuss small computer capabilities in regard to investments with friends who are using them for this purpose in their homes. Computers, for money management purposes, can be real timesavers if the appropriate software programs are used.[23]

This statement is based on my recent experience coauthoring a program (with John Page) titled *How to Use Your Personal Computer to Manage Your Personal Finances* (Englewood Cliffs, N.J.: Prentice-Hall, 1986). It includes a floppy disk and instruction manual.

A POINT OF VIEW

The centerpiece of Dow's Theory is the Dow Jones Industrial Average. Dow deserves much credit for recognizing the potential of the industrials in their formative years before the turn of the century.

What do I think of the Dow Theory? It is an interesting concept. The problem arises as how to interpret its movement. There are forces beyond the stock market that should be considered prior to investing your money. In the charts on the Dow (Chapters 2 to 4 and 7) I refer to political, military, economic, and technological factors. The investor should consider evaluating the impact of these four aspects on the DJIA and individual stocks prior to making any investment.

NOTES

[1]What is now the DJIA was called the Dow Jones Railroad Average through December 31, 1969. Effective January 2, 1970, the 20 stocks comprising the DJTA included 11 railroads, 3 trucking companies, and 6 airlines. Prior to that date it was composed exclusively of railroad issues. This change was in recognition of the growing importance of air and truck transportation and the diminution in the importance of railroads. Nine of the railway stocks were removed at that time. The need for this revision was pointed out in *The Wall Street Journal* on January 5, 1970.

[2]William Hamilton disagreed with Dow's time frame for the categories of movement. His long experience with the averages showed him the primary (main) movement was "rarely three years and oftener less than two," (*The Stock Market Barometer*, pp. 23–4). Subsequent Dow followers have selected different time frames but accepted Dow's basic concept.

[3]Robert Rhea points out that a secondary reaction (trend) is considered to be an important decline in a bull market or advance in a bear market, usually lasting from three weeks to as many months, during which intervals the price movement generally retraces from 33 percent to 66 percent of the primary price change since the termination of the last preceding secondary reaction. These reactions are

frequently erroneously assumed to represent a change of primary trend, because obviously the first stage of a bull market must always coincide with a movement which might have proved to have been merely a secondary reaction in a bear market, the contra being true after the peak has been attained in a bull market. *From* Robert Rhea, *The Dow Theory* (Denver, Col.: Smith, 1932), pp. 13–14.

[4]William Peter Hamilton, *The Stock Market Barometer* (New York: Harper & Row, 1922), p. 22.

[5]Samuel Armstrong Nelson, *The ABC of Stock Speculation* (New York: S. A. Nelson, 1902), preface.

[6]"Pioneer Financial News Trio Recalled By Sole Survivor of 1892 Local Staff," *The Wall Street Journal*, June 27, 1932.

[7]The pure technical analyst relies primarily on charts. By examining price movements, the chartists observe trends in various issues. These patterns made by movements determine whether to buy, sell, or hold.

The fundamentalist examines statistical data and other relevant facts in analyzing the investment merits of a corporation.

[8]*The ABC of Stock Speculation*, preface.

[9]Republished by Fraser Publishing Company, Wells, Vermont, 1964, introduction.

[10]Ibid.

[11]Republished by Robert Rhea (copyright 1937).

[12]William P. Hamilton, *The Stock Market Barometer* (New York: Harper & Row, 1922), p. 250.

[13]Robert Rhea, *The Dow Theory* (Colorado, Springs, Col.: 1932), p. vii.

[14]Ibid., p. ix.

[15]Ibid., p. x.

[16]Ibid., p. x.

[17]George W. Bishop Jr., *Charles H. Dow and The Dow Theory* (New York: Appleton-Century-Crofts, 1960).

[18]Ibid., p. ix.

[19]Pp. 248–354 were copies of the articles Dow wrote in 1879 for the *Providence Journal* and the *Evening Bulletin*. (See Chapter 1 of this book.)

[20]R. J. Briston, *The Stock Exchange and Investment Analysis*, 2d ed. (London: George Allen & Unwin Ltd Inc., 1973), pp. 382–83. By permission of George Allen & Unwin Ltd.

[21]A look at the DJIA charts in Chapters 2 to 4 will reveal that since 1896 the market has usually gone down faster than it has gone up. But I believe short selling is for the professionals.

[22]*The Wall Street Journal*, January 31, 1901, p. 1.

[23]Dow was careful in the editorials on his theory (written between 1899 and 1902) to wisely hedge his bets.

7

The Role of the DJIA in a Lifetime Program of Money Management

Investors sometimes indicate that they would be happy just to achieve the performance of the Standard & Poor's 500 or the Dow Jones Industrial Average—but they almost always make this point after the designated index seems to have provided for an extended period significantly better returns than those achieved by most investors.
—*Walter R. Good, Robert Ferguson, and Jack Treynor*

MONEY MANAGEMENT CONCEPT

One approach to using the DJIA to help you achieve your personal financial goals is to utilize my lifetime money management concept.[1] Figure 7–1 shows that there are four major components to this concept—goals, functions, areas, and the decision-making process. The innermost circle lists goals. Visualize yourself as a manager responsible for all your financial affairs. First it is desirable to establish your financial goals—short, intermediate, and long term. You can then devise a plan, implement the plan, and then check to see that it is being accomplished (second circle).

The third level indicates that there are seven interrelated areas that comprise the field of personal finance. The seven include earning, spending, housing and other real estate, insuring, investing, retiring, and estate planning. The outer ring is titled "Decision-Making Process"—the key to successful money management.

A good decision is rarely made on a whim—you must go through a decision-making process. This process will help you think clearly and allow you to make logical decisions about how to manage your

FIGURE 7–1 Stillman's Lifetime Program of Money Management—A Graphic
Concept

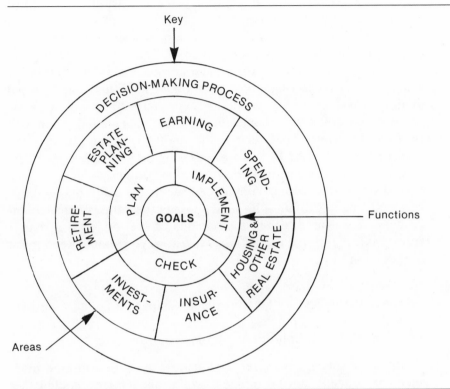

money. As with most decisions, the best place to start is with your
goals (the inner circle of my diagram). It is often helpful to write down
your goals. This exercise will allow you to focus your efforts on desired ends. Your goals must be realistic, and they must be updated if
you modify your lifestyle in a way that might affect your goals.

After you have set yor goals, the next step in the decision-
making process involves the three basic management functions:
planning, implementing, and checking (the second circle in the
model). To effectively accomplish your goals, you must be capable
of performing these three functions:

- Plan what is going to be done.
- Implement the plan.
- Check on what has been accomplished.

We often hear the term *financial planning,* but planning is only one of three functions you must perform. Planning your goals is useless unless you implement what you have planned. The third management function consists of checking on both your plans and your implementation to see if they are being properly accomplished.

The next move toward better-managed money involves appreciating how the other areas of personal finance interact with investments. The third ring in Figure 7–1 points out that your personal finance areas can be divided into seven parts. You will see how these seven areas of personal finance are interrelated when you read the illustration that begins after the next paragraph.

The final ring (the key to successful money management) portrayed in Figure 7–1 is the decision-making process which we have been discussing all along. As you can see the decision-making process is an ongoing affair—this final phase of the money management process draws on all other components of the model to arrive at appropriate solutions. In making a decision, you should keep these questions in mind:

- What is my financial goal?
- Are the necessary facts available to make a sound decision?
- What are the choices?
- Has the most appropriate choice been selected?

An illustration. Now let us illustrate how this money management concept can be utilized. Philip and Grace decided that their primary financial goal for next year was to invest $6,000 in the stock market. They reviewed Figure 7–1 and discussed what to do to achieve their goal.

Philip: We now have adequate savings to meet emergencies. The $10,000 is three months of our combined salaries. In addition, our U.S. Treasury bills approximate $20,000 and, if necessary, can be readily sold. It's time to begin buying stock.

Grace: If we follow my old professor's advice on "investment by progression" and "portfolio balance" we should expand our holdings to include $30,000 in blue chip stocks[2] and $15,000 in real estate. We are covered for the real estate portion as we have a $15,000 equity in our house. That means we can concentrate on stock investments for the next several years to arrive at a 40:60 ratio. I feel comfortable with the distribution of $30,000 in fixed income and building to $45,000 in growth potential. By moving into growth potential stocks it should help us reach our million dollar long-term goal.

Philip: I agree fully about the need for quality stocks. Until we have children, there is no requirement for a larger *home*. But it is essential we *plan* wisely all aspects of this purchase. A management approach also requires us to *implement* the plan and then *check* on how our stock is doing.

Grace: I would like to cut back on some of our *spending* like our weekly splurges at elegant restaurants. Figure 7–1 lists *earnings* as an area to consider in arriving at our investment decision. Perhaps I should accept that weekend job so we can have extra money for securities.

Philip: That may be a good idea to handle the books of RJS Industries. You could do it in six to eight hours. Will our stock purchases impact on other areas?

Grace: Yes, we should have protection (*insurance*) for our certificates. Let's rent a safe deposit box and check our theft coverage. In regard to *retirement* we should continue our IRA commitment. As to *estate planning*, I would like to change our will next year to leave our stockholdings to the university.

Philip: Your points are well taken. I didn't realize what we had to consider in order to make a sound *decision*. But this management approach should really pay off in providing us with a successful investment program.

Prior to examining the place of the Dow industrials in a portfolio, we will touch on two more relevant subjects. We will briefly discuss general investment guidelines and we will also examine the DJIA's performance both in comparison with other averages and alone.

INVESTMENT GUIDELINES

Readers should be cautioned that my approach to money matters is conservative. After 35 years of teaching, writing, and researching in the field I am convinced that sudden roads to riches are seldom successful. In contrast, here is a program that has worked for me.

1. Keep your investment portfolio simple and diversified. One approach is to keep a mix as follows:

Fixed Income 40%
Checking and savings accounts (5–15%)
U.S. Treasury bills and notes (20–35%)
Highest quality municipals (0–15%)
    (if you are in a high enough tax bracket).

Growth Potential. 60%
High quality stocks (40%)
Real estate (15–20%)
Other—gold, silver, etc. (0–5%)

2. Time your purchases and sales. A look at Figure 7–2 presents the wide fluctuations in the DJIA since 1896. A look at the individual Dow issues would also indicate considerable variation in prices—both short and long term. The higher the market (or stock) goes, the more vulnerable it becomes to a sell-off. Conversely, the lower it goes the better the buying opportunity.
3. Buy quality issues and hold them as long as they have a good growth and income record.
4. Prepare and maintain a hypothetical portfolio, whenever practical, in order to determine the credibility of your system (see Figure 7–6 for details on a hypothetical portfolio.)
5. Diversify your stock holdings. Remember what happened recently to Johns-Manville (now Manville Corporation).
6. Support the American way of life that permits us to achieve our financial goals. It pays to invest in the United States.

DJIA'S PERFORMANCE

Versus Other Indexes

A criticism leveled against the DJIA in recent years is its weaker performance when compared with other market indicators. During the 1970 to 1980 period, for example, the results were as follows:

Index	*Rise (percent)*	*Composition*
DJIA	15	30 major industrials (unweighted arithmetic average)
Value Line Composite	39	1,679 companies on the NYSE, AMEX, plus OTC (unweighted—geometric average)

Index	Rise (percent)	Composition
Standard & Poor's (S&P) Composite*	47	500 quality stocks from NYSE, AMEX, OTC (400 industrials; 40 utilities; 40 financial; 20 transportation) (weighted to reflect market value of each stock)
NYSE Composite	56	All common stocks (over 1500) listed on the NYSE (weighted to reflect market value of each stock)

*Most institutions presently use the S&P 500 to measure the yearly performance of their holdings. A Scudder mutual fund, for example, said in 1985 report to shareholders that "For the quarter ended March 31, 1985, Capital Growth Fund's net asset value per share rose 15.3% while the Standard & Poor's 500 Index gained 8.4%. For the twelve-month period ended March 31, there was an 18.3% increase in your Fund versus a 13.8% rise in the S&P 500." (Source: Scudder Capital Growth Fund, Inc., Semiannual Report, March 31, 1985, p.3).

In different time frames, however, the DJIA has compared favorably with other stock barometers. If we look at the most current six-month period (May–November 1985), for example, the DJIA has done better than its competition.

Index	Rise (percent)
DJIA	11.3
Standard & Poor's Composite	7.4
NYSE Composite	7.1
Value Line Composite	4.4

The blue chip issues led the explosive 1985 stock market rise and as a result the DJIA established many new highs. Furthermore, in my Dow strategy only the best (A +) issues have been selected. They have performed better than the DJIA as a whole. And how the market is doing (based on an index) is not as important as how your stocks are doing. Regardless of how the averages move, there are extensive disparities in the progress of individual issues. The DJIA is composed of a much smaller list than the other indexes,

FIGURE 7–2 Dow Jones Industrial Average: 1896–Present (with Stillman's significant political, military, technological, and economic events)

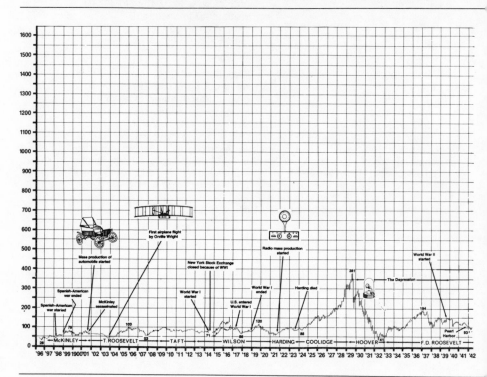

and this makes it much easier to track each stock and select the better performers.

Variations within the DJIA

An examination of Figure 7–3 supports the fact that there has been wide variation in the performance of various Dow Industrials during the past 57 years. Figure 7–3 includes the survivors of the original list of 30 that first appeared in the *Journal* on October 1, 1928. Only 14 of the original members remain on it today. Let us see what happened to two of them.

One share of International Harvester sold for $140 when the DJIA reached its 1929 high of 381.17 on September 3, 1929. It plummeted to $4.875 per share at the DJIA Depression low of 41.22. Note that it paid no dividend at that time in contrast to $2.50 per share paid in 1929. At this writing one share of Harvester is selling for $9 (with no dividend). A person who bought it at the market

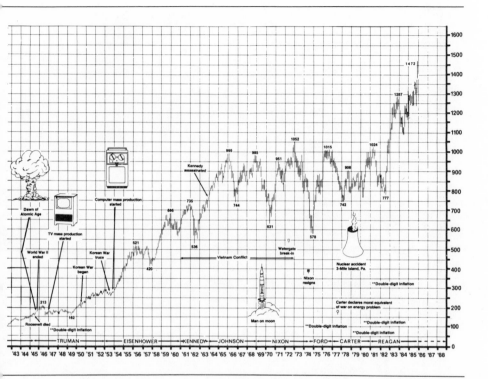

peak in 1929 would have seen Harvester fall from $140 to less than $5—a decline of over 96 percent in less than three years. And if the stock had been retained in a family portfolio from September 3, 1929, until 1985, it would be worth an equivalent of $54. Although presently selling for $9 it had a 3 for 1 split in 1948 and 2 for 1 in 1965. It is selling for less than 40 percent of its 1929 value but more than a 1,000 percent above its 1932 low. And between 1971 and 1985 Harvester has sold between $2.75 per share and $45.50.

General Electric sold for $391 a share on September 3, 1929, and paid a $4 dividend. It split 4 for 1 on January 29, 1930. After this split it fell, in 1932, to a low of $9.375 (equivalent to $37.50 when compared to its September 3, 1929 price). The dividend dropped to 40 cents a share (equivalent of $1.60). It is apparent that the Depression took its toll on General Electric with a drop of over 90 percent in the value of its stock in less than three years. However, the dividend declined only 60 percent. At this writing GE is selling for $60.50 a share and its dividend is $2.20. Since

FIGURE 7–3 Statistical Data on the 14 Stocks That Initially Appeared in the New List of 30 Dow Jones Industrials on October 1, 1928, and Remain on the List Today

	October 1, 1928			*September 3, 1929*			*July 8, 1932*			*May 10, 1985*		
Stock	*Price per share*	*Dividends per share*	*Yield (percent)*	*Price per share*	*Dividends per share*	*Yield (percent)*	*Price per share*	*Dividends per share*	*Yield (percent)*	*Price per share*	*Dividends per share*	*Yield (percent)*
Allied Corporation*	202½	6.00	2.96	354	6.00	1.7	45½	6.00	13.19	44¾	1.80	4.02
American Can	108⅜	2.00	1.84	181	3.00	1.66	31⅜	4.00	12.74	53½	2.90	5.42
Bethlehem Steel	64⅝	—	—	136¾	6.00	4.39	8⅜	—	—	16⅝	.40	2.40
Exxon	45⅞	1.00	2.18	70¾	1.00	1.41	24	1.00	4.17	50	3.40	6.8
General Electric	164	4.00	2.44	391	4.00	1.02	9⅜	.40	4.27	60½	2.20	3.64
General Motors	215	5.00	2.32	71¾	3.00	4.18	7¾	1.00	12.90	68⅜	5.00	7.26
Inco	125⅜	3.00	2.4	54½	1.00	1.83	10½	1.80	17.14	13⅞	.20	1.44
International Harvester	294⅞	6.00	2.03	140	2.50	1.78	4⅞	—	—	9	—	—
Sears Roebuck & Co.	149	2.50	1.68	171	2.50	1.46	10¼	—	—	34¾	1.76	5.06
Texaco	67/2	3.00	4.44	68½	3.00	4.38	9½	1.00	10.53	37	3.00	8.10
Union Carbide	188⅜	6.00	3.18	135¾	2.60	1.91	16⅜	1.20	7.33	38¼	3.40	8.89
U.S.Steel	159½	7.00	4.39	257	7.00	2.72	21½	—	—	28¾	1.00	3.48
Westinghouse	105⅝	4.00	3.79	285⅞	4.00	1.4	15⅞	—	—	32	1.20	3.75
Woolworth	192	5.00	2.6	99	2.40	2.42	23⅛	2.40	10.38	45	2.00	4.44

*Allied merged with Signal September 19, 1985, to become Allied-Signal.
The Dow Jones Industrial Average closed as follows on the four dates used in this chart:

Date	*DJIA*
October 1, 1928	240.01
September 3, 1929	381.17
July 8, 1932	41.22
May 10, 1985	1274.18

FIGURE 7–3 *(concluded)* Stock Splits That Occurred in the 14 Dow Industrials Listed Above

Ticker Symbol	Stock Splits
ALD	4 for 1 (9/5/50) 2 for 1 (1/25/60) 3 for 2 (5/84)
AC	2 for 1 (5/2/52)
BS	3 for 1 (1/19/48) 4 for 1 (2/7/57)
XON	2 for 1 (6/13/51) 3 for 1 (3/19/56) 2 for 1 (7/26/76) 2 for 1 (6/81)
GE	4 for 1 (1/29/30) 3 for 1 (6/14/54) 2 for 1 (6/8/71) 2 for 1 (6/83)
GM	2.5 for 1 (12/13/28) 2 for 1 (10/3/50) 3 for 1 (11/10/55)
N	2 for 1 (5/31/60) 2.5 for 1 (8/19/68)
HR	4 for 1 (12/13/28) 3 for 1 (6/7/48) 2 for 1 (4/12/65)
S	4 for 1 (10/23/45) 3 for 1 (12/19/55) 2 for 1 (3/23/65) 2 for 1 (7/18/77)
TX	2 for 1 (6/12/51) 2 for 1 (6/11/56) 2 for 1 (8/11/61) 2 for 1 (8/11/69)
UK	3 for 1 (5/17/48) 2 for 1 (6/16/65)
X	3 for 1 (6/3/49) 2 for 1 (6/3/55) 3 for 2 (6/2/76)
WX	4 for 1 (5/11/45) 2 for 1 (2/2/60) 2 for 1 (12/16/71) 2 for 1 (5/84)
Z	2.5 for 1 (6/25/29) 3 for 1 (6/18/64)

1929 it has had four stock splits, as shown in Figure 7-3. If a person had bought 100 shares on September 3, 1929, it would have cost $39,100. If the person had waited three years he could have bought 400 shares for $3,750 (there was a 4 for 1 split January 29, 1930). It would have grown to 4,800 shares (worth $290,400) at this writing. In addition, a stream of dividends averaging better than 3 percent annually would have accrued. The price of GE, since 1971, has varied more than $50.

It is apparent from the GE and Harvester examples that *timing* of purchases and sales *is important—very important*. It is also apparent that there are wide variations in the performance of these two stocks. Harvester has slumped badly in recent years while General Electric has had a long-term growth pattern. However, between 1971 and November 22 1985, GE sold at a high of $66.50 and a low of $15.00.

THE ROLE OF THE DJIA IN DEVELOPING AN INVESTMENT STRATEGY

A guideline in a previous section pointed out how important it is to keep your investment program simple. By using Dow Industrial stocks you can reduce the time you need to spend on your investment portfolio. Keep in mind that the editors of *The Wall Street Journal* have devoted considerable effort and study—since 1896—to maintain a list of leading industrial stocks. Capitalize on their efforts. In addition, there is a great amount of information available on these corporations and there is a ready market that permits easy sale or purchase.

How Do You Get Started on a DJIA Stock Purchase Program?

One approach is to make a priority list of Dow stocks that will eventually provide a diversified portfolio. A look back at Chapter 5 (Figure 5-3) indicates that the Dow 30 may be divided into 15 categories. You can easily cut your list from 30 to 15 by choosing what you consider the best selection in each category.

Review the 15 stocks you have chosen and place them in numerical order with the bluest of the blue chips in first place. This selection could be accomplished by using the S&P ranking and obtaining current information on yield, earnings per share, annual dividend, price/earnings ratio, and so on. See Figure 7-4 for factors you may wish to consider as you analyze which stock is best for you. Your analysis can be as simple or complex as you desire. If your work permits little time on your investments you may wish to rely exclusively on the S&P rankings. Figure 7–4 indicates that as of July 1985 only eight stocks had an A+ rating. This rating, membership in the exclusive DJI 30, and your own judgment should provide satisfactory investment results over the long term. Obviously, it is important to keep abreast of S&P rating changes and Dow club membership.

Another alternative is to select the bellwether issues. My top three choices at this writing are as follows:

- IBM
- General Electric (the only issue currently in the DJIA that appeared on the 1896 list)
- McDonald's

If in the beginning, your funds are limited, you may begin by purchasing a minimum of $1,000 of IBM. Next you would buy approximately equal dollar amounts of the other DJI issues as funds become available. Such purchases are predicated on the basis that you would attempt to maintain the 40/60 percent ratio between fixed income and growth holdings.

How to Use My DJIA Charts to Assist Your Analysis

The yearly movement of the Dow Jones Industrial Average during the period from 1896 to 1985 appears on Figure 7–2. It reflects the high and low of the DJIA since its inception. Space has been provided to plot its movement through 1988. Figure 7–5 traces the monthly movement of the DJIA from 1967 to 1985. Space has been provided to plot its monthly movement through 1988. It is desirable to use an extra-fine-point pen (black color) to do your plotting. You may also wish to predict what the DJIA will do in the months ahead. I have found that a pencil with a very fine point is appropriate as each line can be erased easily when the time comes to replace it with the actual high and low for the month. Another approach is to use a transparency (overlay) to plot your projection of where you believe the Dow Industrials will be in the months ahead. The background grid permits you to precisely mark or note material on the poster. Each grid square covers a one year period and 50 points.

It is important to remember that the DJIA only indicates general movement (up, down, sideways) of the 30 stocks that comprise its average. However, time has shown that the Dow Jones Industrials do provide an indication of the general movement of the stock

FIGURE 7-4 Statistical Information on the 30 Dow Industrials
June–August 1985 (by industry)

Name of Company (by industry)	S&P Ranking	Number of Investment Companies Owning Shares	Number of Shares (000) Owned by Investment Company	Common Shares Outstanding (000)	High-Low (1971–1983)	
Aerospace						
United Technologies	A+	574	66,084	122,466	38⅜	5³⁄₁₆†
Automobile, truck and related						
General Motors	B	991	128,979	317,504	91⅛	28⅞
Goodyear	A–	427	01,072	106,840	36⅞	10¾
International Harvester	C	101	15,341	59,557	45½	2¾
Chemicals and other						
Allied Corporation*	A–	341	54,174	83,335	41⅛	15⅜
Dupont	A–	597	84,746	240,311	67⅞	128⅛
Union Carbide	B	378	40,932	70,413	76⅜	129¼
Electrical						
General Electric	A+	1155	224,174	454,876	58⅞	15
Westinghouse Electric	A+	476	72,954	175,051	28³⁄₁₆	4
Electronic						
International Business Machines	A+	1708	313,715	612,686	134¼	37⅝
Financial						
American Express	A	652	134,075	217,963	49⅝	8⅞
Health care						
Merck	A+	683	46,968	71,754	104⅝	46⅝
Manufacturing— steel, aluminum, nickel, and copper						
Aluminum Company of America	B	406	50,678	81,226	47¾	12
Bethlehem Steel	B–	180	22,322	51,657	48	14½
Inco	B–	231	42,187	92,062	46¼	7⅞
U.S. Steel	B–	238	47,458	107,195	59⅞	16

*Allied merged with Signal to become Allied-Signal on September 19, 1985.
†1983 only (new AT&T issue)
The last column of this table has been provided if you wish to include additional data for analysis. Please remember, however, that this information is as of June–August 1985 (except for some Philip Morris and McDonald's data which is current through November 21, 1985). BE SURE TO UPDATE IT PRIOR TO MAKING ANY INVESTMENT DECISION.

High-Low Current 52 Weeks		Current Price per share	Current Dividend per Share	Current Yield	Current Earnings per Share	Current Price Earnings Ratio	Space for Listing Additional Data
45	34	42	1.40	3.3	4.90	11	
85	66	69	.5r	7.2	14.22	6	
30¼	24½	28	1.60	5.7	3.87	8	
11¼	6⅛	9⅜	—	—	d.1.94	—	
46¾	31½	43¼	1.80	4.2	5.03	8	
66⅜	46½	58	3	5.2	5.93	13	
51⅛	32½	50¾	3.40	6.1	4.84	19	
68¼	53	61⅝	2.20	3.6	5.03	12	
36⅜	24	34	1.20	3.5	3.01	11	
133¼	116	127⅜	4.40	3.5	10.77	13	
49⅜	30½	93⅞	1.28	3.0	2.79	15	
117¼	79¾	111¾	3.20	2.9	6.71	16	
39⅞	29¾	34	1.20	3.5	3.13	30	
21⅛	14¼	17¼	.40	1.8	d.3.32	34	
15⅜	9¾	14¾	.20	1.4	d.1.02	—	
31¼	22¼	30	1.20	4.0	2.78	19	

Figure 7–4 *(concluded)*

Name of Company (by industry)	S & P Ranking	Number of Investment Companies Owning Shares	Number of Shares (000) Owned by Investment Company	Common Shares Outstanding (000)	High-Low Recent 10–15 years (1971–1983)	
Manufacturing— containers, and tapes						
American Can	B	202	10,729	24,209	49½	22½
Minnesota Mining & Manufacturing	A	716	70,940	114,802	91⅝	43
Owens-Illinois	B+	234	15,803	29,678	38¾	13¾
Paper and paper products						
International Paper	B	367	26,202	49,942	79¾	28½
Petroleum						
Chevron	A	685	153,182	342,109	58¾	10¹/₁₆
Exxon	A	928	253,029	708,761	44⅜	13¾
Texaco	B+	593	72,802	237,882	54⅜	20
Photography						
Eastman Kodak	A	827	126,272	228,200	101⅛	27⅜
Restaurant, food, tobacco and soap						
McDonald's	A+	540	59,035	85,908	49¾	6⅝
Philip Morris	A+	804	77,386	120,875	72⅜	11¹¹/₁₆
Procter & Gamble	A+	605	73,895	162,392	63⅛	28
Retail stores and other						
Sears Roebuck & Co.	A−	626	171,797	361,610	61⅝	14⅜
Woolworth	B	191	18,283	31,430	55¾	8
Utility						
American Telephone & Telegraph	A−	832	181,434	1,050,493	214*	17⅜†

High-Low Current 52 Weeks		Current Price per share	Current Dividend per Share	Current Yield	Current Earnings per Share	Current Price Earnings Ratio	Space for Listing Additional Data
60⅛	45½	58⅛	2.90	5.0	4.74	11	
86	73⅛	79¾	3.50	4.4	6.27	13	
51⅜	37	49⅛	1.80	3.7	4.70	10	
57¾	47⅛	49	2.40	4.9	1.88	57	
39	29¼	36⅞	2.40	6.5	4.48	9	
54¼	38¼	51¼	3.40	6.6	6.77	8	
10¼	37⅜	35¾	3	8.4	1.03	32	
52	41¼	44¼	2.20	5.0	3.81	13	
74¼	50	75	.90	1.2	4.39	16	
95⅛	72	75¾	4.00	5.3	7.24	8	
54⅞	50⅜	57⅝	2.60	4.5	5.35	14	
39⅛	29¾	35¼	1.76	5.0	4.01	9	
48	33⅝	44¼	2	4.5	14.45	10	
24⅝	17¾	21⅛	1.20	5.7	1.25	16	

FIGURE 7–5 Dow Jones Industrial Average, 1967–1988 (with Stillman's significant political, military, technological and economic events)

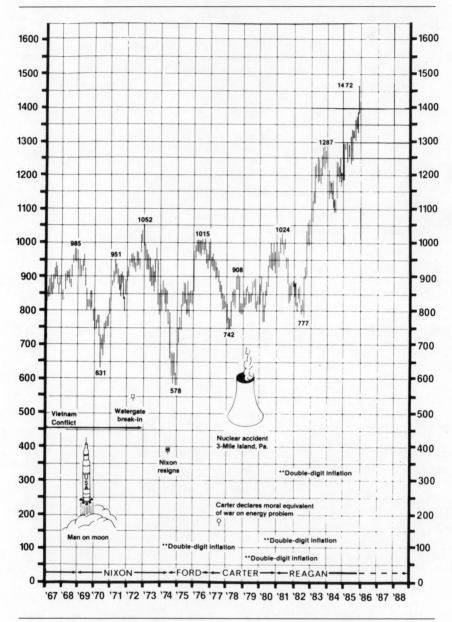

market. But it does not reflect either the true dollar value of corporate stocks or the actual dollar increase or decrease. With this in mind, you may wish to plot the movement of your stock in order to compare it with the DJIA. A transparency can be useful in making the comparison. If you own gold, silver, or any other investment, you may wish to plot its progress either on Figure 7–2 or on a transparency.

One yellow metal enthusiast traced the movement of his investment on Figure 7–2. He said, "I used a gold color pen to show its movement and made my scale from 0 to 1200. It is interesting to analyze the DJIA and gold. The different timing in fluctuations was readily apparent. Likewise, the differing impact of important happenings on gold in contrast to the DJIA."

Now let us turn from the movement of the DJIA in order to examine the other material appearing on Figure 7–2. Significant political, military, technological, and economic events appear in black. The time frame of all wars involving the United States are portrayed. Note the decline of the DJIA in the gloomy aftermath of Pearl Harbor as compared to its strong advance as the United States gained military supremacy in World War II. Political events are centered on U.S. presidents since 1896. You can determine, for example, if election years have been good for the stock market. Economic and technological events include the first airplane flight, the dawn of the atomic age, years of double-digit inflation, man on the moon, and initial mass production of cars, radios, TV, and computers. You may wish to add your own significant events to Figure 7–5 or project those which you believe will occur through 1988.

The information on these charts, coupled with your own input, should be helpful in arriving at your investment decisions. If time permits you can use my PEMT and Vulnerability Indexes, discussed in Chapter 6.

Maintaining Your Portfolio

A splendid way to gain experience and test the Dow investment strategy, at no cost to you, is to simulate the purchase and sale of securities, perhaps for a one-year period or until you actually have funds to invest. Assume you have received $100,000. How would you go about investing it to meet your financial goals (growth, income, safety, or a combination thereof)? You may wish to keep a record of your "transactions" by using a format similar to that presented in Figure 7–6. At the end of a year, or other period, you can determine how well you did in comparison with the Dow Jones Industrials. This comparison can be made in regard to both growth and income. You can also use this format to maintain your actual stock records. Keeping it on a calendar-year basis can be useful for income tax purposes.

Comparison of Your Stocks with the DJIA

One way to find out how your Dow stocks (or others) did during the past year is to compare their results with the Dow Jones Industrial Average. In order to make a valid comparison, you will want to convert the Dow Jones Industrial Average and the price of your securities[3] into a percentage basis. This can be accomplished yearly as follows:

1. Determine the difference in the price of the DJIA at the beginning of the previous year and its price at the beginning of the present year. The difference should then be divided by the price at the beginning of the previous year.

Formula:
$$\frac{\text{Difference between price at beginning of previous year and price at beginning of present year}}{\text{Price at the beginning of previous year}}$$

= Percentage increase or decrease over the previous year

Example:
$$\frac{300}{900} = 33\frac{1}{3}\% \text{ increase}$$

900 = Price of DJIA at beginning of previous year
1,200 = Price of DJIA at beginning of present year
300 = Difference

2. Each of your stocks should then be converted to a percentage basis using the formula presented above. Once you have completed all computations, the results can be posted to Figure 7–7 to point up the performance of your stocks vis-à-vis the DJIA.

This type of comparison can be helpful in deciding whether to hold, sell, or buy more shares of a particular stock in your portfolio. Obviously, if growth is your primary objective and one of your securities does worse than the DJIA over a considerable period of time, you should sell it. Conversely, if it does better you may wish to purchase additional shares.

Stock Indexes—An Alternative Strategy

A recent development in the marketplace has been the introduction of stock indexes (options and futures). It provides an alternative investment strategy for individuals interested in using a more speculative approach for a portion of their portfolio. First let us look at background information on stock options.

Options on stocks have become big business since April 1973. At that time the Chicago Board Options Exchange (CBOE) opened, creating a central marketplace where listed options can be bought or sold. The CBOE is a registered national securities exchange with all the regulatory and price dissemination capabilities associated with exchange trading. And CBOE options are registered securities. Prior to that date, firms specializing in puts and calls did very limited volume in the over-the-counter markets. A call may be defined as "the right to buys shares of a certain stock, if desired, at a set price within a given period of time as specified in the contract." A put is the opposite of a call and thus is "the right to sell shares of a certain stock, if desired, at a set price within a given period of time." In view of the CBOE success, the American, Philadelphia, New York, and Pacific exchanges have established similar central marketplaces for dealing in options.

The CBOE dealt only in call options between 1973 and 1976. In 1977 it began dealing in put options. The growth of the option business has been remarkable. Its success had been due to the fact that it provided the first organized mechanism for individuals and institutions to deal in options. In 1974, there were 32 companies whose common stock had been approved as underlying stock for option transactions. Now there are over 500 on five different exchanges (CBOE, NYSE, AMEX, Philadelphia, and Pacific). Information on various options are listed daily in the financial section of major newspapers.

The primary attractions for a purchaser of call options (and sellers of put options) are (1) the opportunity to make a large amount of money with a small investment and (2) predetermined risk. As pointed out in the definitions, a call is the right to buy shares and a put is the right to sell shares. However, an option

FIGURE 7-6 Format for a $100,000 Portfolio

of _____

as of _____

Name of Company	Ticker Symbol*	Number of Investment Companies Owning Shares*	Number of Shares (000) Owned by Investment Company*	Common Shares Outstanding* (000)	High-Low (Recent 10–15 years)*	High-Low (current 52 weeks)*	Number of Shares Bought	Date Purchased	Price per Share†	Broker's Commission to Buy

Name of Company	Total Cost	Current Dividend per Share*	Total Dividend	Current Yield†	Current Earnings per Share*	Current Price Earnings Ratio*	Gross Selling Price	Date Sold	Number of Shares Sold	Broker's Commission to Sell	Net Proceeds of Sale

*Available in current Standard & Poor's Stock Guide.
†Available in The Wall Street Journal or financial section of many newspapers.

FIGURE 7–7 Format for Comparison of the DJIA with the Stocks of (name) as of (date)

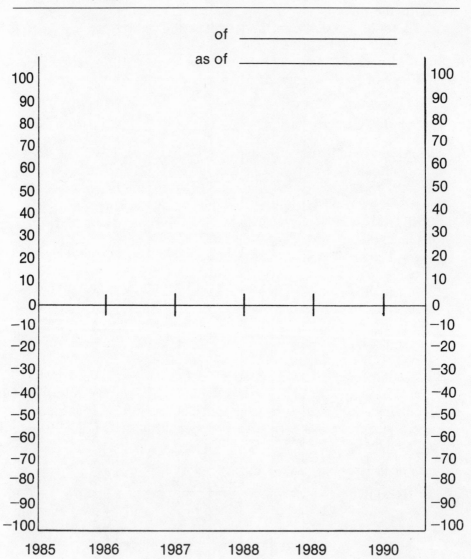

only costs a small portion of what it would take to buy 100 shares of the stock itself, and the investor's risk exposure is limited to the price paid for the option. This cost usually ranges from 5 to 20 percent with the length of the option varying from one to nine months. This leverage feature permits a large profit, but it also has a major risk factor that can easily result in the total loss of the investment.

Stock Index Options

The newest option kid on the block is the stock index. In 1983 the Chicago Board Option Exchange introduced the Standard & Poor's 100 stock market index (S&P 100). Since that date 10 more stock indexes have been introduced by five stock exchanges (CBOE, NYSE, AMEX, Philadelphia, and Pacific). Information on the various indexes can be found in the financial section of major newspapers. Figure 7–8 lists the data provided daily by *The Wall Street Journal*.

In lieu of the right (option) to buy (sell) a single stock an index option contains a group of stocks. The size of the group may vary from 20 issues to nearly 1,700. Figure 7–9 lists the composition, name, relationship to the DJIA, and exchange of the different index options.

The American Stock Exchange's Major Market Index (MMI) is the closest approximation to the Dow Jones Industrial Average. It contains a list of 20 high-quality stocks in nine different industries. Sixteen of these stocks are included in the DJIA and are so indicated by an asterisk.[4]

*American Express

*American Telephone & Telegraph

*Chevron

 Coca-Cola

 Dow Chemical

*Du Pont

*Eastman Kodak

*Exxon

*General Electric

*General Motors

*International Business Machines

FIGURE 7–8 Index Options Information (May 15,1985)

INDEX OPTIONS

Wednesday, May 15, 1985

Chicago Board

S&P 100 INDEX

Strike	Calls–Last			Puts–Last		
Price	May	Jun	Jul	May	Jun	Jul
160	18¾	....	20½	....	....	1/16
165	....	....	....	....	1/16	....
170	9½	10½	12½	1/16	3/16	5/16
175	4½	6¼	7¾	1/16	⅝	1⅛
180	½	2¾	4¼	1 1/16	2 7/16	3
185	1/16	⅞	2	5¾	6	6⅜
190	1/16	3/16	¾	....	10	....
195	....	1/16	....	16½	....	....

Total call volume 267,231 Total call open int. 663,861
Total put volume 123,246 Total put open int. 470,725
The index: High 180.42; Low 178.50; Close 179.32, +0.81

S&P 500 INDEX
(No Trades)

Total call volume 0 Total call open int. 55
Total put volume 0 Total put open int. 37
The index: High 185.43; Low 183.86; Close 184.54, +0.67

American Exchange

MAJOR MARKET INDEX

Strike	Calls–Last			Puts–Last		
Price	May	Jun	Jul	May	Jun	Jul
235	....	....	....	....	1/16	....
240	....	....	....	....	⅛	⅜
245	8⅛	9¾	....	1/16	½	1
250	3⅛	5⅛	7¼	3/16	1 11/16	2½
255	¼	2 11/16	4½	2 7/16	4	4
260	1/16	1	2 3/16	....	....	....
265	....	5/16	1	....	....	....
270	....	⅛	....	....	....	....

Total call volume 31,529 Total call open int. 88,033
Total put volume 17,198 Total put open int. 68,164
The index: High 254.42; Low 252.08; Close 253.11, +0.94

AMEX MARKET VALUE INDEX

Strike	Calls–Last			Puts–Last		
Price	May	Jun	Jul	May	Jun	Jul
220	....	11⅜	....	....	....	....
225	....	....	8¼	⅛	....	....
230	¼	....	....	1½	3⅝	....
235	....	1⅛	....	....	....	....

Total call volume 81 Total call open int. 393
Total put volume 56 Total put open int. 383
The index: High 228.96; Low 227.54; Close 228.73, +0.97

COMPUTER TECHNOLOGY INDEX

Strike	Calls–Last			Puts–Last		
Price	May	Jun	Jul	May	Jun	Jul
90	....	7¼	....	....	....	¾
95	4⅝	3¾	....	3/16	1⅜	....
100	1/16	1⅝	....	3⅜	4	....
105	....	⅜	....	....	....	....

Total call volume 265 Total call open int. 3,907
Total put volume 36 Total put open int. 568
The index: High 97.13; Low 95.89; Close 96.35, +0.35

OIL INDEX

Strike	Calls–Last			Puts–Last		
Price	May	Jun	Jul	May	Jun	Jul
135	1¾	2⅞	....	....	1⅝	2⅜
140	....	....	2	....	....	....

Total call volume 50 Total call open int. 746
Total put volume 6 Total put open int. 1,078
The index: High 136.94; Low 135.97; Close 136.40, +0.38

TRANSPORTATION INDEX

Strike	Calls–Last			Puts–Last		
Price	May	Jun	Jul	May	Jun	Jul
140	....	....	....	¼	....	....
150	....	2¾	....	....	....	....

Total call volume 2 Total call open int. 26
Total put volume 2 Total put open int. 33
The index: High 150.01; Low 148.48; Close 149.27, +0.69

N.Y. Stock Exchange

NYSE OPTIONS INDEX

Strike	Calls–Last			Puts–Last		
Price	May	Jun	Jul	May	Jun	Jul
100	6¾	7⅜	8	....	1/16	3/16
105	1 13/16	2⅞	3¾	1/16	½	15/16
110	....	9/16	1⅛	3⅜	3⅜	3¾
115	....	1/16	¼	....	....	....

Total call volume 9,119. Total call open int. 48,646.
Total put volume 3,803. Total put open int. 31,940.
The index: High 107.28; Low 106.47; Close 106.87, +0.39

NYSE DOUBLE INDEX

Strike	Calls–Last			Puts–Last		
Price	May	Jun	Jul	May	Jun	Jul
200	....	....	....	....	1/16	....
205	8⅛	....	11⅜	....	⅛	9/16
210	3⅝	5½	....	1/16	15/16	1½
215	¼	2⅞	4⅜	2 1/16	2⅝	3⅝
220	1/16	1 1/16	2 3/16	....	5¾	....
225	....	¼	1⅛	....	....	....

Total call volume 3,670. Total call open int. 21,867.
Total put volume 1,551. Total put open int. 14,743.
The index: High 214.56; Low 212.94; Close 213.74, +0.78

Philadelphia Exchange

GOLD/SILVER INDEX

Strike	Calls–Last			Puts–Last		
Price	May	Jun	Jul	May	Jun	Jul
70	....	....	....	....	1/16	....
75	....	....	....	....	3/16	....
80	....	....	....	....	7/16	1⅜
85	4¼	....	....	....	1⅝	....
90	½	....	4⅝	1⅜	....	4⅞
95	1/16	15/16	2⅜	....	....	....
100	....	11/16	....	....	....	....

Total call volume 366 Total call open int. 2,231
Total put volume 110 Total put open int. 3,436
The index: High 89.92; Low 88.77; Close 88.91, −0.94

VALUE LINE INDEX OPTIONS

Strike	Calls–Last			Puts–Last		
Price	May	Jun	Jul	May	Jun	Jul
185	....	....	....	....	1/16	⅜
190	5⅞	8	....	1/16	½	1 1/16
195	1⅛	4⅛	5⅞	5/16	1 13/16	....
200	1/16	1 13/16	3	4¼	4½	....
205	....	⅝	1½	....	....	....
210	....	⅛	....	....	....	....

Total call volume 8,055 Total call open int. 34,488
Total put volume 3,693 Total put open int. 23,983
The index: High 196.08; Low 195.22; Close 195.78, +0.33

Pacific Exchange

TECHNOLOGY INDEX

Strike	Calls–Last			Puts–Last		
Price	May	Jun	Jul	May	Jun	Jul
95	....	....	....	1/16	⅜	....
100	2¼	5⅛	....	⅞	1⅜	2⅛
105	⅛	2 3/16	....	3¼	....	....
110	....	1 1/16	....	....	....	....
115	....	⅜	....	....	....	....

Total call volume 198 Total call open int. 2,732
Total put volume 134 Total put open int. 1,331
The index: High 102.69; Low 101.67; Close 101.96, +0.24

FIGURE 7–9 Major Stock Index Options (cash)

Name	Ticker Symbol	Exchange	Composition	Relationship to DJIA (approximate ratio)
AMEX market value index	XAM	American Stock Exchange	All stocks on stock exchange (over 800) (unweighted index)	none
Major market index	XMI	American Stock Exchange	20 leading industrials (unweighted index)	5 to 1
NYSE composite index	NYA	New York Stock Exchange	All stocks on the NYSE (over 1500 weighted index)	6.5 to 1
NYSE double index	NDX	New York Stock Exchange	All stocks on the NYSE (over 1500 weighted index)	13 to 1
S&P 100 index	OEX	Chicago Board Options Exchange	100 high quality stocks on which CBOE currently lists equity options (weighted index)	7.5 to 1
Value line composite index	XVL	Philadelphia Stock Exchange	Nearly 1,700 stocks selected by value line (weighted index—geometric average)	none

These are six stock option indexes that provide a perspective on how the stock market is doing.

*International Paper

Johnson & Johnson

*Merck & Company

*Minnesota Mining & Manufacturing

Mobil

*Philip Morris

*Procter & Gamble

*Sears Roebuck & Co.

*U.S. Steel

Past experience has indicated that the correlation of the MMI with the movement of the DJIA is quite close. Such a correlation permits Dow theorists to test the merits of their strategy.

The two most popular indexes are the S&P 100 and the Major Market Index. This is apparent from an examination of Figure 7–10, which lists the most active options. The popularity of stock index options exceeds that of options on individual issues.

Let us see how a stock index option works using the MMI as an example. Assume that on May 15, 1985, you believed the stock market (as reflected in the DJIA) would go up markedly in the next several months. In order to profit from this possibility you decide to buy one MMI index option contract call (100 shares).[5] You have three different expiration months from which to make a selection. A look at Figure 7–8 indicates the premiums on the Major Market Index 255 striking price are ¼(May); 2 ¹¹⁄₁₆(June); 4½(July).[6] Your decision is to buy one July 255 MMI contract. Assume the MMI closed at 262 on July 12, 1985, and you exercised the call on that date. Here would be the result:

$262	MMI close on July 12, 1985
− 255	Strike (exercise) price
7	
× 100	Trading unit
700	
− 450	Premium
250	
− 71	Brokerage fee
$179	Gain

Keep in mind that the *commission alone is expensive*. A regular commission on such a transaction, at this writing, would approximate $71 (includes both purchase and exercise of call).

A discount broker may charge the following:

Options

Dollar Amount of Transaction	Commission Rate*
Under $3,000	$25 + .014 of $ amount
$3,000–$9,999	$25 + .010 of $ amount
$10,000 and over	$25 + .007 of $ amount

*This is the USAA Brokerage Services commission rate as of May 1985. If no more than a single contract is purchased or written, the maximum charge is $25.00 per contract and the minimum charge is $2.50 per contract.

FIGURE 7–10   Closing Prices of Most Active Options (May 15, 1985)

MOST ACTIVE OPTIONS

Chicago Board

		Sales	Last	Chg.	N.Y. Close
CALLS					
SP100	May180	114261	½	+	⅛ 179.32
SP100	May175	51633	4½	+	⅞ 179.32
SP100	Jun180	31026	2¾	+	5-16 179.32
SP100	Jun185	21496	⅞	+	1-16 179.32
SP100	Jun175	15038	6¼	+	⅝ 179.32
PUTS					
SP100	May180	61532	1 1-16	−	¾ 179.32
SP100	Jun180	21042	2 7-16	−	⅜ 179.32
SP100	Jun175	20393	⅝	−	¼ 179.32
SP100	May175	4130	1-16	......	179.32
SP100	Jun170	3541	3-16	......	179.32

American Exchange

		Sales	Last	Chg.	N.Y. Close
CALLS					
MMIdx	May255	10783	¼	+	1-16 253.11
MMIdx	May250	7903	3⅛	+	⅞ 253.11
MMIdx	Jun255	5945	2 11-16	+	⅜ 253.11
Arkla	May25	4237	1-16	−	⅛ 22¾
Sonat	Jul40	3218	2⅜	+1	11-16 39¼
PUTS					
MMIdx	May250	6264	3-16	−	¼ 253.11
MMIdx	Jun250	3793	1 11-16	−	⅜ 253.11
MMIdx	Jun245	2639	½	−	3-16 253.11
MMIdx	May255	2609	2 7-16	−11-16	253.11
Dig Eq	Jul100	1297	2 7-16	−	3-16 104⅝

Philadelphia Exchange

		Sales	Last	Chg.	N.Y. Close
CALLS					
Wst Un	Jul10	6827	1¾	+	1 11
Wst Un	Jul15	3011	5-16	+	3-16 11
VL idx	May195	2949	1⅛	+	⅛ 195.78
PhibroS	Jul45	2508	1	......	41⅜
Wlwrth	Aug40	2500	5¾	......	44¾
PUTS					
Alld C	Jul40	3314	1⅞	+	1⅝ 40
Wst Un	Jul10	2422	⅝	−	⅝ 11
VL Idx	May195	2009	5-16	−	⅛ 195.78
Coleco	Jul10	968	⅛	......	14⅛
Coleco	Jul15	935	1½	+	1-16 14⅛

Pacific Exchange

		Sales	Last	Chg.	N.Y. Close
CALLS					
Signal	May40	3886	¼	−	1¼ 38⅞
Signal	Aug40	3509	1½	−	1¾ 38⅞
Signal	May35	3002	3⅞	−	⅞ 38⅞
Signal	Aug35	2773	4½	−	1¾ 38⅞
Unocal	Jul45	1662	2⅝	+	⅛ 46⅛
PUTS					
Unocal	Jul40	3164	3¼	+	⅛ 46⅛
Unocal	Jul45	2022	6½	+	¼ 46⅛
A M D	Jul30	1920	2 11-16	−	3-16 28¼
Unocal	Jul50	1185	10⅜	+	¼ 46⅛
Unocal	Jul35	866	13-16	−	1-16 46⅛

N.Y. Stock Exchange

		Sales	Last	Chg.	N.Y. Close
CALLS					
NY Idx	Jun105	2898	2⅞	−	⅛ 106.87
NY Idx	May105	2740	1 13-16	+	5-16 106.87
Dbl Idx	May215	1770	¼	−	1-16 213.74
NY Idx	Jun110	1645	9-16	+	1-16 106.87
NY Idx	Jul115	651	¼	......	106.87
PUTS					
NY Idx	Jun105	2484	½	−	1-16 106.87
NY Idx	Jul105	516	15-16	−	1-16 106.87
NY Idx	Sep100	420	¼	−	⅛ 106.87
Dbl Idx	Jun210	393	15-16	−	⅛ 213.74
Dbl Idx	May215	365	2 1-16	−	1-16 213.74

SOURCE   *The Wall Street Journal,* May 16, 1985, p.52.

In contrast, if the MMI failed to advance more than the premium and commission cost, there would be no profit. The most, however, a call (or put) buyer would lose is the premium ($450 plus the initial commission of $31).[7] But as apparent in the example above this can be sizable, particularly with a series of losers over a short period of time. Time can be the enemy of the option trader and the ally of the broker. The reason for this is that the life of the stock index option is relatively short (three months or less), and the broker always obtains his initial commission as well as a commission on stock options closed out prior to the expiration date of the transaction.

Note that in the profitable example above the MMI must advance nearly six points within three months to make a profit. This is comparable to about 30 points in the DJIA based on an approximate ratio of 5 to 1. It is apparent that the market has to make a sizable move for the speculator to make a profit.

Futures Contracts

There is another vehicle for speculating in stock indexes. The Futures Markets currently trade five stock index futures. They are traded on four exchanges:

Index	Margin Requirement (initial)	Exchange	Ticker Symbol
S&P 500 Futures Index	$6,000	Chicago Mercentile Exchange (CME)	SP
S&P 100 Stock Futures	6,000	Chicago Mercentile Exchange (CME)	SX
Major Market Index	1,750	Chicago Board of Trade (CBT)	MX
NYSE Composite Futures	3,500	New York Futures Exchange (NYFE)	YX
KC Value Line Futures	6,500	Kansas City Board of Trade (KCBT)	KV

Daily pricing and open interest data on futures can be found in *The Wall Street Journal* (see Figure 7–11) and financial sections of major newspapers. Prices, as shown in Figure 7–11, are quoted in points and eighths of one point. An eighth of a point is $12.50 per

FIGURE 7–11   Information on Stock Index Futures (appear daily in
The Wall Street Journal)

FUTURES PRICES

Monday, May 20, 1985.
Open Interest Reflects Previous Trading Day.

	Open	High	Low	Settle	Chg	Discount Settle	Open Chg	Open Interest

S&P 500 FUTURES INDEX (CME) 500 Times Index
June   190.00 191.00 189.35 190.40 + 2.40 191.00 155.10 50,348
Sept   193.90 194.55 193.25 194.10 + 2.35 194.55 158.10 12,165
Dec   197.50 198.00 196.95 197.55 + 2.35 198.00 175.40   231
   Est vol 72,793; vol Fri 67,858; open int 62,765, +2,518.
   S&P 500 STOCK INDEX (Prelim.)
   189.33 189.98 187.50 189.72 + 2.30   ....
   MAJOR MARKET INDEX (CBT) $100 Times Index
June   257⅜ 259⅝ 257⅜ 259¼ + 3⅜ 265⅜ 243   5,413
   Est vol 18,000; vol Fri 17,679; open int 11,826, +134.
   MAJOR MARKET INDEX (Prelim.)
   254.92 259.59 254.92 259.05 + 4.13   ....
   NYSE COMPOSITE FUTURES (NYFE) 500 Times
Index
June   110.00 110.90 109.80 110.50 + 1.50 110.90 90.00 9,187
Sept   112.45 113.20 112.30 112.80 + 1.40 113.20 91.35 1,899
Dec   114.45 115.15 114.35 114.95 + 1.40 115.15 101.20   625
   Est vol 15,203; vol Fri 13,564; open int 11,803, +663.
   NYSE COMPOSITE STOCK INDEX
   108.43 109.84 108.43 .109.72 + 1.24   ....
   KC VALUE LINE FUTURES (KC) 500 Times Index
June   201.90 203.85 201.80 203.30 + 3.10 210.70 170.10 5,799
Sept   207.20 208.90 207.10 208.50 + 3.50 213.50 185.75   918
   Est vol 5,650; vol Fri 4,160; open int 6,727, +116.
   KC VALUE LINE COMPOSITE STOCK INDEX
   198.13 199.90 ¹98.13 199.81 + 1.75   ....

OTHER FUTURES MARKETS

S&P 100 Stock Futures Index (CME) 500 Times Index
Jun 180.75 ; Est. vol. 0; Open Int. 35

SOURCE   *The Wall Street Journal,* May 21, 1985, p.42.

contract. Thus, a one-point move on the Major Market Index represents a $100 price change. On the other futures indexes (i.e., S&P, NYSE, Value Line), one point reflects a $500 price change.

Until recently, futures contracts required delivery of the item agreed to in the contract (i.e., silver, corn, foreign currency, etc.) at some future date at a specific price. However, with the advent of stock index futures a cash settlement is made in lieu of the index itself.

What are the risks and rewards facing the futures markets speculator? A splendid statement of the risks involved is this one:

Commodity speculation . . . is a high-risk business and suitable only for a relatively small group of people. In order to be successful, indeed in order to survive at all, the speculator must be astute, a proficient student of the commodity, and have considerable nerve and money and a great deal of pure luck! What the wise speculator has going for him, however, is that he can play known odds, which are fundamentally in his favor.[8]

The risks in commodity trading should be apparent. But the rewards may be king-size for a small investment. Handsome profits are possible through "money leverage." For example, one Major Market Index Futures contract may require, for speculators, a minimum margin of $1,750.[9] If we assume that you bought the contract at $260, the $1,750 is controlling $26,000 (260 × $100). A change in price of even one point represents a profit, or loss, of $100 (not including the healthy commission that approximates $84). It is good to keep in mind, however, that a similar decline results in a comparable loss. And unlike stock index options that limit losses to a specified amount, the losses on futures could be unlimited.

The Chicago Board of Trade provides the following profitable examples in their brochure:[10]

> If an investor believes the market as a whole is on the upswing, he can go long (buy) MMI futures to capitalize on that expectation. For instance, if MMI futures are trading at 220 and the investor believes a bull market move is imminent, he may go long one (1) MMI futures contract. Now suppose the market advances to 232; the investor may offset the long position for a twelve(12) point or $1,200 profit (minus commission costs).

Go long (buy) @ 220 or ($22,000)
Go short (sell) @ 232 or $23,200
Profit $ 1,200

> Or if the investor believes the market is likely to decline, he can go short (sell) MMI futures. But unlike the stock market, MMI futures traders are not required to short "on an uptick." So assume a trader goes short MMI futures at 220 and the MMI declines to 210; the trader may offset the short position for a ten (10) point or $1,000 profit (minus commission costs).

Go short (sell) @ 220 or $22,000
Go long (buy) @ 210 or ($21,000)
Profit $ 1,000

This brief explanation provides only an introduction to understanding stock index options and futures. It has been presented primarily to point out how it is now possible to speculate on what the market will do based on a variety of stock indicators. It can be used for both speculating and hedging. To hedge, for example, assume you have a group of stocks that move comparable to a particular index (or indexes) and they have made a sharp advance. You can retain your stocks and take an opposite position with an option (buy a put) to protect your profit. But prior to putting money into this arena read on.

A Word of Caution

If you decide to place a portion of your funds in stock index options and/or futures, take time to become thoroughly familiar with this subject. Max G. Ansbacher has written an informative book titled *The New Stock Index Market: Strategies for Profit in Stock Index Futures and Options*. It has chapters on both basic and complex trading strategies. An appendix includes a glossary of terms and "The Eight Biggest Mistakes in Stock Index Trading." Two pamphlets prepared by the five exchanges and The Options Clearing Corporation are "a must" reading: *Understanding The Risks and Uses of Listed Options* and *Listed Options on Stock Indexes*. A brochure on each stock option index is prepared by the stock exchange listing it. AMEX, for example, has a pamphlet called *Stock Index Options: An Introduction to the Major Market Index*. The Chicago Board Option Exchange has a booklet on *S&P 100 Index Options: The Index Edge*. *The Future is Here: Futures Trading & The Value Stock Index* is published by the Kansas City Board of Trade. The New York Stock Exchange has a brochure titled *Introducing New York Stock Exchange Index Futures*. In order to keep abreast of current activities it is important to read publications like *The Wall Street Journal, Barron's,* and the *New York Times*. Information on trading strategies (including recommendations) can be found in *CMI's Options Trader,* which is published 48 times a year ($230 for 12 months). In addition to the six-page pamphlet, subscribers have access to a daily telephone hotline which is updated every market day. *Stock Options Guide* is published weekly and contains graphic and statistical data on stock indexes ($160 annually).

Recommendation

My recommendation in regard to stock index options and stock index futures in not—repeat—not to consider them in your investment portfolio. However, if you must speculate in this arena first acquire considerable market experience and be prepared to devote ample time to it. Finally, ask yourself if you could use this time more profitably in your business or other pursuits.

A POINT OF VIEW

The Dow Jones Industrials can be used in a conservative investment strategy. A diversified list of the highest quality members of the DJIA should provide satisfactory results over the long run. However, it is desirable to keep up-to-date on economic, political, military, and technological events that may affect your portfolio. Selection of Dow stocks enables you to obtain an abundance of information. However, this information is only helpful if you use it. If time permits take advantage of these sources:

- Visit a stock brokerage firm or library (public or university) and look over the material published by Standard & Poor's (26 Broadway, New York, NY 10004) and Moody's Investors Service, Inc. (99 Church Street, New York, NY 10007).
- Obtain the annual reports of companies that interest you.
- Read the financial section of a good daily newspaper. The *Journal* may be your best bet—after all, the Dow is their baby. It will have the most information on the DJIA and its list of 30.
- Subscribe to several of the publications listed in Appendix D.

As mentioned earlier, you may not have the time to delve into all the material available. If not, you can rely on the efforts of *The Wall Street Journal* editors and the rankings of the *Standard & Poor's* to maintain your portfolio.

The historical perspective of the DJIA that has been presented in the previous chapters illustrates the numerous modifications that have been made since 1896. The 1928 to 1985 list of 30, for example, has been modified 15 times and involved 36 companies (Chapter 4, Figure 4–2). Since 1979 the *Journal* editors have made the following changes:

Added
IBM
Merck
American Express
McDonalds
Phillip Morris

Deleted
Chrysler
Esmark
Johns Manville
American Brands
General Foods

It is fair to assume that other changes, such as the case of International Harvester, are being scrutinized. Likewise under study should be the long-term impact of the shift from a smokestack to a service economy.

The following question may be asked in regard to changes made in the Dow. Will the removal be made only after a precipitous decline that would result in financial loss to shareholders?[11] This has happened in the past. The way to help avoid this problem, as mentioned earlier, is to buy only the highest S&P-ranked DJI issues. And to consider selling them on any sign of major weakness, such as a lowered S&P rating. As a further protection, it is desirable to eventually diversify into 15 securities in 15 different industries (See Figure 7–4).

There are numerous investment strategies. You must decide if the Dow strategy will work best for you.

A PARTING THOUGHT

Manage your investments so that they are a source of enjoyment in life and a source of benefit when you are gone.

NOTES

[1] The Stillman concept on money management was first used in my personal finance classes. It was later published in *Guide to Personal Finance: A Lifetime Program of Money Management* (Englewood Cliffs, N.J.: Prentice Hall, 1972). The latest edition was published in 1984.

[2] You may wish to buy quality stock concurrently with T-bills and/or notes. But it is desirable to establish an emergency fund first.

[3] You may also wish to check the results of your total stock portfolio against the Dow.

[4] Dow Jones does not permit its index to be used because of the speculative nature of options.

[5] A put would be purchased if you anticipated the stock market would decline.

[6] The *striking (or exercise) price* is the price a purchaser of a call (put) can buy (sell) the stock index during the life of the call (put).

[7]It is assumed the buyer of the call lets it expire and, therefore, does not pay any terminal commission cost.

[8]*How Businessmen Use Commodity Futures Trading* (New York: New York Coffee and Sugar Exchange, Inc., n.d.), pp. 10–11.

[9]The minimum margin for stock index futures is established by the commodity exchanges. Individual brokers may require a greater amount. In additions to the initial amount the speculator will be required to furnish additional funds if the value of the contract falls. Failure to provide it will result in the broker closing out the contract.

[10]CBOT, *Major Market Index Futures,* pamphlet published by Chicago Board of Trade, 1984.

[11]Conversely, if the new member of the Dow fits into your portfolio, you may wish to consider buying it. After all, the *Journal* editors spend considerable time in selecting a quality replacement.

Appendixes

Appendix A: Monthly movement of the Dow (1885–1985)

1. Monthly Movement of the Dow Combined Railroad and Industrial Average (11–14 stocks, 1885–1896)
2. Monthly Movement of the Dow Combined Railroad and Industrial Average (20 stocks, 1889–1896)
3. Monthly Highs and Lows of the Dow Jones Industrial Average (12 stock series 1896–1916)
4. Monthly Highs and Lows of the Dow Jones Industrial Average (20 Stock series, 1916–1928)
5. Monthly Highs and Lows of the Dow Jones Industrial Average (12 and 20 Stock Series, 1914–1916)
6. Monthly Highs and Lows of the Dow Jones Industrial Average (30 stock series, 1928–1985)

Appendix B: DJIA Charts (with Stillman's significant political, military, technological, and economic events)

1. 1884–1896: Dow Combined Railroad and Industrial Series—11–14 Stocks
2. 1896–1916: Dow Jones Industrial Average—12 Stock Series
3. 1914–1916: Dow Jones Industrial Average—12 and 20 Stock Series

4. 1916–1928: Dow Jones Industrial Average—20 Stock Series
5. 1928–1985: Dow Jones Industrial Average—30 Stock Series
6. 1896–1985: 12, 20,and 30 Stock Series
7. 1986–2000: Plot Your Own Projection and Significant Political, Military, Technological, and Economic Events.

Appendix C: Bibliography
Appendix D: Financial Periodicals and Services
Appendix E: Thomas Woodlock Article

APPENDIX A

Monthly Movement of the Dow (1885–1985)

1. Monthly Movement of the Dow Combined Railroad and Industrial Average (11–14 stocks, 1885–1896)
2. Monthly Movement of the Dow Combined Railroad and Industrial Average (20 stocks, 1889–1896)
3. Monthly Highs and Lows of the Dow Jones Industrial Average (12 stock series, 1896–1916)
4. Monthly Highs and Lows of the Dow Jones Industrial Average (12 and 20 stock series, 1914–1916)
5. Monthly Highs and Lows of the Dow Jones Industrial Average (20 stock series, 1916–1928)
6. Monthly Highs and Lows of the Dow Jones Industrial Average (30 stock series, 1928–1985)

FIGURE A-1 Monthly Movement of the Dow Combined Railroad and Industrial Average (11–14 stocks, 1885–1896)*

	1885		1886		1887		1888		1889		1890	
	Low	High	Low	High	Low	High	Low	High	Low	High	Low	High
January			80.28	86.33	86.55	89.85	81.38	83.38	85.38	87.13	91.13	93.16
February	62.76	66.67	83.62	86.83	86.11	90.03	80.98	82.66	86.59	87.77	90.10	92.90
March	61.87	65.99	79.75	84.92	88.34	90.80	75.85	81.47	83.59	87.54	90.11	91.71
April	61.59	65.12	78.93	82.71	90.50	91.77	75.28	83.09	84.17	86.83	90.67	96.30
May	61.91	63.97	77.28	82.51	90.87	93.27	78.50	83.54	86.80	90.44	96.53	99.14
June	61.73	64.65	81.81	85.59	86.69	92.49	77.12	79.22	89.38	91.38	95.84	98.66
July	61.49	68.85	83.03	86.20	82.51	88.50	78.35	84.37	86.28	89.67	95.40	96.88
August	67.61	72.10	83.52	87.08	81.21	85.63	83.76	86.51	87.80	91.57	91.78	95.30
September	66.92	69.68	84.86	90.68	81.19	86.30	84.51	87.80	92.03	93.67	91.38	94.70
October	68.92	78.25	88.94	91.86	77.44	83.15	85.24	88.10	89.86	92.75	86.56	91.47
November	77.64	82.75	91.60	93.34	80.13	84.42	83.62	86.86	90.30	92.70	78.86	87.06
December	76.95	81.12	86.46	94.25	80.38	83.66	81.88	86.68	90.25	92.21	76.77	81.68

	1891		1892		1893		1894		1895		1896	
	Low	High	Low	High	Low	High	Low	High	Low	High	Low	High
January	82.21	85.82	88.11	91.21	86.56	90.38	71.11	75.38	69.83	72.53	69.45	74.82
February	85.16	86.89	89.64	93.71	84.47	89.69	73.64	75.40	68.68	71.81	74.30	78.11
March	83.13	85.66	91.62	94.65	82.75	85.92	74.89	78.22	68.77	72.97	74.47	77.18
April	84.56	89.15	90.81	94.58	82.70	86.76	76.45	78.77	71.82	75.46	75.48	78.69
May	83.79	88.71	90.93	93.47	76.37	81.84	73.39	77.58	75.45	79.17	76.15	78.20
June	82.20	85.28	89.60	91.80	75.40	78.80	72.41	75.64	77.40	79.37		
July	80.82	84.55	89.21	92.48	61.94	76.47	71.60	73.90	77.66	81.60		
August	81.01	89.23	89.89	92.42	64.82	69.59	72.31	78.93	80.55	82.81		
September	87.82	92.95	86.19	89.33	70.01	73.59	74.44	78.56	79.53	84.23		
October	88.08	90.75	88.05	90.50	70.39	78.63	70.65	74.21	78.59	82.60		
November	86.19	89.03	86.06	90.30	75.25	78.46	70.66	75.05	77.00	78.83		
December	88.15	91.47	85.76	88.31	71.39	78.75	71.23	73.59	67.93	77.89		

During the period from July 3, 1884 to May 25, 1896, Dow published a list of stocks composed of both railroad and industrial issues. The industrials included only 2 companies but the railroads varied from 9 to 12. Dow also compiled a 20-stock average between September 23, 1889, and October, 24, 1896. It consisted of 18 railroad stocks and 2 industrials. Beginning October 26, 1896, he published a list of 20 stocks containing only railroads.

*In 1922, William P. Hamilton wrote that "The first average found in the files, of these 11 stocks, 9 of which were rails, was 69.93 as of July 3, 1884. It appeared irregularly until February 16, 1885." *The Stock Market Barometer.* (New York: Harper & Row, 1922), p. 281.

FIGURE A–2   Monthly Movement of the Dow Combined Railroad and Industrial
Average (20 stocks, 1889–1896)

	1889		1890		1891		1892	
	Low	High	Low	High	Low	High	Low	High
January			71.86	73.35	62.75	66.25	70.78	73.51
February			70.76	73.13	65.03	66.48	72.01	75.34
March			70.65	71.89	63.49	65.56	72.78	75.68
April			70.95	75.31	64.76	69.05	72.02	74.85
May			75.65	78.04	64.47	68.68	71.28	73.84
June			74.93	78.38	62.67	65.61	70.29	72.38
July			74.64	75.93	61.50	65.11	70.06	72.99
August			71.78	74.68	62.16	69.89	70.78	73.08
September	72.56	73.26	70.70	74.01	68.71	73.21	67.97	70.36
October	70.72	73.18	67.09	70.86	69.41	71.63	69.54	71.43
November	70.96	72.91	59.25	67.78	68.61	70.49	67.58	71.75
December	70.96	72.60	58.10	62.21	69.86	73.25	66.86	69.11

	1893		1894		1895		1896	
	Low	High	Low	High	Low	High	Low	High
January	67.14	70.87	50.73	54.31	49.70	51.95	49.10	54.11
February	64.25	70.09	52.95	54.36	48.77	51.21	53.68	56.79
March	62.80	65.59	54.21	56.82	48.75	52.46	52.96	55.65
April	62.66	66.31	55.25	57.27	51.63	54.88	53.67	56.18
May	56.52	61.85	52.45	56.18	54.91	58.59	53.45	55.63
June	54.78	58.33	51.97	54.55	57.07	59.05	50.96	55.26
July	43.47	55.91	51.59	52.98	57.80	60.93	45.64	51.69
August	45.90	50.60	51.45	57.60	60.02	62.71	41.82	46.51
September	50.27	54.08	53.60	57.13	59.66	63.77	45.97	50.21
October	50.75	57.82	51.24	53.90	58.62	62.24	47.51	51.98
November	54.48	56.90	50.99	54.78	56.77	58.65	52.76	56.68
December	51.15	57.35	50.99	53.22	48.56	57.88	49.98	54.35

During the period from September 23, 1889 to October 24, 1896, Dow published a list of stocks composed of both railroad and industrial issues. The industrials included 2 companies and the railroads, 18. Dow also compiled a smaller stock average between July 3, 1884, and May 25, 1896. It consisted of 2 industrial stocks, and the railroads varied between 9 and 12. Beginning October 26, 1896, he published a list of 20 stocks containing only railroads.

FIGURE A–3 Monthly Highs and Lows of the Dow Jones Industrial Average (12 stocks, 1896–1916)

	1896 Low	1896 High	1897 Low	1897 High	1898 Low	1898 High	1899 Low	1899 High	1900 Low	1900 High	1901 Low	1901 High
January			40.37	43.25	48.00	50.67	60.41	65.02	63.27	68.13	64.77	70.44
February			39.72	42.38	44.67	50.23	61.95	67.52	63.35	68.36	67.00	70.78
March			39.13	42.29	42.00	47.47	65.90	74.70	61.11	66.02	67.18	69.92
April			38.49	40.43	43.27	46.32	72.60	77.28	60.47	66.15	70.91	75.89
May	40.20	40.94	38.67	39.95	48.30	52.74	67.51	76.04	56.62	61.36	67.38	75.93
June	35.53	40.60	40.01	44.61	50.87	53.71	68.40	72.08	53.68	59.38	76.07	78.26
July	30.50	35.60	43.60	47.95	52.27	54.20	70.55	73.73	55.48	59.02	69.46	77.08
August	28.48	31.97	48.84	54.81	54.60	60.97	73.68	76.23	57.06	58.90	69.05	73.83
September	32.02	36.75	50.98	55.82	53.44	60.50	72.39	77.61	52.96	58.58	66.22	73.27
October	34.74	39.53	48.42	52.66	51.56	55.43	70.95	74.97	54.42	60.79	63.48	66.07
November	40.93	44.90	45.65	49.11	54.51	57.20	73.06	75.93	59.18	69.07	64.48	66.52
December	38.59	42.22	48.14	49.81	58.14	60.52	58.27	75.68	63.98	71.04	61.52	64.87

	1902 Low	1902 High	1903 Low	1903 High	1904 Low	1904 High	1905 Low	1905 High	1906 Low	1906 High
January	62.57	65.17	64.19	66.33	47.07	50.50	68.76	71.33	94.44	103.00
February	64.58	65.58	65.53	67.70	46.71	49.03	70.91	76.16	93.94	101.71
March	64.77	67.52	62.86	66.01	46.41	49.12	75.92	80.02	92.90	96.96
April	65.95	68.44	60.79	64.56	48.62	49.98	76.08	83.75	88.70	98.19
May	64.73	67.11	60.27	64.06	47.43	48.71	71.37	78.05	86.45	93.77
June	63.67	66.26	56.65	59.90	48.08	49.47	72.53	77.78	87.01	95.21
July	64.25	67.28	49.08	58.81	49.31	53.14	77.48	81.70	85.18	92.41
August	65.33	66.78	47.38	53.88	52.68	54.61	80.63	82.82	91.67	96.08
September	64.07	67.77	45.09	52.75	54.94	57.59	78.60	81.91	93.31	96.07
October	63.84	66.58	42.25	47.62	57.59	64.54	80.83	83.77	92.76	96.75
November	60.62	65.80	42.15	45.46	63.72	72.36	80.83	89.89	92.38	95.33
December	59.57	64.29	44.35	49.35	65.77	73.23	89.50	96.56	92.94	95.89

FIGURE A–3 *(concluded)*

	1907		1908		1909		1910		1911	
	Low	High	Low	High	Low	High	Low	High	Low	High
January	90.77	96.37	59.61	65.84	84.09	86.95	90.66	98.34	81.70	84.93
February	89.75	93.39	58.62	62.14	79.91	86.72	85.03	91.34	84.33	86.02
March	75.39	90.12	60.97	69.92	81.64	86.12	89.47	94.56	81.80	84.53
April	81.40	84.80	67.04	70.29	85.37	88.29	86.20	92.62	81.32	83.65
May	77.30	85.02	69.78	75.12	88.32	92.18	84.72	89.66	82.60	86.40
June	77.40	80.36	71.70	74.38	89.66	94.46	81.18	86.28	85.79	87.06
July	78.87	82.52	72.76	80.34	92.82	96.79	73.62	81.64	85.28	86.47
August	69.25	78.87	80.57	85.40	96.30	99.26	76.14	81.41	78.93	85.47
September	67.16	73.89	77.07	84.55	95.86	100.12	78.35	79.72	72.94	80.28
October	57.23	67.95	79.50	83.55	95.70	100.50	79.95	86.02	74.82	78.66
November	53.00	58.48	82.90	88.38	95.89	100.53	82.52	85.85	77.69	81.86
December	56.85	61.77	83.46	87.67	96.66	99.28	79.68	82.16	79.19	82.48

	1912		1913		1914		1915		1916	
	Low	High	Low	High	Low	High	Low	High	Low	High
January	80.19	82.36	81.55	88.57			74.65	78.41	120.23	128.19
February	80.15	81.57	78.72	83.64			73.18	76.58	120.15	126.02
March	81.96	88.62	78.25	81.69			74.76	82.14	118.15	125.64
April	88.72	90.93	78.39	83.19			82.51	90.91	109.92	122.84
May	87.59	90.48	78.38	79.95			82.46	90.78	112.91	127.77
June	88.32	91.09	72.11	77.27			84.16	91.94	119.84	129.42
July	87.97	91.69	75.23	79.06			87.27	93.12	116.72	125.28
August	89.84	92.06	78.21	81.81			92.92	99.51	121.53	132.60
September	90.38	94.15	80.27	83.43			100.12	114.05	126.21	156.67
October	90.35	94.12	77.09	81.43			111.91	121.29		
November	89.58	91.94	75.94	78.42			116.79	127.04		
December	85.25	90.85	75.27	78.85	73.48	76.86	125.28	134.00		

FIGURE A—4 Monthly Highs and Lows of the Dow Jones Industrial Average (12 and 20 stocks, 1914–1916)

	1914–20 Stocks		1914–12 Stocks		1915–20 Stocks		1915–12 Stocks		1916–20 Stocks		1916–12 Stocks	
	Low	High	Low	High	Low	High	Low	High	Low	High	Low	High
January					54.63	58.52	74.65	78.41	90.58	98.81	120.23	128.19
February					54.22	57.83	73.18	76.58	90.89	96.15	120.15	126.02
March					55.29	61.30	74.76	82.14	90.52	96.08	118.15	125.64
April					61.05	71.78	82.51	90.91	84.96	94.46	109.92	122.84
May					60.38	71.51	82.46	90.78	87.71	92.62	112.91	127.77
June					64.86	71.90	84.16	91.94	87.68	93.61	119.84	129.42
July					67.88	75.79	87.27	93.12	86.42	90.53	116.72	125.28
August					76.46	81.95	92.92	99.51	88.15	93.83	121.53	132.60
September					80.40	90.58	100.12	114.05	91.19	103.73	126.21	156.67
October					88.23	96.46	111.91	121.29				
November					91.08	97.56	116.79	127.04				
December	53.17	56.76	73.48	76.86	94.78	99.21	125.28	134.00				

FIGURE A–5 Monthly Highs and Lows of the Dow Jones Industrial Average (20 stocks, 1916–1928)

	1916		1917		1918		1919		1920	
	Low	High	Low	High	Low	High	Low	High	Low	High
January			95.13	99.18	73.38	79.80	79.88	83.35	101.90	109.88
February			87.01	94.91	77.78	82.08	79.15	85.68	89.98	103.01
March			91.10	98.20	76.24	79.93	84.04	89.05	91.68	104.17
April			90.66	97.06	75.58	79.73	88.84	93.51	93.16	105.65
May			89.08	97.58	78.08	84.04	93.26	105.50	87.36	94.75
June			94.78	99.08	77.93	83.02	99.56	107.55	90.16	93.20
July			90.48	95.31	80.51	83.20	107.16	112.23	86.85	94.51
August			83.40	93.85	80.71	83.18	98.46	107.99	83.20	87.29
September			81.20	86.02	80.29	84.68	104.99	111.42	82.95	89.95
October	98.94	105.28	74.50	83.58	83.36	89.07	108.90	118.92	84.00	85.73
November	105.63	110.15	68.58	74.23	79.87	88.06	103.60	119.62	73.12	85.48
December	90.16	106.81	65.95	74.38	80.44	84.50	103.55	107.97	66.75	77.63

	1921		1922		1923		1924	
	Low	High	Low	High	Low	High	Low	High
January	72.67	76.76	78.59	82.95	96.96	99.42	94.88	100.66
February	74.34	77.14	81.68	85.81	97.71	103.90	96.33	101.31
March	72.25	77.78	85.33	89.05	102.36	105.36	92.54	98.86
April	75.06	78.86	89.08	93.46	98.38	102.70	89.18	94.69
May	73.44	80.03	91.50	96.41	92.77	98.19	88.33	92.47
June	64.90	73.51	90.73	96.36	87.85	97.24	89.19	96.37
July	67.25	69.86	92.90	97.05	86.91	91.72	96.38	102.14
August	63.90	69.95	96.21	100.78	87.20	93.70	101.51	105.57
September	66.83	71.92	96.30	102.05	87.89	93.61	100.76	104.95
October	69.46	73.93	96.11	103.43	85.76	90.45	99.18	104.08
November	73.44	78.01	92.03	99.53	88.41	92.88	103.89	111.38
December	78.12	81.50	95.03	99.22	92.64	95.61	110.44	120.51

	1925		1926		1927		1928	
	Low	*High*	*Low*	*High*	*Low*	*High*	*Low*	*High*
January	119.46	123.60	153.20	159.10	152.73	156.56	194.50	203.35
Feburary	117.96	122.86	154.45	162.31	154.31	161.96	191.33	199.35
March	115.00	125.68	135.20	153.13	158.41	161.78	194.53	214.45
April	117.40	122.02	136.27	144.83	160.66	167.36	207.94	216.93
May	121.10	129.95	137.16	143.43	164.55	172.96	211.73	220.88
June	126.75	131.01	142.30	154.03	165.73	171.98	201.96	220.96
July	131.33	136.59	153.01	160.58	168.06	182.61	205.10	216.62
August	134.45	143.18	160.41	166.64	177.13	190.63	214.08	240.41
September	137.22	147.73	156.26	166.10	191.56	198.97	236.86	241.72
October	144.77	156.52	145.66	159.69	179.78	199.78		
November	148.18	159.39	150.51	157.37	181.65	198.21		
December	152.11	157.01	156.65	161.86	193.58	202.40		

FIGURE A–6 Monthly Highs and Lows of the Dow Jones Industrial Average (30 stocks, 1928–1985)

	1928 Low	1928 High	1929 Low	1929 High	1930 Low	1930 High	1931 Low	1931 High	1932 Low	1932 High
January			296.98	317.51	244.20	267.14	161.45	173.04	71.24	85.88
February			295.85	322.06	262.47	272.27	168.71	194.36	71.80	85.98
March			296.51	321.18	270.25	286.19	172.36	187.72	73.28	88.78
April			299.13	319.29	276.94	294.07	143.61	172.43	55.93	72.18
May			293.42	327.08	258.31	275.07	128.46	154.41	44.74	59.01
June			299.12	333.79	211.84	274.45	121.70	156.93	42.84	50.88
July			335.22	347.70	218.33	240.81	135.39	155.26	41.22	54.26
August			337.99	380.33	217.24	240.42	133.77	145.80	53.16	75.61
September			343.45	381.17	204.90	245.09	96.61	140.13	65.06	79.93
October	237.75	257.13	230.07	352.86	183.35	214.18	86.48	109.70	58.47	72.09
November	254.16	295.62	198.69	257.68	171.60	190.30	90.02	116.79	56.35	68.04
December	257.33	300.00	230.89	263.46	157.51	186.82	73.79	91.77	55.83	61.93

	1933 Low	1933 High	1934 Low	1934 High	1935 Low	1935 High	1936 Low	1936 High	1937 Low	1937 High
January	59.29	64.35	96.73	108.99	100.49	105.88	143.11	149.49	177.72	186.90
February	50.16	60.09	103.12	110.74	100.23	107.17	149.58	154.43	186.01	190.29
March	52.54	62.95	98.76	105.79	96.71	103.27	150.42	158.75	179.82	194.40
April	55.66	77.66	100.49	106.55	100.39	110.47	143.65	161.99	170.13	185.19
May	76.63	90.02	91.81	100.62	108.71	116.81	146.41	152.64	167.46	176.30
June	88.87	98.74	91.41	100.42	109.74	120.75	149.26	160.66	165.51	175.14
July	88.42	108.67	85.51	99.02	118.69	126.56	155.60	167.01	170.13	185.61
August	92.55	105.07	87.47	95.71	124.93	128.99	160.80	169.10	175.91	190.02
September	93.18	105.74	86.69	93.65	127.27	134.11	165.16	169.55	147.38	173.08
October	83.61	99.72	90.41	95.60	128.06	141.47	168.26	177.63	125.73	154.08
November	89.62	101.28	93.46	103.08	141.07	148.44	176.67	184.90	113.64	135.94
December	95.28	102.92	99.59	104.04	138.94	144.47	175.85	182.18	118.93	129.98

1938–1942

	1938 Low	1938 High	1939 Low	1939 High	1940 Low	1940 High	1941 Low	1941 High	1942 Low	1942 High
January	120.14	134.35	136.42	154.85	144.65	152.80	124.05	133.59	108.94	114.22
February	118.49	132.41	142.43	147.30	145.00	148.94	117.66	124.76	105.10	110.80
March	98.95	130.47	131.84	152.28	145.59	148.37	120.30	123.92	99.21	106.97
April	103.02	121.00	121.44	132.83	146.80	151.29	115.54	124.65	92.92	102.50
May	107.74	119.43	127.83	138.18	113.94	148.17	115.30	117.82	95.83	101.09
June	109.71	135.87	130.05	140.14	111.84	123.86	116.18	123.97	101.30	106.29
July	134.56	144.91	131.73	144.71	120.96	126.14	122.85	130.06	102.69	108.91
August	136.21	145.67	131.33	144.26	121.24	129.42	124.90	128.22	104.80	107.55
September	129.91	143.08	135.25	155.92	127.74	135.10	125.81	129.32	106.03	109.56
October	143.13	154.17	149.60	155.48	130.39	135.09	117.82	126.85	109.65	115.29
November	146.14	158.41	145.69	152.64	129.78	138.12	114.23	119.85	114.10	117.30
December	147.39	154.76	146.34	150.24	128.41	132.35	106.34	116.65	114.61	119.71

1943–1947

	1943 Low	1943 High	1944 Low	1944 High	1945 Low	1945 High	1946 Low	1946 High	1947 Low	1947 High
January	119.26	125.58	135.92	138.65	151.35	155.85	190.90	205.35	171.95	180.44
February	125.07	130.11	134.22	137.45	153.79	160.40	186.02	206.97	177.22	184.49
March	128.60	136.82	136.44	141.00	152.27	161.52	188.46	200.56	172.37	181.88
April	131.18	136.93	135.00	139.11	154.99	165.44	199.19	208.31	166.69	177.45
May	136.20	142.06	137.06	142.24	163.09	169.08	200.65	212.50	163.21	174.21
June	138.79	143.38	141.62	148.63	164.57	168.92	200.52	211.47	168.00	177.44
July	135.95	145.82	145.58	150.50	160.91	167.09	195.22	207.56	179.88	186.85
August	134.00	138.45	144.90	148.96	161.55	174.29	189.19	204.52	177.57	183.81
September	136.91	141.75	142.96	147.16	173.90	181.71	165.17	181.18	174.86	179.81
October	136.39	140.33	145.83	148.92	183.06	187.06	163.12	175.94	178.10	185.29
November	129.57	138.50	145.60	148.08	186.41	192.27	163.55	174.40	179.40	183.17
December	130.68	136.24	147.30	152.53	189.07	195.82	167.50	178.32	175.74	181.16

FIGURE A–6 *(continued)*

	1948		1949		1950		1951		1952	
	Low	High	Low	High	Low	High	Low	High	Low	High
January	171.18	181.04	175.03	181.54	196.81	201.98	238.99	249.58	268.08	275.40
February	165.65	174.92	171.10	180.39	201.69	205.03	250.76	255.71	258.49	272.51
March	165.39	177.20	173.66	178.45	202.33	210.62	243.95	253.61	260.08	269.46
April	177.32	183.78	173.24	177.16	206.37	215.31	246.02	259.13	257.63	267.22
May	180.28	191.06	168.36	176.63	214.87	223.42	245.27	263.13	256.35	264.22
June	187.90	193.16	161.60	168.15	206.72	228.38	242.64	254.03	262.09	274.26
July	181.20	191.62	168.08	176.46	197.46	210.85	243.98	260.70	272.58	279.56
August	179.27	183.60	176.84	182.02	211.26	221.51	259.89	270.25	273.17	280.29
September	175.99	185.36	178.04	183.29	218.10	226.78	270.63	276.37	268.38	277.15
October	179.87	190.19	181.98	190.36	225.01	231.81	258.53	275.87	263.06	271.40
November	171.20	189.76	187.98	193.62	222.52	235.47	255.95	264.06	270.23	283.66
December	173.22	177.92	192.71	200.52	222.33	235.42	262.29	269.23	281.63	292.00

	1953		1954		1955		1956		1957	
	Low	High	Low	High	Low	High	Low	High	Low	High
January	285.24	293.79	279.87	292.85	388.20	408.89	462.35	485.78	474.59	499.20
February	281.14	290.19	289.54	294.54	405.70	413.99	465.72	485.71	454.82	477.22
March	270.87	290.64	296.40	303.51	391.36	419.68	486.69	513.03	468.91	475.01
April	270.73	280.09	304.26	319.33	412.97	430.64	503.02	521.05	474.98	494.36
May	271.48	278.79	317.93	327.49	414.12	426.30	468.81	516.44	494.68	506.04
June	262.88	269.84	319.27	336.90	424.08	451.38	475.29	492.78	497.08	513.19
July	268.06	275.38	334.12	347.92	453.82	468.45	491.92	517.81	503.29	520.77
August	261.22	276.74	335.80	350.38	448.84	468.18	495.96	520.95	470.14	506.21
September	255.49	265.48	338.13	363.32	455.56	487.45	475.25	509.82	456.30	486.13
October	264.26	276.31	352.14	364.43	438.59	461.14	468.70	490.19	419.79	465.82
November	273.88	281.37	353.96	388.51	454.89	487.38	466.10	495.37	427.94	449.87
December	279.26	283.54	384.04	404.39	480.72	488.40	480.61	499.47	425.65	449.55

	1958 Low	1958 High	1959 Low	1959 High	1960 Low	1960 High	1961 Low	1961 High	1962 Low	1962 High
January	438.68	451.16	583.15	597.66	622.62	685.47	610.25	650.64	689.92	726.01
February	436.89	458.65	574.46	603.50	611.33	636.92	637.04	662.08	702.54	717.55
March	443.38	455.92	601.71	614.69	599.10	626.87	661.08	679.38	706.63	723.54
April	440.09	455.86	602.94	629.87	601.70	630.77	672.66	696.72	665.33	705.42
May	455.45	463.67	615.64	643.79	599.61	625.50	677.05	705.96	576.93	675.49
June	466.11	478.97	617.62	643.60	624.89	656.42	680.68	703.79	535.76	611.05
July	476.89	504.37	650.88	674.88	601.68	646.91	679.30	705.37	571.24	597.93
August	502.67	512.42	646.53	678.10	608.69	641.56	710.46	725.76	588.35	616.00
September	511.77	532.09	616.45	655.90	569.08	626.10	691.86	726.53	574.12	607.63
October	530.94	546.36	625.59	646.60	566.05	596.48	697.24	708.49	558.06	589.77
November	540.52	567.44	634.46	659.18	585.24	612.01	703.84	734.34	597.13	652.61
December	556.08	583.65	661.29	679.36	593.49	617.78	720.10	734.91	640.14	653.99

	1963 Low	1963 High	1964 Low	1964 High	1965 Low	1965 High	1966 Low	1966 High	1967 Low	1967 High
January	646.79	683.73	766.08	787.78	869.78	902.86	968.20	994.20	786.41	849.89
February	662.94	688.96	783.04	800.14	881.35	906.30	950.66	995.15	836.64	860.97
March	659.72	684.73	802.75	820.25	887.82	901.91	911.08	938.19	841.76	876.67
April	684.27	718.33	810.77	827.33	890.33	922.31	931.29	954.73	842.43	897.05
May	712.55	726.96	817.10	830.17	913.22	939.62	864.14	931.95	852.56	909.63
June	706.03	726.87	800.31	831.50	840.59	908.53	870.10	903.17	847.77	886.15
July	687.71	716.45	837.35	851.35	861.77	883.23	847.38	894.04	859.69	909.56
August	694.87	729.32	823.40	842.83	878.89	896.18	767.03	852.39	893.72	926.72
September	732.02	745.96	844.00	875.74	893.60	937.88	772.66	814.30	901.18	943.08
October	737.94	760.50	868.44	881.50	929.65	960.82	744.32	809.57	879.74	933.31
November	711.49	753.77	870.64	891.71	946.38	961.85	791.59	820.87	849.57	884.88
December	751.82	767.21	857.45	874.13	939.53	969.26	785.69	820.54	879.16	905.11

FIGURE A-6 (continued)

	1968 Low	1968 High	1969 Low	1969 High	1970 Low	1970 High	1971 Low	1971 High	1972 Low	1972 High
January	855.47	908.92	921.25	951.89	744.06	811.31	830.57	868.50	889.15	917.22
February	831.77	863.56	899.80	952.70	746.44	777.59	868.98	890.06	901.79	928.13
March	825.13	843.22	904.03	935.48	763.60	791.05	882.39	916.83	928.66	950.18
April	861.25	912.22	917.51	950.18	724.33	792.50	903.04	950.82	940.92	968.92
May	891.60	919.90	936.92	968.85	631.16	733.63	905.78	939.92	925.12	971.25
June	897.80	917.95	869.76	933.17	682.91	720.43	873.10	923.06	926.25	961.39
July	883.00	923.72	801.96	886.12	669.36	735.56	858.43	903.40	910.45	942.13
August	869.65	896.13	809.13	837.25	707.35	765.81	839.59	908.37	930.46	973.51
September	900.36	938.28	811.84	837.78	747.47	773.14	883.47	920.93	935.73	970.05
October	942.32	967.49	802.20	862.26	753.56	783.68	836.38	901.80	921.66	955.52
November	946.23	985.08	807.29	863.05	754.24	794.09	797.97	843.17	968.54	1025.21
December	943.75	985.21	769.93	805.04	794.29	842.00	846.01	893.66	1000.00	1036.27

	1973 Low	1973 High	1974 Low	1974 High	1975 Low	1975 High	1976 Low	1976 High	1977 Low	1977 High
January	992.93	1051.70	823.11	880.69	632.04	705.96	858.71	975.28	954.37	999.75
February	947.92	996.76	803.90	863.42	707.60	749.77	950.57	994.57	931.52	958.36
March	922.71	979.98	846.68	891.66	743.43	786.53	970.64	1009.21	919.13	968.00
April	921.43	967.41	827.68	869.92	742.88	821.34	968.28	1011.02	914.60	947.76
May	886.51	956.58	795.37	865.77	815.00	858.73	965.57	1007.48	898.66	943.44
June	869.13	927.00	802.41	859.67	819.31	878.99	958.09	1007.45	903.04	929.70
July	870.11	936.71	757.43	806.24	824.86	881.81	979.29	1011.21	888.43	923.42
August	851.90	912.78	656.84	797.56	791.69	835.34	960.44	999.34	854.12	891.81
September	880.57	953.27	607.87	677.88	793.88	840.11	978.64	1014.79	834.72	876.39
October	948.83	987.06	584.56	673.50	784.16	855.16	932.35	979.89	801.54	851.96
November	817.73	948.83	608.57	674.75	825.72	860.67	924.04	966.09	800.85	845.89
December	788.31	851.14	577.60	616.24	818.80	859.81	946.64	1004.65	806.22	831.17

	1978		1979		1980		1981	
	Low	High	Low	High	Low	High	Low	High
January	763.34	817.74	811.42	859.75	820.31	881.91	938.61	1004.69
February	742.12	782.66	807.00	840.87	854.44	903.84	931.57	974.58
March	742.72	773.82	815.95	871.36	759.98	856.48	964.62	1015.22
April	751.04	837.32	854.90	878.72	759.13	817.06	989.10	1024.05
May	822.07	858.37	822.16	857.59	805.20	860.32	963.44	995.59
June	812.28	866.51	821.21	849.10	843.77	887.54	976.88	1011.99
July	805.79	862.27	825.51	852.99	872.27	936.18	924.66	967.66
August	860.71	900.12	846.16	887.63	929.78	966.72	881.47	953.58
September	857.16	907.74	866.13	893.94	921.93	974.57	824.01	884.23
October	792.45	901.42	805.46	897.61	917.75	972.44	830.96	878.14
November	785.26	827.79	796.67	831.74	932.42	1000.17	844.08	888.98
December	787.51	821.90	819.62	844.62	908.45	974.40	868.25	892.69

	1982		1983		1984		1985*	
	Low	High	Low	High	Low	High	Low	High
January	838.95	882.52	1027.04	1092.35	1220.58	1286.64	1184.96	1292.62
February	811.26	852.55	1059.79	1121.81	1134.21	1213.88	1275.84	1297.92
March	759.47	828.39	1114.45	1145.90	1139.76	1184.36	1247.35	1299.36
April	833.24	865.58	1113.49	1226.20	1130.55	1175.25	1252.98	1284.78
May	819.54	869.20	1190.02	1232.59	1101.24	1186.56	1242.05	1315.41
June	788.62	816.88	1185.50	1248.30	1086.90	1133.84	1290.10	1335.46
July	796.99	833.43	1189.90	1243.69	1086.57	1134.28	1321.91	1359.54
August	776.92	901.31	1163.06	1206.50	1134.61	1239.73	1312.50	1355.62
September	895.05	934.79	1206.81	1260.77	1197.99	1237.52	1297.94	1339.27
October	903.61	1036.98	1223.48	1284.65	1175.13	1225.93	1324.37	1375.57
November	990.99	1065.49	1214.84	1287.20	1185.29	1244.15	1389.68	1475.69
December	990.25	1070.55	1236.79	1275.10	1163.21	1211.70	1457.91	1553.10

*Through December 17, 1985.

APPENDIX B

DJIA Charts (with Stillman's significant political, military, technological, and economic event)

1. 1884–1896: Dow Combined Railroad and Industrial Series—11–14 stocks
2. 1896–1916: Dow Jones Industrial Average—12 Stock Series
3. 1914–1916: Dow Jones Industrial Average—12 and 20 Stock Series
4. 1916–1928: Dow Jones Industrial Average—20 Stock Series
5. 1928–1985: Dow Jones Industrial Average—30 Stock Series
6. 1896–1985: Dow Jones Industrial Average—12, 20, and 30 Stock Series
7. 1986–2000: Plot Your Own Projection and Significant Political, Military, Technological, and Economic Events.

FIGURE B–1 1884–1896: Dow Railroad and Industrial Average —11 to 14 Stocks (with Stillman's significant political, military, technological, and economic events)

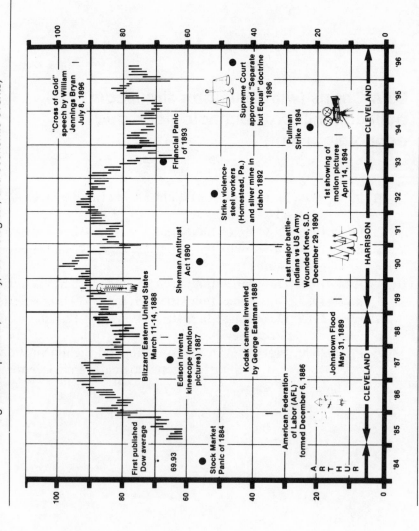

FIGURE B–2   1896–1916: Dow Jones Industrial Average—12 Stock Series (with Stillman's significant political, military, economic, and technological events)

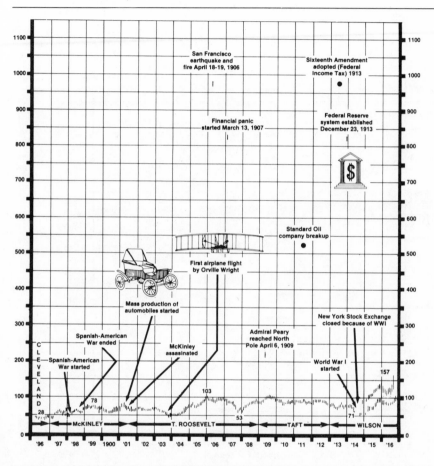

FIGURE B–3 1914–1916: Dow Jones Industrial Averages—12 and 20 Stock Series

□ 12 Stocks ▮ 20 Stocks

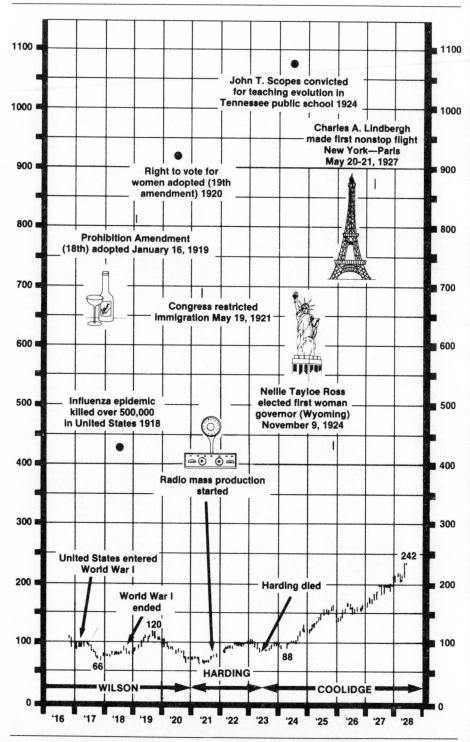

FIGURE B–4 1916–1928: Dow Jones Industrial Average—20 Stock Series (with Stillman's significant political, military, economic, and technological events)

John T. Scopes convicted for teaching evolution in Tennessee public school 1924

Charles A. Lindbergh made first nonstop flight New York—Paris May 20-21, 1927

Right to vote for women adopted (19th amendment) 1920

Prohibition Amendment (18th) adopted January 16, 1919

Congress restricted immigration May 19, 1921

Influenza epidemic killed over 500,000 in United States 1918

Nellie Tayloe Ross elected first woman governor (Wyoming) November 9, 1924

Radio mass production started

United States entered World War I

World War I ended

120

Harding died

242

66

88

HARDING

WILSON

COOLIDGE

'16 '17 '18 '19 '20 '21 '22 '23 '24 '25 '26 '27 '28

FIGURE B–5 1928–1985: Dow Jones Industrial Average—30 Stock Series (with Stillman's significant political, military, economic, and technological events)

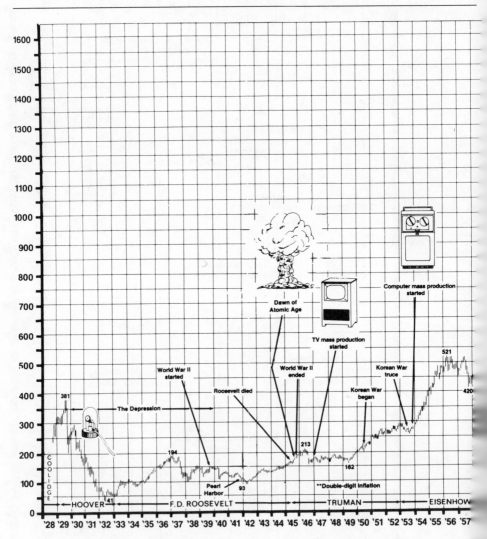

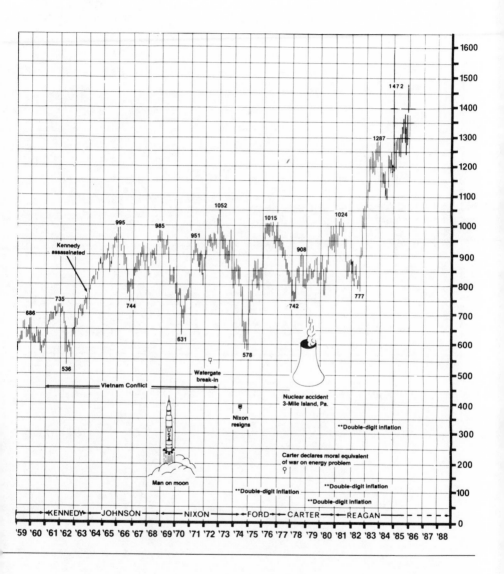

FIGURE B–6 1896–1985: Dow Jones Industrial Average—12, 20, and 30 Stock Series (with Stillman's significant political, military, technological, and economic events)

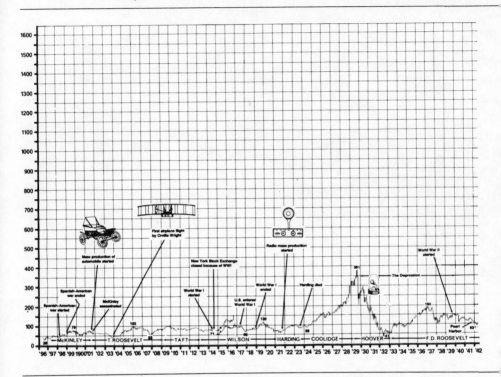

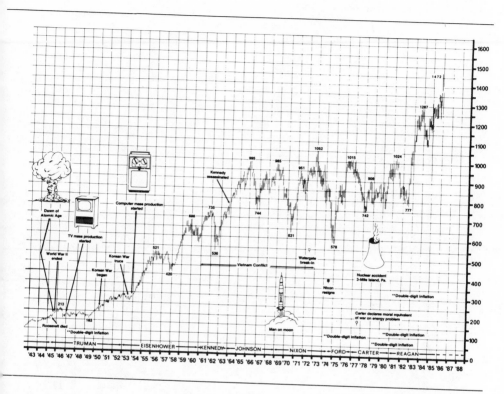

1600
1500
1472
1400
1287
1300
1200
1100
1052
1000
995 985 1015 1024
961
906
900
Kennedy
assassinated
800
735
777
688 744 742
700
631
600
578
521
536
500
420
Vietnam Conflict
Watergate
break-in
400
Nixon
resigns
Nuclear accident
3-Mile Island, Pa.
300
213
**Double-digit inflation
182
200
Roosevelt died
Man on moon
Carter declares moral equivalent
of war on energy problem
100
**Double-digit inflation
**Double-digit inflation
**Double-digit inflation
**Double-digit inflation
0

Dawn of
Atomic Age

TV mass production
started

Computer mass production
started

World War II
ended

Korean War
truce

Korean War
began

TRUMAN — EISENHOWER — KENNEDY — JOHNSON — NIXON — FORD — CARTER — REAGAN

'43 '44 '45 '46 '47 '48 '49 '50 '51 '52 '53 '54 '55 '56 '57 '58 '59 '60 '61 '62 '63 '64 '65 '66 '67 '68 '69 '70 '71 '72 '73 '74 '75 '76 '77 '78 '79 '80 '81 '82 '83 '84 '85 '86 '87 '88

FIGURE B–7   Dow Jones Industrial Average, 1986–2000: Plot Your Own
Projection and Significant Political, Military, Technological, and
Economic Events.

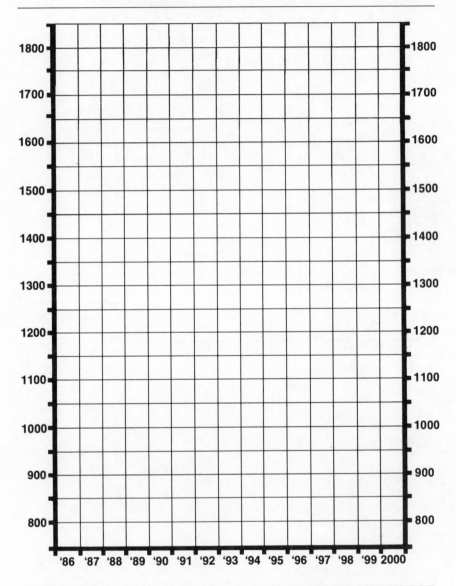

This chart enables you to plot your projection of the monthly movement of the DJIA
and significant events between now and the year 2000. Each grid square covers a one-
year period and 50 points. You may also wish to plot the movement of your stock(s) in
order to compare its movement with the DJIA. A transparency can be useful in making
the comparison. If you own gold, silver, or any other investment, you may wish to plot its
progress either on the chart or on a transparency.

SOURCE © Copyright 1986 by Richard J. Stillman. All Rights Reserved.

APPENDIX C

Bibliography

Books

ABY, CARROLL D., Jr., and DONALD F. VAUGHN. *Investment Classics*. Santa Monica, Calif.: Goodyear Publishing, 1979.

AMLING, FREDERICK, *Investments*. 5th ed. Englewood Cliffs, N.J.: Prentice-Hall, 1982.

BISHOP, GEORGE W., Jr. *Charles H. Dow: Economist*. Princeton, N.J.: Dow Jones & Co., 1967.

——— *Charles H. Dow and the Dow Theory*. New York: Appleton-Century-Crofts, 1960.

BOLTON, STEVEN E. *Security Analysis and Portfolio Management: An Analytical Approach to Investments*. New York: Holt, Rinehart Winston, 1972.

BRISTON, R. J. *The Stock Exchange and Investment Analysis*. 2d ed. London: George Allen & Unwin Ltd Inc., 1973.

BROOKS, JOHN. *Once in Golconda: A True Drama of Wall Street 1920–1938*. New York: Harper & Row, 1969.

BURTCHETT, FLOYD F. *Investments and Investment Policy*. New York: Longmans, Green and Co., 1938.

CHRISTY, GEORGE H., and JOHN C. CLENDENIN. *Introduction to Investments*. New York: McGraw-Hill, 1982.

COHEN, JEROME B.; EDWARD D. ZINBARG; and ARTHUR ZEIKEL. *Investment Analysis and Portfolio Management*. Homewoood, Ill.: Richard D. Irwin, 1982.

DICE, CHARLES A. *The Stock Market*. New York: A.W. Shaw and Co., 1926.

DOW, CHARLES H. *History of Steam Navigation between New York & Providence*. Providence, R.I.: William Turner & Company, 1877.

―――――

Newport, the City by the Sea. Providence, R. I.: John P. Sanborn, 1880.

DOW, ROBERT PIERCY. *The Book of Dow*. Rutland, Vt.: The Tuttle Company, 1929.

DREW, GARFIELD A. *New Methods for Profits in the Stock Market*. Boston, Mass.: Metcalf Press, 1941.

EDWARDS, ROBERT D., and JOHN MAGEE. *Technical Analysis of Stock Trends*. Springfield, Mass.: John Magee, 1958.

ELLINGER, A. G. *The Art of Investment*. 3d ed., London: Bowes & Bowes, 1971.

ELTON, EDWIN J., and MARTIN J. GRUBER. *Modern Portfolio Theory and Investment Analysis*. 2d ed. New York: John Wiley & Sons, 1984.

FARRELL, MAURICE L., ed. *The Dow Jones Averages, 1885–1970*. Homewood, Ill.: Dow Jones-Irwin, 1972.

―――――

The Dow Jones Investor's Handbook. Homewood, Ill.: Dow Jones-Irwin, 1973.

FINLEY, HAROLD M. *Everybody's Guide to the Stock Market*. Chicago, Ill.: Henry Regnery Co., 1956.

FISHER, DONALD E. and RONALD J. JORDAN. *Security Analysis and Portfolio Management*. Englewood Cliffs, N.J.: Prentice-Hall, 1983.

FRANCIS, JACK CLARK; CHENG-FEW LEE; and DONALD E. FARRAR: *Readings in Investments*. New York: McGraw-Hill, 1980.

GALBRAITH, JOHN KENNETH. *The Great Crash 1929*. Boston: Houghton Mifflin, 1954.

GORDON, WILLIAM. *The Stock Market Indicators*. Palisades Park, N.J.: Investor's Press, 1968.

GRAHAM, BENJAMIN, and DAVID L. DODD.*Security Analysis*. 2d ed. New York: McGraw-Hill, 1940.

GRANVILLE, J. E. *A Strategy for Daily Stock Market Timing for Maximum Profit.* Englewood Cliffs, N.J.: Prentice-Hall, 1960.

GREINER, PERRY P., and HALE C. WHITCOMB, *The Dow Theory and the Seventy-Year Forecast Record.* New York: Investors Intelligence, 1969.

HAMILTON, WILLIAM PETER. *The Stock Market Barometer.* New York: Harper & Row, 1922. Republished by Robert Rhea in 1937.

HIRST, FRANCIS W. *The Stock Exhcange: A Short Study of Investment and Speculation.* London: Oxford University Press, 1948.

JONES, CHARLES P. *Investments: Analysis and Management.* New York: John Wiley & Sons, 1985.

KERBY, WILLIAM F. *A Proud Profession: Memoirs of a Wall Street Journal Reporter, Editor, and Publisher.* Homewood, Ill.: Dow Jones-Irwin, 1981.

LORIE, JAMES H.; PETER DODD; and MARY H. KIMPTON. *The Stock Market: Theories and Evidence.* 2d ed. Homewood, Ill: Richard D. Irwin, 1985.

MARKOWITZ, HARRY M. *Portfolio Selection.* New York: John Wiley & Son, 1976.

Moody's Handbook of Common Stocks. New York: Moody's Investors Service, Inc., published quarterly.

Nelson, Samuel Armstrong. *The ABC of Options and Arbitrage.* New York: S. A. Nelson, 1904.

———

The ABC of Stock Speculation. New York: S. A. Nelson, 1902. Reprinted in 1903. Republished in 1934 by Stock Market Publications and in 1964 by Fraser Publishing Company.

———

The ABC of Wall Street. New York: S. A. Nelson, 1900.

ORMEROD, C. B. *Dow Theory: Applied to the London Stock Exchange.* London: Sir Isaac Pitman & Sons, Ltd., 1939.

PIERCE, PHYLLIS S. (ed). *The Dow Jones Averages 1885–1980.* Homewood, Ill.: Dow Jones-Irwin, 1982.

PRATT, SERENO S. *The Work of Wall Street.* New York: D. Appleton & Company, 1921.

PRING, MARTIN J. *Technical Analysis,* 2d ed. New York: McGraw-Hill, 1985.

RHEA, ROBERT. *Dow's Theory Applied to Business and Banking.* New York: Simon & Schuster, 1938.

_____

The Dow Theory. Denver, Col.: Smith, 1932. Republished in 1959 by Rhea, Greiner & Co.

_____

The Story of the Averages. Colorado Springs, Col.: Robert Rhea, 1934.

SCHABACKER, R. W. *Stock Market Profits.* New York: B. C. Forbes, 1934.

_____

Stock Market Theory & Practice. New York: B. C. Forbes, 1930.

SHARPE, WILLIAM F. *Investments.* 3d ed. Englewood Cliffs, N.J.: Prentice-Hall, 1985.

SMITH, CHARLES. *The Mind of the Market : A Study of Stock Market Philosophy, Their Uses and Their Implications.* New York: Harper, 1983.

STANSBURY, CHARLES B. *The Dow Theory Explained.* New York: Barron's Publishing Co., 1938.

STILLMAN, RICHARD J. *Guide to Personal Finance: A Lifetime Program of Money Management.* 4th ed. Englewood Cliffs, N.J.: Prentice-Hall, 1984.

_____

Small Business Management: How to Start and Stay in Business. Boston: Little, Brown, 1983.

Six Steps to Your Financial Success: A Guide to Personal and Family Budgeting. Alexandria, Va.: Pentagon Federal Credit Union, 1985.

STILLMAN, RICHARD J., and JOHN PAGE. *How to Use Your Personal Computer to Manage Your Personal Finances.* Englewood Cliffs, N.J.: Prentice-Hall, 1986. A computer software program.

_____

WENDT, LLOYD. *The Wall Street Journal.* Chicago: Rand McNally, 1982.

WOODLOCK, THOMAS F. *The Anatomy of a Railroad Report and Ton Mile Cost.* New York: S. A. Nelson, 1900.

Pamphlets

STILLMAN, RICHARD J., and Khalil Dibee. *Barron's in Investments and Personal Finance.* Homewood, Ill.: Dow Jones-Irwin, 1981.

The Dow Jones Averages: A Non-professional's Guide. Homewood, Ill.: Dow Jones-Irwin, 1984.

ZWEIG, MARTIN E. *The ABC's of Market Forecasting: How to Use Barron's Market Laboratory Pages. Homewood, Ill.: Dow Jones-Irwin, 1985.*

Articles

"A Closer Look at Dow Jones Average." *U.S. News & World Report.* September 13, 1982, p. 79.

BAIDA, PETER. "The Centennial of Charles Dow's Captivating Index." *The Wall Street Journal,* July 3, 1984, p. 18.

BALCH, W. F. "Market Guides: Indexes of Stock Prices Lately Have Multiplied." *Barron's,* September 26, 1966, p. 9.

BARBOUR, JUSTIN F. "An Analysis of the Conclusions of the Cowles Studies with Respect to the Dow Theory." *Financial Analysts Journal,* 4 Quarterly 1946, p. 11.

"Security Market Outlook." *Financial Analysts Journal,* 1 Quarterly 1949, p. 7.

BISHOP, GEORGE W., Jr. "Evolution of the Dow Theory." *Financial Analysts Journal,* September–October 1961, p. 23.

"New England Journalist: Highlights in the Newspaper Career of Charles H. Dow." *Business History Review,* Fall 1960, p. 77.

BLEIBERG, ROBERT M. "Salute to Dow Theory." *Barron's,* May 18, 1981, p. 7.

"Way Above Average: For a Century Dow Theory Has Served Investors Well." *Barron's,* July 9, 1984, p. 9.

BUTLER, H. L., Jr., and M. B. DECKER. "A Security Check on the Dow Jones Industrial Average." *Financial Analysts Journal,* February 1953, p. 37.

BUTLER, HARTMAN L., Jr., and ALLEN J. DEVON, "The Dow Jones Industrial Average Re-Reexamined." *Financial Analysts Journal,* November–December 1979, p. 23.

CARTER, E. E. and K. J. COHEN. "Stock Averages, Stock Splits and Bias." *Financial Analysts Journal,* May–June 1967, p. 77.

———

"Bias in the DJIA Caused by Stock Splits." *Financial Analysts Journal,* November–December 1966, p. 90.

COLLINS, CHARLES J. "The Dow–Jones Industrial Average." *Financial Analysts Journal,* March–April 1961, p. 7.

COMER, HARRY D. "The Market-Backward and Forward." *Financial Analysts Journal,* August 1952, p. 142.

COOTNER, PAUL H. "Stock Market Indexes: Fallacies and Illusions." *Commercial and Financial Chronicle,* September 29, 1966 (reprint), p. 18.

———

"Deep Inside the Dow." *Forbes,* October 8, 1984, p. 256.

DE GOUMOIS, MARC. "Predetermined Resistance Levels for the Dow-Jones Industrial Average." *Financial Analysts Journal,* September 1960, p. 59.

Dow Charles H. "Temples of Learning." *The Providence Journal,* September 2, 1878, p. 3.

———

"The State Farm." *The Providence Journal,* July 14, 1978, p. 2.

———

"Prisons and Prisoners." *The Providence Journal,* January 20, 1878, p. 2.

EDGERTON, JERRY. "How You Can Forecast the Market." *Money,* June 1982, p. 40.

EDWARDS, WILLIAM F. "Judgement versus Mechanical Investment Plans." *Financial Analysts Journal,* 1 (Quarterly 1946), p. 3.

FISHER, LAWRENCE. "Some New Stock Market Indexes." *Journal of Business Security Prices: A Supplement,* January 1966, p. 191.

GORDON, C. E. II, and S. C. LEUTHOLD. "Margin for Error: The American Stock Exchange Index Has Exceeded It." *Barron's,* March 1, 1971, p. 14.

JOHNSON, GREG. "Changing Times Chip Away at an Institution." *Industry Week,* October 4, 1982, p. 73.

KEKISH, BOHDAN J. "Moody's Averages." *Financial Analysts Journal,* May–June 1967, p. 65.

LAFARGE, FRANCIS W. "Methods of Evaluating Future Price Levels of the Dow-Jones Industrial Average." *Financial Analysts Journal,* October 1945, p. 45.

LATANE, HENRY A.; Donald L. Tuttle; and William E. Young. "Market Indexes and Their Implications for Portfolio Management." *Financial Analysts Journal,* September–October 1971, p. 75.

LAUBSHER, HARRY W. "Thoughts about Theories." *Financial World,* August 1, 1982, p. 50.

LEUTHOLD, S. C., and K. I. BLAICH. "Warped Yardstick." *Barron's, September 18, 1972, p. 9.*

"Looking at the Dow." New York Times, March 14, 1983, p. 22.

MALABRE, A. L. "When Forecasters Go Wrong." *Money,* November 1975, p. 46.

MENNIS, EDMUND A. "Security Prices and Business Cycles." *Financial Analysts Journal,* February 1955, p. 79.

MILNE, ROBERT D. "The Dow Jones Industrial Average Re-Examined." *Financial Analysts Journal,* November–December 1966, p. 86.

MOLODOVSKY, NICHOLAS. "Building a Stock Market Measure— A Case Story." *Financial Analysts Journal,* May–June 1967, p. 43.

"Dow Jones Industrials—A Reappraisal." *Financial Analysts Journal,* March–April 1961, p. 13.

REILLY, FRANK K. "Price Changes in NYSE, AMEX, and OTC Stocks Compared." *Financial Analysts Journal,* March–April, 1971, p. 54.

RENSHAW, EDWARD F., and PAUL J. FELDSTEIN. "The Case for an Unmanaged Investment Company." *Financial Analysts Journal,* January 1960, p. 43.

ROLO, CHARLES J. "Anticipating Major Ups and Downs." *Money,* June 1982, p. 44.

"Predicting How the Market Will Move." *Money,* June 1977, p. 61.

RUDD, ANDREW T. "The Revised Dow Jones Industrial Average: New Wine in Old Bottles?" *Financial Analysts Journal,* November–December 1979, p. 57.

SCHELLBACH, LEWIS, L. "Yardsticks for the Market." *Financial Analysts Journal,* November 1955, p. 33.

————

"When Did the DJIA Top 1200?" *Financial Analysts Journal,* May–June 1967, p. 71.

SCHLOSS, WALTER J. "The Dow Jones Industrial Average Amended." *Financial Analysts Journal,* February 1953, p. 35.

SCHOOMER, B. ALVA, Jr. "The American Stock Exchange Index System." *The Financial Analysts Journal,* May–June 1967, p. 57.

"Stock Market Cues Technicians Use." *Changing Times,* March 1983, p. 74.

SELIGMAN, D. "Playing the Market With Charts." *Fortune,* February 1962, p. 118.

————

"The Mystique of Point and Figure." *Fortune,* March 1962, p. 113.

SHAW, ROBERT B. "The Dow Jones Industrials versus the Dow Jones Industrial Average." *Financial Analysts Journal,* November 1955, p. 37.

SITT, IRVING. "Mechanical Investment Plans versus Judgement." *Financial Analysts Journal* 2 (Quarterly 1946), p. 30.

The Wall Street Journal. Daily editions between 1889 and 1929 for the writings of Charles H. Dow and William P. Hamilton.

WEST, STAN, and NORMAN MILLER. "Why the New NYSE Common Stock Indexes?" *Financial Analysts Journal,* May–June 1967, p. 49.

APPENDIX D

Financial Periodicals and Services

The financial periodicals and services listed here may provide helpful information for maintaining your investment program. The rapidity of change in the world today can have a significant impact on an investment portfolio. In order to be well informed, the individual responsible for managing his/her money should establish and maintain a personal library. This should include a copy of the author's three recent publications: *Guide to Personal Finance* 4th ed. (1984); *How to Use Your Personal Computer to Manage Your Personal Finances (1986);* and *Six Steps to Your Financial Success (1985).* Keep up-to-date by reading such publications as *The Wall Street Journal, Barron's, Forbes,* and a major newspaper like *the New York Times.* Also listen to such TV programs as "Nightly Business Report" and "Wall Street Week."

Periodicals

Periodical	Frequency of Publication	Publisher	Type Information
Barron's	Weekly	Dow Jones & Co. Inc., Chicopee, Mass.	General Business and financial newspaper with market quotations
Business Week	Weekly	McGraw-Hill, New York, N.Y.	Business publication covering many economic areas
Changing Times	Monthly	The Kiplinger Washington Editors, Inc., Washington, D.C.	Articles of consumer interest
Financial Analysts Journal	Bimonthly	Financial Analysts Federation, New York, N.Y.	Articles and transcripts of speeches of interest to securities analysts
Forbes	Semimonthly	Forbes, Inc., New York, N.Y.	Articles concerning companies and industries as investments
Fortune	Semimonthly	Time, Inc., New York, N.Y.	Various comprehensive business articles
Harvard Business Review	Bimonthly	Harvard Graduate School of Business Administration, Boston, Mass.	General business articles; some articles on investments
Money	Monthly	Time, Inc., Los Angeles, Calif.	Timely articles on a variety of personal finance subjects
New York Times	Daily	N.Y. Times Publishing Co., New York, N.Y.	Daily business and financial news, appearing as a separate section in the New York Times.
The Wall Street Journal	Daily Monday through Friday	Dow Jones & Co. Inc., New York, N.Y.	General business and financial newspaper with market quotations
U.S. News & World Report	Weekly	U.S. News & World Report, Inc., Washington, D.C.	Articles of general business interest

Services

Service	Frequency of Publication	Publisher	Type Information
Babson's Reports	Weekly	Babson's Reports, Inc., Wellesley Hills, Mass.	Views on the stock market to include recommendations
Dow Theory Letters	Weekly	Dow Theory Letters, La Jolla, Calif.	Dow theorist Richard Russell discusses trends in stocks, bond, gold, silver, etc.
Edison Gould's Findings & Forecasts	24 times a year	New York, N.Y.	Forecast of stock market trends suspported by technical material
Granville Market Letter Inc.	46 times a year	The Granville Market Letter Inc., Kansas City, Mo.	Joseph Granville discusses market turns and the probabilities of when they may occur
Holt Investment Advisory	Weekly	T. J. Holt Company, Inc., 290 Post Road West, Westport, Conn.	Provides specific guidelines in regard to the stock and options market
Mansfield Chart Service	Weekly	Mansfield chart Service, Jersey City, N.J.	3500 Mansfield charts with buy/sell signals
Moody's Investors Service	Varies depending on individual publication	Moody's Investor's Service Inc., New York, N.Y.	Numerous services of interest to the investor
Standard & Poor's Corp.	Varies depending on individual publication	Standard & Poor's Corporation, New York, N.Y.	Numerous services of interest to the investor
The Astute Investor	Weekly	The Astute Investor, Paoli, Penn.	Weekly market letter—comprehensive analytic approach; Robert Nurock, publisher, appears as a panelist on the TV program "Wall \$treet Week"

Services

Service	Frequency of Publication	Publisher	Type Information
Value Line Investment Survey	Weekly	Arnold Bernhard & Co., Inc., New York, N.Y.	Continuous analysis and review of numerous stocks; also special situations in various industries
Zweig Forecast	18 times a year	Zweig Forecast, New York, N.Y.	Emphasizes the importance of timing based on technical indicators; Martin, Zeig appears as a panelist on TV program, "Wall $treet Week"
The Elliot Wave Theorist	Monthly	New Classics Library, Inc. P.O. Box 1518–B Gainesville, Ga.	Forecasting letter covering stocks, bonds, gold, and interest rates; Editor Robert Prechler analyzes Elliot waves.

APPENDIX E

Thomas Woodlock Article

The Woodlock article was titled "Pioneer Financial News Trio Recalled By Sole Survivor of 1892 Local Staff" and appeared in *The Wall Street Journal* June 27, 1932, first page, third section.

Pioneer Financial News Trio Recalled
By Sole Survivor of 1892 Local Staff

BY THOMAS F. WOODLOCK

The present writer joined the staff of Dow Jones & Co., Inc., September 28, 1892. His knowledge of the first ten years of the firm's operations, being hearsay, is not evidence. It was, however, impressed upon him that he was becoming part of a very highly organized and perfected organization at what was really the kid glove stage of its existence. At that time the firm consisted of Charles H. Dow, Edward D. Jones and Charles M. Bergstresser. In addition to the firm, there was a local reporting staff consisting of Frank B. Phelps, who specialized in coal and metals, and this writer, to whom was assigned the department of money and foreign exchange. John Boyle was representative in Washington—he is still with the organization—and, there were correspondents in Chicago and two or three other western cities of smaller dimensions. In these cases the correspondent was of the "occasional" type. The Exchange Telegraph Co. represented Dow Jones & Co. then as now in London. Last, but assuredly not least, there was the Boston News Bureau, which in those days was Mr. Barron, as Boston correspondent with a special leased wire.

The plant, consisting of three Mergenthaler linotypes, one old-fashioned flat bed press, on which "The Wall Street Journal" was printed, a couple of small hand-driven rotary presses for the news slips and a couple of job presses for the printing of brokers' market letters was assembled on a single floor in an old building at 41 Broad Street. Power was furnished by an antiquated type Babcock & Wilcox engine in the cellar. The messenger boys who delivered the news slips were also lodged on the same floor. Light was furnished by gas. At the back of the building was a cosy little cubbyhole with one old-fashioned walnut desk of probable "vintage 1860" and three chairs. This was the firm's private room, wherein "conferences" were daily held at the close of business. From this brief description it will be seen that the plant and organization were quite up-to-date, representing the very last word in mechanical perfection and efficiency.

SOURCE *The Wall Street Journal*, June 27, 1932, section 3, p. 1.

Four Full Beards and a Walrus Mustache

Memory is a whimsical thing, especially when it travels back forty years and its offerings follow no particular rule of importance. In 1893 Charles H. Dow was 41 years old; Edward D. Jones, 36 Clarence W. Barron 37; Charles M. Bergstresser, 33, and the present writer, 26--yet in the five there were four full beards and one mustache, "walrus type" the latter owned by Jones Perhaps this will serve to date the era as well as anything else. Dow was termed by Jones a "Connecticut Yankee" and Jones used to characterize himself as a "New England Baptist" from Providence; Bergstresser, coming from Lykens Valley, was, of course, a "Pennsylvania Dutchman." Mr. Barron was "Boston" through and through. Merely to complete the record, Phelps owned Jamesville, Wisconsin, as his home and the present writer first saw the light on the banks of the Liffey in County Dublin. Seeing that he joined the staff sixteen days after his arrival in the United States, it will not seem over strange that he found himself in distinctly unfamiliar company and surroundings. The three men, whose partner he was to become four years later, were three as unlike each other—and for that matter as unlike any one whom he had ever met as could be imagined. The one and only thing that Dow and Jones and Bergstresser had in common was "the business"; in every other particular they were of totally diverse types.

Dow was a tall, black bearded, slightly stooping man, with the grave air and the measured speech of a college professor. Jones was tall and ruddy, swift in his motions, high-strung as a race horse, tempestuous in temper and speech, with a mind quick as a lightning flash and a nose for "news" as keen as that of a thoroughbred bird dog. Bergstresser was of shorter build, but stocky, placid, imperturbable, with a thick brown beard, a photographic memory, a capacity for penetrating recesses where no other reporter could gain access, and an acquaintance with everyone of any importance in the entire financial district. People would talk to Bergstresser who would talk to no other newspaperman and no one ever asserted that Bergstresser had misquoted him. No rebuff availed against his calm friendly glance (through thick lenses) and his obvious confidence that he was a welcome caller. Jones used to say that Bergstresser could make a wooden Indian talk and furthermore tell the

Continued on Fourteenth Page Fourth Section

Woodlock Writes of Early Days

Continued from First Page Third Section

truth. With Mr. Barron this writer became acquainted only some years later; suffice it at this point to say that he was in nothing at all like the three thus roughly sketched.

Dow and Jones Came From Providence

Dow and Jones had worked together as young men on the Providence Journal. Which of them came first to New York to join the old Kiernan News Agency in Wall Street this writer does not know, but whoever came first persuaded the other to join him. Both were capable newspapermen when they joined Kiernan. Whatever may have been the reason why Dow and Jones elected to go into the news business on their own account, the fact is that they broke away fifty years ago and established the firm of Dow and Jones

Bergstresser was hired as a stenographer and "flimsy" writer, for in those pioneer days the news was circulated on sheets known by that name, manifolded by stylograph and carbon paper. His capacity for getting and reporting news and statements developed at an early stage and he soon became a member of the firm.

At the time when this writer joined up and the business had developed into the compact organization above described, the division of work in general was such that Jones acted as the "desk man" or "city editor" while Dow, Bergstresser, Phelps and this writer did the "leg work" and the reporting. Jones had a special faculty for editing news and devising assignments. He was also peculiarly adept at figures and their analysis. It is fair to say that he was probably the first of the "corporation analysts" in Wall Street. He could disembowel a railroad report—they were about the only reports in those days, for there were very few so called industrials that interested Wall Street— with the speed and accuracy of a skilled surgeon. Dow attended to the stock market end of the news and wrote the stock market gossip. He was well and favorably known in all of the important stock broker offices of the day. Bergstresser circulated the district in search of "statements" and "interviews" and the like, and was relied upon to catch any important railroad or corporation visitor who could be tracked down when he came to New York.

Phelps busied himself with coal—in those days it was mainly anthracite that was of interest—metals, hides and leather and such miscellaneous matters, while to this writer were left the banks and the foreign exchange houses. At this point it may perhaps be permitted to him to recall the fact that when Mr. Dow suggested that money and foreign exchange would be a good department for him to undertake and he had in a burst of frankness informed Mr. Dow that he knew little or nothing about either subject, Mr. Dow said that a good way to find out about them was to write about them. To which he may add that whatever information he possesses on these subjects today he acquired by that method.

Local Staff Numbered Five

The above five men constituted the entire local staff and produced daily the bulletin news service, the matter of which—with elaborate but it must be confessed occasionally inaccurate statistical tables—furnished the meat for a four page Wall Street Journal each afternoon at the close of business and circulating some 1,500 copies every day. On a very busy day the news output would be at a liberal estimate perhaps as much in quantity as one-fifth of that now turned out on a very quiet day in the dead season of the year. To complete the tale of mechanical efficiency it may be stated that a single telephone instrument and a single typewriter filled all the requirements of the organization. Both were attended to by a young lady. It was whispered that one reason why she was engaged was that Dow thought that the presence in the office of a lady might help to restrain the vivid varieties of (in point of fact quite harmless) profanity to which Jones under stress of business would occasionally give way. Miss Egan up to her marriage and retirement from the staff took all the copy that Dow, Bergstresser and Jones produced; she was a remarkably rapid operator and took dictation straight on the machine. Thus the reader will observe that there was at the command of Dow Jones & Co. every possible resource and convenience that a thoroughly up-to-date and complete organization would really use.

Dow could make more interesting lines out of a given fact or idea than any newspaperman that this writer ever knew or heard of. This, perhaps, may be accounted for by the fact that on the Providence Journal his job was to produce daily a column of local items. He worked noiselessly, never raised his voice and habitually practiced that rhetorical figure which Englishmen use so generally and is known as meiosis. Jones liked action and noise, plenty of both. To

see him handle a "rush" item was to see an
elemental force of nature at work. Bergstresser worked more in Dow's fashion. The three
men teamed perfectly; it was, as this writer
later found, an ideal partnership.

All important actions affecting the business
were discussed in common, and however many
were the opinions before conference there was
but one afterwards. It happened one day in
Jones' absence that Dow and Bergstresser determined upon some course of action and Jones
remonstrated. Whereupon Dow informed him
quite seriously that he had represented Jones
in the conference and had voted no for him but
that he was in a minority. When something
untoward happened Jones would explode like a
dynamite cartridge and that would be all there
was from him. Dow, on the other hand, used
to say that it took him a good 24 hours to get
really angry and once angry he stayed angry.
This writer does not recall ever having seen
Bergstresser either angry or excited. One single
instance may perhaps suffice to indicate the re-
spective characteristics of the firm; it occurred
in December, 1895 and this writer was eyewit-
ness. In the early afternoon President Cleveland's famous Venezuela message came over the
wires from Washington. Dow, Bergstresser and
the present writer happened to be at the desk
when the message came in to Jones. The question was what would be the effect. This writer
did not regard the affair as of more than passing moment, in which Bergstresser agreed with
him. Dow said that is seemed to him as if it
might have some unpleasant implications. Jones
emphatically said, "this means panic" and panic
it was, but it took the Street several hours to
realize and reflect its implications.

Moved to 44 Broad in 1893

Thus constituted and equipped the firm of
Dow Jones & Co. went through the panic of
1893 and the difficult years immediately following. Gradually, however the staff commenced
to enlarge a little and when in 1899 Jones retired from the firm, the basement of the old
Edison Building at 44 Broad Street—to which
the plant had removed in the spring of 1893—
housed a considerably increased population
That was the year when The Wall Street Journal started to grow. The old press was ex-
changed for a Hoe Perfecting Press with a
stereotype plant and a Philadelphia special wire
was added to the Boston wire and correspondents were taken on in additional places. The
single telephone instrument gave place to r
small switchboard, the late "W. P. Hamilton
joined the local staff, a page printing ticker
had been installed and the entire outfit had

started to grow in substantial fashion. By that time this writer had become acquainted with Mr. Barron.

The first impression that he had remained ever after as the strongest. It was one of an extraordinarily dynamic personality. Energy was his dominant characteristic. Somewhat later this writer in fact charged Mr. Barron with being in effect a sort of "vampire" in that he seemed to absorb vital energy from everyone around him.

This was hardly just, but traveling with Mr. Barron in the news business was an exciting pastime which did in fact make considerable demands on an ordinary person's reserves physically and mentally. Everything seemed to interest him and when Mr. Barron was interested it meant work. This writer will not now attempt any appraisal of Mr. Barron further than to say that he was without doubt the most picturesque and forceful personality that has thus far appeared in the field of financial journalism. He had his own way of stating things. He was no believer in qualified utterances; there was no "on the other hand" about him, but he was very seldom caught in any important inaccuracy, notwithstanding the dogmatic way in which he expressed his views.

The most important and colorful portions of his career, however, fell outside the period during which this writer was associated with him. He became the owner of the Dow Jones & Co. business in April, 1902 and this writer sought other pastures three years later. It is for other people to judge his work in the following years. There are some people, not many perhaps, of whom one gets an impression that is best summed up in the word "personality"; Mr. Barron was one of these. Whether it was work in Boston or New York or whether it was play at Cohasset, the entire energy of the man was centered on the matter in hand. This writer has memories of sea fishing trips off Minot's Light, of yacht racing in which he shipped as unable seaman with Mr. Barron as skipper in a light Herreshoff sloop and got his orders mixed, thereby loosing thunderbolts of good sea talk from the skipper, and he has a picture of Mr. Barron in the water near his own dock in Cohasset which suggests a more definitely amphibian performance than he ever saw before or since by human being. Keen, able, energetic and competent, as are the men engaged in financial journalism today, it will be long before another Clarence W. Barron shall appear—if ever.

Hamilton Joined Staff in 1899

Hamilton came to The Wall Street Journal in 1899 and was engaged to write paragraphs about the stock market. He was a Scotchman who had lived mainly in England where as a clerk on the stock exchange and a very young man he had dabbled not a little in Liberal politics and numbered among his friends a good ~~many men whose names are still known in con~~ nection with the party. To this writer Hamilton used to confide the intense irritation with which he underwent drilling in his job at the hands of Mr. Dow. He was assured that if Mr. ~~Dow had not recognized what was in him he~~ would neverd have taken the trouble thus to educate him.

At this point it is perhaps useful to state how the editorial column of The Wall Street Journal originated. For some time prior to 1902 it had been the custom for the top left hand column of the paper to carry a couple of paragraphs under the head "Review and Outlook." These paragraphs generally concerned themselves with the financial situation (as a whole) and the stock market, very much like the ordinary "lead" to financial articles in the daily press. In the early autumn of 1902 the great anthracite coal strike developed ! Dow, who wrote the Review and Outlook, developed a very strong opinion on the strike against the side of the coal operators and wrote several editorials in Review and Outlook which attracted much attention. These were in fact the first strictly editorial utterances of The Wall Street Journal, and they had a curious sequel.

Theodore Roosevelt, then President, as will be remembered, appointed the famous anthracite coal Commission to inquire into the merits of the controversy. It so happened that these editorials were almost the last work that Mr. Dow did for The Wall Street Journal—he/died early in December, 1902—and after his death the present writer took up the editorial column. One Saturday afternoon there came into his office three men. One was Mr. Walter Weyl, afterwards well known in the economic field. They announced themselves as advisory counsel for Mr. John Mitchell, head of the anthracite miners' union and said that they had observed the course of The Wall Street Journal on the strike. They wished the paper to undertake the preparation of the statistics for the side of the miners. Naturally this could not be done, but it has always seemed to this writer that no higher compliment was ever paid to the paper than was paid upon that occasion.

From that time on the editorial column became a considerable feature of the Journal and shortly afterwards Mr. Barron engaged the late Sereno S. Pratt, for years the New York correspondent of the Philadelphia Ledger under the famous owner, George W. Childs. Pratt had written a standard book known as "The Work of Wall Street" which still remains a classic on the subject. He was engaged to act as this writer's assistant in the production of editorials. Pratt was a singularly earnest and forceful writer and it was no uncommon experience for the present scribe to receive letters warmly commending editorials which Pratt had written. Upon the present writer's resignation from the paper in 1905, Pratt became its editor, resigning at the end of 1909 to become Secretary of the New York State Chamber of Commerce. Hamilton succeeded him.

Hamilton Editorials Widely Quoted

The choice was really inevitable. Hamilton had from time to time, both under the editorship of this writer and of Pratt, contributed occasional editorials to the Journal which were marked by a peculiarly flavorful style and, in the language of the prize ring, "packing a punch." It is not too much to say that in the following nearly 20 years during which he was its editor, Hamilton's editorials made the paper known from end to end of the United States. Like all other powerful editorial writers, he had his own views on many controversial matters which he could state in highly epigrammatic fashion. These editorials were very widely quoted. Naturally, at times they stirred up violent reactions and sharp replies. In controversy with Hamilton, however, one had to be quick of eye and sure of foot, for whether it was mace or rapier that he was handling at the time, he was dangerous with both

Dow, Jones, Bergstresser, Barron, Pratt and Hamilton all have passed on. The present writer is the sole survivor of the crew of 40 years ago and he has written obituary notes for each of his former associates. Coming back after 20 years to The Wall Street Journal he finds himself, so far as he knows, the oldest man in the entire organization. At this time when the organization is celebrating its fiftieth anniversary it has been a pleasant task for him to recall the men with whom as a young man beginning life in the United States he threw his lot 40 years ago. He feels a degree of sympathetic understanding of the mind of Rip Van Winkle when he came down from the Catskills to find his old village a bustling town, and in coming home again at eventide he too has been happy.

INDEX